when

HEAVEN

invades

EARTH

EXPANDED EDITION

DESTINY IMAGE BOOKS BY BILL JOHNSON

A Life of Miracles

Dreaming With God

Center of the Universe

Momentum

Release the Power of Jesus

Strengthen Yourself in the Lord

The Supernatural Power of a Transformed Mind

Hosting the Presence

Bill Johnson

when

HEAVEN

invades

EARTH

A PRACTICAL GUIDE TO
A LIFE OF MIRACLES

EXPANDED EDITION

Some of the names of the people mentioned in this book have been changed. The author has done so where he felt anonymity is essential.

DESTINY IMAGE® PUBLISHERS, INC.

P.O. Box 310, Shippensburg, PA 17257-0310

"Promoting Inspired Lives."

This book and all other Destiny Image, Revival Press, MercyPlace, Fresh Bread, Destiny Image Fiction, and Treasure House books are available at Christian bookstores and distributors worldwide.

For a U.S. bookstore nearest you, call **1-800-722-6774.**

For more information on foreign distributors, call **717-532-3040.**

Reach us on the Internet: **www.destinyimage.com.**

ISBN 13 TP: 978-0-7684-4210-6

ISBN 13 Ebook: 978-0-7684-8736-7

For Worldwide Distribution, Printed in the U.S.A.

1 2 3 4 5 6 7 8 / 17 16 15 14 13

DEDICATION

I dedicate this book to the two churches I have pastored: Mountain Chapel of Weaverville, California, and Bethel Church of Redding, California. You both embraced a life of discomfort—living with continual risk—and were willing to endure the unexplainable to obtain the unforgettable. I owe you more than I could ever repay. Thanks. I love you so much.

ACKNOWLEDGMENTS

Mom and Dad—thanks for honestly believing I could do anything.

Mark Sanders, John Montgomery, Kris Vallotton, Diane Brown, and Dr. Andre Van Mol—thanks for the consistent exhortation and encouragement to write. Diane—your ideas were very helpful.

Elders of Mountain Chapel—thanks for giving me room to grow, encouraging me to follow my vision, and for buying me a Mac.

Staff and Elders of Bethel Church—you are my heroes. Your willingness to pay the price for revival has paved the way for fruit beyond our wildest dreams. You are the Dream Team.

Dann Farrelly—thanks for honest evaluation of the materials written, and for your tireless efforts in editing my stuff.

Guy Chevreau—thanks for your candid suggestions and editing efforts. They were invaluable to me!

Bobby and Carolyn Conner—thanks for the use of the Angel Cabin for many days of writing.

Bob and Claudia Perry—thanks for the use of your Shasta Hilton as a writing hideaway.

To my wife Beni—you are for me a taste of heaven on earth. Thanks.

ENDORSEMENTS

Bill Johnson's book *When Heaven Invades Earth* is changing lives around the world!

We require everyone who attends our Iris Harvest School of Missions in Pemba, Mozambique, to read and practice it! It is a profound and moving teaching resource on life in the supernatural. While practicing the truths revealed in this powerful book, we discover that we are created to live every day in the miraculous Kingdom realms of God. All over the world as I travel, I find people whose lives have been transformed as they have begun to practice Bill's teachings.

It is a great privilege for my husband Rolland and I to know the remarkable man who authored this book and to count him as one of our dearest friends. One of my personal goals in life is to be a woman who demonstrates on every level the truths of Bill's Kingdom teachings!

Heidi Baker, PhD
Founding Director, Iris Global

Bill has written a book that is absolutely revolutionary. We have prayed the Lord's Prayer for over 2,000 years, but now we are seeing the realities of "on earth as it is in heaven." Bill's book, *When Heaven Invades Earth*, has been used as a catalyst into the supernatural for the average believer—like no other book that I know of. This book is already a classic that will impact generations to come.

Dr. Ché Ahn
Senior Pastor, HRock Church, Pasadena, CA
President, Harvest International Ministry
International Chancellor, Wagner Leadership Institute

This book has brought a vital revelation to the Body of Christ, and in its early editions was read by many thousands. I'm excited to hear that it's being reprinted and offered again because this life-changing message needs to saturate the Body of Christ; and who better to present it than Bill Johnson?

John Arnott

There have been few books written in the past 20 years that have had as great an impact upon the Church and the Kingdom than Bill Johnson's *When Heaven Invades Earth*. When it first came out, it seemed like everywhere in the English-speaking world I went, they were reading *When Heaven Invades Earth*. It is an honor to write this endorsement for the 10th anniversary edition. It has become a modern-day classic. If you haven't read it, don't put this book down. Instead, buy it and read it.

Randy Clark

CONTENTS

DEVOTIONAL

FOREWORD

WHEN I AM INTERESTED IN READING A NEW BOOK, I always have two questions: Is the life of the author consistent with the message of the book? Is his (or her) ministry supportive of the declarations of the book? If both questions are not answered in the affirmative without resounding definition, I will pass on reading the book.

In the case of *When Heaven Invades Earth* and Bill Johnson, I had prior knowledge of the author and his ministry before I read the manuscript. Therefore, with the aforementioned questions already answered in the affirmative, I happily read the treatise.

I first ministered in Bethel Church of Redding, California—which is pastored by Bill Johnson—in 2001, a few months after my wife died. I had heard several tapes by Bill Johnson a few months previous to going to Bethel. Being very much in the grieving process over the loss of my wife of more than 47 years, I found myself being greatly ministered to while I was ministering. I taught in the School of Supernatural Ministry and was exposed to a large group of radical seekers after the Kingdom of God. I was informed that their subject was the Kingdom of God and that these sessions were only a part of their training. The sessions were geared toward preparing for Kingdom ministry. After the session the instructor told the students, "You have studied the Kingdom; now go out and do the Kingdom stuff!" And they did...in the malls, on the streets, in the bookshops and coffeehouses! They expected results and results happened!

I got the impression that this group represented the spirit of Bethel Church, which seemed to say, "Let's seek the Kingdom, find it, declare what we've found, and give it away!"

When I returned to visit Bethel Church and Bill Johnson a second time, I had just learned that my fiancé, Jerry, had cancer. Jerry, who is now my wife, was scheduled to undergo major surgery a few days after our visit to Bethel Church. At Bethel, two separate healing teams and a staff member and his wife joined us in powerful seasons of prayer, each group without knowledge of the content and impressions of the others. The experience was joyful, faith-giving, and confidence-building as they all agreed, "She will live and join you in an enhanced ministry." The surgery took place a few days later, and today Jerry is my wife and she ministers with me cancer free. To us this experience at Bethel was a demonstration of the validity of the message of this book.

The direction and perspective of this volume is essentially, "What happens when heaven invades earth?" This book you are holding is literally out of this world! It is about something unseen yet more real than the eyes reading these words. It is about the eternal realm, not yet fully seen or expressed but presently accessible and awaiting the obedience of anyone or any group to "seek first the kingdom of God and His righteousness" (Matt. 6:33).

I love *When Heaven Invades Earth* and am excited that it is about to break upon the Christian scene. I love this book because it points us toward primary reality in a world almost totally preoccupied with secondary reality. The reader of Scripture is aware that it ultimately defines primary reality as "unseen and eternal" while secondary reality is temporal, that is, it doesn't last (see 2 Cor. 4:18). Bill Johnson's beliefs, teachings, and ministry center on primary or Kingdom reality and finds that reality sufficient to change the face of "that which is seen."

I love this book because it declares unapologetically that Kingdom living and power are a part of the normal Christian life. What is described in this volume is not some exotic and rare expression, only to be viewed on infrequent occasions; instead, it is the very heartbeat of the Kingdom believer's life and ministry.

I love this book because it includes the necessity of repentance or "change of mentality" as a prerequisite to seeing and entering the Kingdom. This is approached in the brief but pungent material in Chapter 1 and somewhat enlarged in Chapter 3.

I love this book because it is a call to spiritual revolution to change the face of the earth, and it reports on how one church is doing it by changing its neighborhood, city, and region "one person at a time."

I love this book because practical faith (is there any other kind?) is clearly presented as being anchored in the unseen and living from the invisible to the visible. Once we repent we see the Kingdom, and, upon that view, faith comes. This is ably presented in Chapter 4.

I love this book because it is framed in a setting of the miraculous! Its opening pages are taken up (much like Jesus at Cana) with a miracle at a wedding and its concluding pages narrate the healing of a child.

I love this book because it challenges me to Kingdom prayer as the gateway to power and the means of getting heaven down to earth. As the Kingdom of God sheds true and new light on all other truths, so it does to prayer.

I love this book because it makes clear the practical results and fruit of signs and wonders. We do not seek such things but are promised that signs and wonders will follow those who believe.

Finally, I love this book because it leaves me with an intense desire to know God better, to fellowship with Him more intimately, and to minister with Him in more power than ever before. This is coupled with a standing-on-tiptoe excitement about what the future holds for myself in particular, and the Body of Christ in general, in sharing Christ with the world.

I now read this volume with a real but fading regret that something like this was not presented to me 55 years ago when I began ministry. It is a fading regret because I know that God can make up for the years lost or limited by a lack of knowledge of these things.

It is with no small measure of expectation of what reading this work may affect in your life that I recommend it to you without reservation. Read it slowly, read it thoroughly, and walk out what God teaches you through it. The results, I believe, will be heaven invading earth in your life!

Jack R. Taylor
President, Dimensions Ministries
Melbourne, Florida

FOREWORD

BILL JOHNSON'S BOOK, *When Heaven Invades Earth*, contains a message greatly needed for the Church today. It challenges many of our "sacred cows." Like Gideon, Johnson had to begin by tearing down the Asherah poles in the backyard of the Church. He is a man with a mission to wake up the Church. Not since I first met John Wimber have I been so taken with someone's understanding of the significance of the Kingdom of God message. I have yet to meet a pastor who is more committed to "power evangelism" than Bill Johnson. The stories of the healings and miracles done through the "little ole me's" in his local church are truly amazing. This book is not about some theoretical possibility, nor some pie-in-the-sky theology, nor some rationale for the lack of power in the Church. No, instead it offers practical, tried-and-proven strategies for pushing back the kingdom of darkness and advancing the Kingdom of Light. I wish I had met Pastor Bill Johnson earlier in my life. I feel I would be farther along on the road to moving in the power of the Kingdom of God than I presently am at this time.

When Heaven Invades Earth is a must-read for every pastor and leader in the Church today. This book was written by a fifth-generation pastor from the

Pentecostal perspective—and, what better perspective to hear from when it comes to the working of the Holy Spirit, especially regarding the gifts of healings. I have had the privilege of meeting many pastors from the United States and Canada over the past nine years of traveling. Pastor Bill Johnson, I believe, has more to say regarding the concepts of "power evangelism" than any other pastor I have met. Though he is an Assembly of God pastor and not a Vineyard pastor, he carries the DNA of John Wimber more than anyone else I know, especially when it comes to his passion for healing and the activity of the Holy Spirit. He is a radical pastor, a great teacher, and an apostolic voice in the Church today. His message is not the sound of an echo; it is a voice of one crying in the wilderness, "Prepare the way for the Lord's kingdom, which is at hand."

This book is full of powerful statements I wish I had written. So many wonderful quotes will be taken from this book—quotes such as the following: "One of the tragedies of a weakened identity is how it affects our approach to Scripture. Many, if not most, theologians make the mistake of taking all the good stuff contained in the prophets and sweeping it under that mysterious rug called *the Millennium*....We are so entrenched in unbelief that anything contrary to this world view (the dispensationalist's view of a weak end-time Church) is thought to be of the devil."

Other great quotes from this book are: "Unbelief is anchored in what is visible or reasonable apart from God. It honors the natural realm as superior to the invisible.... Unbelief is faith in the inferior"; and "Faith comes by hearing.... It does not say that it comes from having heard. It is the listening heart, in the present tense, that is ready for heaven's deposit of faith.... Hearing now is a key to faith."

When Heaven Invades Earth is a wake-up call to the Church. It is a death-blow to "cessationism," a challenge to "dispensationalism," and it is a call to those within the Pentecostal heritage to return to their roots. The book is solidly based in Scripture and reveals the heart of a man who loves not only the Spirit, but also loves the Word of God. With fresh revelation Bill Johnson takes us to Scripture and lets Scripture speak a fresh word to us.

He forces us to see what the Scriptures actually say, instead of only seeing what our theologically correct blinders allow us to see.

I have been waiting for Bill to finish this book so I could offer it at my book table at my meetings. He has so much to say that I avoid missing any of his speaking times when we minister together. They are too rich to miss. In this day of so many principles and strategies, it is refreshing to hear one call us back to the strategy of Jesus for evangelism.

Randy Clark
Global Awakening Ministries
International Conference Speaker
Author, *God Can Use Little Ole Me*

INTRODUCTION

A FEW YEARS AGO I overheard a conversation that stirred me beyond words. It was during my uncle David Morken's 90th birthday party. Along with a sizable crowd of family members, several of his peers in ministry had gathered for the celebration. As a young man, Uncle David had been a soloist for Aimee Semple McPherson before becoming a missionary to China and Sumatra, and later he became a right-hand man to Billy Graham. His accomplishments are stunning, but are a subject for another time.

Toward the end of the evening I saw a few of the older saints sitting together, talking. Noticing the subject was the outpouring of the Spirit during Aimee Semple McPherson's ministry, I couldn't help but eavesdrop. With youthful enthusiasm one said to the other, "It was like heaven on earth." There they were, some 70 years after the fact, with eyes brightened by the memory of things that others seldom dream of. Their experience became the standard by which all other days were to be measured. I was pierced through.

My heart burns for the coming move of God. I live for the revival that is unfolding and believe it will surpass all previous moves combined, bringing more than 1 billion souls into the Kingdom. Yet, for this one moment, I wished I could go back in time.

As a fifth-generation pastor on my dad's side of the family, and fourth on my mom's, I grew up hearing of the great moves of God. My grandparents sat under the ministry of Smith Wigglesworth and other notable revivalists. (I remember Grandpa telling me, "Not everyone liked Wigglesworth." Of course he is well loved today. Israel also loved their prophets after they were dead.)

Grandpa and Grandma Morken received the baptism in the Holy Spirit in 1901 and 1903, respectively, and they loved to talk about what they had seen and experienced. They've been in heaven now for over 25 years. I only wish I had another chance to hear their stories and to ask them the questions I never had asked as a young man. It would mean so much more to me now.

The quest described in this book began in me many years ago. I needed to see the gospel in life as it is in print. For me it was an issue of being faithful to God. However, it quickly became clear to me that such a pursuit was costly. Many misunderstandings come when we pursue what others ignore.

I could not limit my values and pursuits to what makes others comfortable. Being possessed by a promise I live without options. I will spend the rest of my life exploring what could happen through the life of one who is willing to cultivate the God-given appetite to see impossibilities bow to the name of Jesus. All my eggs are in one basket. There is no "Plan B." And it's from this posture that I write.

Chapter I

THE NORMAL
CHRISTIAN LIFE

*It is abnormal for a Christian not to have an appetite for the impossible.
It has been written into our spiritual DNA to hunger for the
impossibilities around us to bow at the name of Jesus.*

ON A COLD AND RAINY SATURDAY, church buses were sent to the neediest parts of our city, Redding, to find the homeless and the poor. The bride and groom eagerly anticipated their return and prepared a meal in their honor. The needy were to be the distinguished guests of their wedding.

Ralph and Colleen met while working in our ministry to the poor. They shared a passion for God and a love for the needy. Although it is common for the bride and groom to register for gifts at fine department stores, Ralph and Colleen did so at Target; and all they put on their *wish list* were coats, hats, gloves, and sleeping bags...to be given to their *guests*. This was not going to be a typical wedding.

In our pre-wedding meeting the bride and groom encouraged me to be sensitive to the Holy Spirit in case He wanted to heal people during the wedding. If I received a word of knowledge for healing, I was to stop the ceremony and pray for the sick. As a pastor I was excited to see what might happen. They had created far too great a *miracle opportunity* for God not to do something extraordinary.

The wedding began. Apart from an extended time of worship, followed by an evangelistic message and a prayer for salvation, the ceremony ended up quite normal.

It's very different to see among family and friends of the bride and groom people who are there simply to get a meal. It wasn't wrong. It was just different. Following the ceremony, the newly married couple went directly to the reception hall, got behind the serving table, and dished the food for their guests. The meal was excellent. The hungry became satisfied. God was pleased.

But before the wedding ever started, two or three people came to me with excitement in their voice. "There is somebody here who only has two-and-a-half to three years to live!" We had crossed a milestone. Miracles of healing had become more common...to the point that a life-threatening disease seemed more like a potential miracle than it did something to fear. That in itself is a dream come true for me—people in North America *expecting* something supernatural from God!

THE MIRACLE CONTINUES

His name was Luke. Like most of the folks from the streets, he and his wife Jennifer had come to the wedding because food would be served. Luke walked with difficulty, needing the help of a cane. He wore braces on each arm, and a large brace around his neck.

Following the meal, my brother Bob and I brought them into the church kitchen, asking him about the braces on each arm. He told us his problem was carpal tunnel syndrome. I asked him if he would take the braces off and let us pray. He said yes. (Whenever it's possible, I like to remove whatever that person might trust in other than God.) He did so, and we laid our hands on his wrists, commanding the *tunnel* to open and all numbness and pain to be gone. He then moved his hands freely, experiencing the healing he had just received.

When we asked him about his cane and the obvious problem with his leg, he described how he had suffered a horrible accident. As a result he had an artificial shin and hip and had even lost half a lung. His walk was labored and painful. When the surgeons put him back together, his leg was an inch too short. I had him sit down and encouraged both him and his wife to watch what God was about to do. I held his legs in such a way that they could see the problem and would be able to recognize any change. We commanded the leg to grow. It did. When he stood, he shifted his weight from side to side, almost as though he were trying on a new pair of shoes, saying, "Yeah, that's about right." The response of the unchurched is very matter of fact...and very refreshing. I asked him to walk across the room, which he did gladly, without a limp and without pain. God was at work. He replaced one inch of missing bone and removed all the pain caused by Luke's accident.

Next we asked about Luke's neck. He told me he had cancer and was given a couple of years to live. He went on to explain that the brace was necessary because of the loss of the muscles in his neck. The brace held his head in place. By this time a group had gathered, not to watch, but to participate. At my request he removed the brace while another man in our church, a medical doctor, safely held his head. As we began to pray I heard the doctor command new muscles to grow. He called them by their Latin names. I was impressed. When we were finished, Luke turned his head from side to side. All was restored. He then placed his hand on the side of his neck and exclaimed, "The lumps are gone!"

His doctor gave him a clean bill of health, and the miracles continued long past the physical healing. Luke and Jennifer began to serve Jesus as their Lord and Savior. Within weeks Luke got a job, the first time he had worked in 17 years. Jesus heals the whole person.

JUST ANOTHER DAY

Although that kind of wedding remains unusual, our church's deliberate pursuit of the poor and the miracles are common. This story is true, and it is closer to the normal Christian life than what the Church *normally* experiences. The lack of miracles isn't because it is not in God's will for us. The problem exists between our ears. As a result, a transformation—a *renewing of the mind*—is needed, and it's only possible through a work of the Holy Spirit that typically comes upon desperate people.

The aforementioned bride and groom, although noble, are ordinary people who serve an extravagant Father. There wasn't a great person involved, except for Jesus. All the rest of us simply made room for God, believing Him to be good 100 percent of the time. The risks that the bride and groom took were more than God could pass up. In the midst of this marriage celebration, God invaded a home marked by hellish disease and established a testimony for His glory.

Stories of this nature are becoming the norm, and the company of people who have joined this quest for an authentic gospel—*the gospel of the Kingdom*—is increasing. Loving God and His people is an honor. We will no longer make up excuses for powerlessness because powerlessness is inexcusable. Our mandate is simple: raise up a generation that can openly display the raw power of God. This book is all about that journey...the quest for the King and His Kingdom.

> *The kingdom of God is not a matter of talk but of power* (I Corinthians 4:20 NIV).

> *Seek first the kingdom of God...* (Matthew 6:33).

Chapter 2

COMMISSION
RESTORED

Jesus of Nazareth, a Man attested by God to you by miracles, wonders, and signs which God did through Him in your midst... (Acts 2:22).

JESUS COULD NOT HEAL THE SICK. Neither could He deliver the tormented from demons or raise the dead. To believe otherwise is to ignore what He said about Himself, and more importantly, to miss the purpose of His self-imposed restriction to live as a man.

Jesus Christ said of Himself, "The Son can do nothing" (John 5:19). In the Greek language that word *nothing* has a unique meaning—it means *nothing*, just like it does in English! He had *no* supernatural capabilities whatsoever! While He is 100 percent God, He chose to live with the same limitations that man would face once he was redeemed. He made that point over and over again. Jesus became the model for all who would embrace the invitation to invade the impossible in His name. He performed *miracles, wonders, and signs* as a man in right relationship to God...not as God. If He performed miracles because He was God, then they would be unattainable for us. But if He did them as a man, I am responsible to pursue His lifestyle. Recapturing this simple truth changes everything...and makes possible a full restoration of the ministry of Jesus in His Church.

What were the distinctions of His humanity?

1. He had no sin to separate Him from the Father.

2. He was completely dependent on the power of the Holy Spirit working through Him.

What are the distinctions of our humanity?

1. We are sinners cleansed by the blood of Jesus. Through His sacrifice He has successfully dealt with the power and effect of sin for all who believe. Nothing now separates us from the Father. There remains only one unsettled issue—

2. How dependent on the Holy Spirit are we willing to live?

THE ORIGINAL COMMISSION

The backbone of Kingdom authority and power is found in the *commission*. Discovering God's original commission and purpose for mankind can help fortify our resolve to a life of history-changing significance. To find that truth we must go back to the beginning.

Man was created in the image of God and placed into the Father's ultimate expression of beauty and peace: the Garden of Eden. Outside of that garden it was a different story. It was without the order and blessing contained within and was in great need of the touch of God's delegated one—Adam.

Adam and Eve were placed in the garden with a mission. God said, "Be fruitful and multiply; fill the earth and subdue it" (Gen. 1:28). It was God's intention that as they bore more children, who also lived under God's rule, they would be extending the boundaries of His garden (His government) through the simplicity of their devotion to Him. The greater the number of people in right relationship to God, the greater the impact of their leadership. This process was to continue until the entire earth was covered with the glorious rule of God through man.

But in Genesis chapter 1 we discover it's not a perfect universe. Satan had rebelled and had been cast out of heaven, and with him a portion of the fallen angels took dominion of the earth. It's obvious why the rest of the planet needed to be subdued—it was under the influence of darkness (see Gen. 1:2). God could have destroyed the devil and his host with a word, but instead He chose to defeat darkness through His delegated authority— those made in His image who were lovers of God by choice.

A ROMANCE STORY

The Sovereign One placed us—Adam's children—in charge of planet earth. "The heaven, even the heavens, are the Lord's; but the earth He has given to the children of men" (Ps. 115:16). This highest of honors was chosen because love always chooses the best. That is the beginning of the romance of our creation...created in His image, *for intimacy*, that dominion might be expressed through love. It is from this revelation that we are to learn to walk as His ambassadors, thus defeating the "prince of this world." The stage was set for all of darkness to fall as man exercised his godly influence over creation. But instead, man fell.

Satan didn't come into the Garden of Eden violently and take possession of Adam and Eve. He couldn't! Why? He had no dominion there. Dominion empowers. And since man was given the keys of dominion over the planet, the devil would have to get his authority from them. The suggestion to eat the forbidden fruit was simply the devil's effort to get Adam and Eve to agree with him in opposition to God, thus empowering him. Through that agreement he is enabled to *kill, steal, and destroy*. It's important to realize that even today satan is empowered through man's agreement.

Mankind's authority to rule was forfeited when Adam ate the forbidden fruit. Paul said, "You are that one's slaves whom you obey" (Rom. 6:16). In that one act mankind became the slave and possession of the evil one.

All that Adam owned, including the title deed to the planet with its corresponding position of rule, became part of the devil's spoil. God's predetermined plan of redemption immediately kicked into play, "I will put enmity between you and the woman, and between your seed and her Seed; He shall bruise your head, and you shall bruise His heel" (Gen. 3:15). Jesus would come to reclaim all that was lost.

THERE WERE NO SHORTCUTS TO HIS VICTORY

God's plan of rulership for man never ceased. Jesus came to bear man's penalty for sin and recapture what had been lost. Luke 19:10 says that Jesus came "to seek and to save that which was lost." Not only was mankind lost to sin, his dominion over planet earth was also lost. Jesus came to recapture both. Satan tried to ruin that plan at the end of Jesus' 40-day fast. The devil knew he wasn't worthy of Jesus' worship, but he also knew that Jesus had come to reclaim the authority that man had given away.

Satan said to Him, "All this authority I will give You, and their glory; for this has been delivered to me, and I give it to whomever I wish. Therefore, if You will worship before me, all will be Yours" (Luke 4:6-7). Notice the phrase "for this has been delivered to me." Satan could not steal it. It had been relinquished when Adam abandoned God's rule. It was as though satan was saying to Jesus, "I know what You came for. You know what I want. Worship me and I'll give You back the keys." In effect, satan offered Jesus a shortcut to His goal of recapturing the keys of authority that man lost through sin. Jesus said "no" to the shortcut and refused to give him any honor. (It was this same desire for worship that caused satan's fall from heaven in the first place. See Isaiah 14:12.) Jesus held His course, for He had come to die.

The Father wanted satan defeated by man...one made in His image. Jesus, who would shed His blood to redeem mankind, emptied Himself of His rights as God and took upon Himself the limitations of man. Satan was defeated by a man—the Son of Man—who was rightly related to God. Now, as people receive the work of Christ on the cross for salvation, they become grafted into that victory. Jesus defeated the devil with His sinless life, defeated him in His death by paying for our sins with His blood, and again, in the resurrection, rising triumphant with the keys of death and hell.

WE ARE BORN TO RULE

In redeeming man, Jesus retrieved what man had given away. From the throne of triumph He declared, "All authority has been given to Me in heaven and on earth. Go therefore…" (Matt. 28:18-19). In other words: *I got it all back. Now go use it and reclaim mankind.* In this passage, Jesus fulfills the promise He made to the disciples when He said, "I will give you the keys of the kingdom of heaven" (Matt. 16:19). The original plan was never aborted; it was fully realized once and for all in the resurrection and ascension of Jesus. We were then to be completely restored to His plan of ruling as a people made in His image. And as such we would learn how to enforce the victory obtained at Calvary: "The God of peace will soon crush Satan under your feet" (Rom. 16:20 NIV).

We were born to rule—rule over creation, over darkness—to plunder hell and establish the rule of Jesus wherever we go by preaching the gospel of the Kingdom. *Kingdom* means *King's domain.* In the original purpose of God, mankind ruled over creation. Now that sin has entered the world, creation has been infected by darkness, namely, disease, sickness, afflicting spirits, poverty, natural disasters, demonic influence, etc. Our rule is still over creation, but now it is focused on exposing and undoing the works of the devil. We are to give what we have received to reach that end (see Matt. 10:8). If I truly receive power from an encounter with the God of power, I am equipped to give it away. The invasion of God into impossible situations comes through a people who have received power from on high and learn to release it into the circumstances of life.

THE KEY OF DAVID

The gospel of salvation is to touch the whole man: spirit, soul, and body. John G. Lake called this a *Triune Salvation.* A study on the word *evil* confirms the intended reach of His redemption. That word is found in Matthew 6:13 (KJV), "Deliver us from evil." The word *evil* represents the entire curse of sin upon man. *Poneros,* the Greek word for evil, came from the word *ponos,* meaning pain. And that word came from the root word *penes,* meaning poor. Look at it: *evil*-sin, *pain*-sickness, and *poor*-poverty. Jesus destroyed the power of sin, sickness, and poverty through His redemptive work on the cross. In Adam and Eve's commission to subdue the earth, they were without sickness, poverty, and sin. Now that we are restored to His original purpose, should we expect anything less? After all, this is called the better covenant!

We were given the keys to the Kingdom (see Matt. 16:19)—which in part is the authority *to trample over all the powers of hell* (see Luke 10:19). There is a unique application of this principle found in the phrase *key of David,* which is mentioned in both Revelation and Isaiah (see Isa. 22:22; Rev. 3:7). *Unger's Bible Dictionary* states, "The power of the keys consisted not only in the supervision of the royal chambers, but also in deciding who was and who was not to be received into the King's service."[1] All that the Father has is ours through Christ. His entire treasure house of resources, His royal chambers, is at our disposal in order to fulfill His commission. But the more sobering part of this illustration is found in *controlling who gets in to see the King.* Isn't that what we do with this gospel? When we declare it, we give opportunity for people to come to the King to be saved. When we are silent, we have chosen to keep those who would hear away from eternal life. Sobering indeed! It was a costly key for Him to purchase, and it's a costly key for us to use. But it's even more costly to *bury it and not obtain an increase for the coming King.* That price will be felt throughout eternity.

A REVOLUTION IN IDENTITY

It's time for a revolution in our vision. When prophets tell us, *Your vision is too small,* many of us think the antidote is to increase whatever numbers we're expecting. For example: if we're expecting 10 new converts, let's change it to 100. If we were praying for cities, let's pray instead for nations. With such responses, we're missing the sharp edge of the frequently repeated word. Increasing the numbers is not necessarily a sign of a larger vision from God's perspective. Vision starts with identity and purpose. Through a revolution in our identity, we can think with divine purpose. Such a change begins with a revelation of Him.

One of the tragedies of a weakened identity is how it affects our approach to Scripture. Many, if not most theologians, make the mistake of taking all the *good stuff* contained in the prophets and sweeping it under that mysterious rug called the *Millennium.* It is not my desire to debate that subject right now. But I do want to deal with our propensity to put off those things that require courage, faith, and action to another period of time. The mistaken idea is this: if it is good, it can't be for now.

A cornerstone in this theology is that the condition of the Church will always be getting worse and worse; therefore, tragedy in the Church is just another sign of these being the last days. In a perverted sense, the weakness of the Church confirms to many that they are on the right course. The worsening condition of the world and the Church becomes a sign to them that all is well. I have many problems with that kind of thinking, but only one I'll mention now—*it requires no faith!*

We are so entrenched in unbelief that anything contrary to this worldview is thought to be of the devil. So it is with the idea of the Church having a dominating impact before Jesus returns. It's almost as though we want to defend the right to be small in number and make it by the *skin of our teeth.* Embracing a belief system that requires no faith is dangerous. It is contrary to the nature of God and all that the Scriptures declare. Since He plans to do *above all we could ask or think,* according to Ephesians 3:20, His promises by nature challenge our intellect and expectations. "[Jerusalem] did not consider her destiny; therefore her collapse was awesome" (Lam. 1:9). The result of forgetting His promises is not one we can afford.

We are often more convinced of our *unworthiness* than we are of His *worth*. Our *inability* takes on greater focus than does His *ability*. But the same One who called *fearful Gideon* a Valiant Warrior and *unstable Peter* a Rock has called us the Body of His beloved Son on earth. That has to count for something.

In the next chapter we'll see how to use a gift to manifest His Kingdom—causing heaven to touch earth.

ENDNOTE

1. *Unger's Bible Dictionary*, "Key," (Chicago, IL: Moody Press, 1957), 629.

Chapter 3

REPENT TO SEE

Most Christians repent enough to get forgiven,
but not enough to see the Kingdom.

ISRAEL EXPECTED THEIR MESSIAH to come as the King who would rule over all other kings. And He did. But their misunderstanding of greatness in His Kingdom made it difficult for them to grasp how He could be born without earthly fanfare and become the servant of all.

They expected Him to rule with a rod of iron. In doing so they would finally have revenge on all those who had oppressed them throughout the ages. Little did they realize that His vengeance would not be aimed so much at the enemies of Israel as it would be toward the enemies of man: sin, the devil and his works, and the self-righteous attitudes fostered by religion.

Jesus the Messiah came…full of surprises. Only the contrite in heart could keep up with His constant *coloring outside the lines* and stay unoffended. His purpose was revealed in His primary message: "Repent, for the kingdom of heaven is at hand" (Matt. 4:17). Now there's something that caught them completely off guard; He brought His world with Him!

MORE THAN TEARS

Repentance means much more than weeping over sin, or even turning from those sins to follow God. In fact, turning from sin to God is more the *result* of true repentance than it is the actual act. Repentance means you *change your way of thinking*. And it's only in changing the way we think that we can discover the focus of Jesus' ministry—the Kingdom.

This is not just a heavenly mandate to have happy thoughts. Obeying this command is possible only for those who surrender to the grace of God. The renewed mind is the result of a surrendered heart.

AN ABOUT-FACE

Repentance is often defined as *doing an about-face*. It implies that I was pursuing one direction in life and I change to pursue another. Scripture illustrates it like this, "Repentance from dead works...faith toward God" (Heb. 6:1). Faith then is both the crown and the enabler of repentance.

This command has been preached strongly in recent years. The message is greatly needed. Hidden sin is the *Achilles' heel* of the Church in this hour. It has kept us from the purity that breeds boldness and great faith. But as noble as that target is, the message has fallen short. God wants to do more than just *getting us out of the red*. He wants to *get us into the black!* Repentance is not complete until it envisions His Kingdom.

CO-LABORERS WITH CHRIST

The focus of repentance is to change our way of thinking until the presence of His Kingdom fills our consciousness. The enemy's attempt to anchor our affections to the things that are visible is easily resisted when our hearts are aware of the presence of His world. Such awareness aids us in the task of being *co-laborers* with Christ (see I Cor. 3:9)—*destroying the works of the devil* (see I John 3:8).

If the Kingdom is *here and now*, then we must acknowledge it's in the invisible realm. Yet being *at hand* reminds us that it's also *within reach*. Paul said that the invisible realm is eternal, while that which is seen is only temporal (see 2 Cor. 4:18). Jesus told Nicodemus that he'd have to be born again to *see* the Kingdom (see John 3:3). That which is unseen can be realized only through *repentance*. It was as though He said, "If you don't change the way you perceive things, you'll live your whole life thinking that what you see in the natural is the superior reality. Without changing the way you think you'll never see the world that is right in front of you. It's My world, and it fulfills every dream you've ever had. And I brought it with Me." All that He did in life and ministry, He did by drawing from that *superior* reality.

LIVING FROM THE UNSEEN

"It is the glory of God to conceal a matter, but the glory of kings is to search out a matter" (Prov. 25:2). Some things are only discovered by the *desperate*. That highly valued Kingdom attitude (see Matt. 5:6) is what marks the heart of true *Kingdom royalty* (see Rev. 1:5). The God who put the gold in the rocks brought His Kingdom with Him, but left it unseen.

Paul dealt with this in his letter to the Colossians. There he informs us that God hid our abundant life *in Christ* (see Col. 3:3). Where is He? *Seated at the right hand of the Father, in heavenly places* (see Eph. 1:20). Our abundant life is hidden in the Kingdom realm. And only faith can make the withdrawals.

THE KING'S DOMAIN

Look at the word *Kingdom*—King-dom. It refers to the *King's domain*, implying authority and lordship. Jesus came to offer the benefits of His world to all who surrender to His rule. The realm of God's dominion, that realm of all sufficiency, is the realm called the Kingdom. The benefits of His rule were illustrated through His works of forgiveness, deliverance, and healing.

The Christian life has been harnessed to this goal, verbalized in the Lord's Model Prayer: "Your kingdom come. Your will be done on earth as it is in heaven" (Matt. 6:10). His dominion is realized when what happens here is *as it is in heaven*. (This will be dealt with more thoroughly in Chapter 4.)

THE GREATEST SERMON

In Matthew chapter 4, Jesus first declared the repentance message. People came from all over, bringing the sick and diseased, the tormented and handicapped. Jesus healed them all.

After the miracles He gave the most famous sermon of all time: the Sermon on the Mount. It is important to remember that this group of people just saw Jesus heal all kinds of sicknesses and perform mighty deliverances. Is it possible that instead of giving commands on the new way of thinking, Jesus was actually identifying for them the transformation of heart they had just experienced?

"Blessed are the poor in spirit, for theirs is the kingdom of heaven" (Matt. 5:3). How would you describe a people who left cities for days at a time, traveling great distances on foot, abandoning all that life involves, only to follow Jesus to some desolate place? And there He would do what they had thought impossible. The hunger of their hearts pulled a reality from the heart of God that they didn't even know existed. Can their condition be found in the Beatitudes? I think so. I call them "poor in spirit." And Jesus gave them the promised manifestation of the Kingdom with healing and deliverance. He then followed the miracles with the Sermon, for it was common for Jesus to teach so He could explain what He had just done.

In this case, the actual presence of the Spirit of God upon Jesus stirred up a hunger for God in the people. That hunger brought a change in their attitudes without their being told it should change. Their hunger for God, even before they could recognize it as such, had created a new perspective in them that even they were unaccustomed to. Without an effort to change, they had changed. How? The Kingdom comes in the presence of the Spirit of God. It was His presence they detected, and it was His presence they longed for. For them it didn't matter if He was doing miracles or just giving another sermon, they just had to be where He was. Hunger humbles. Hunger for God brings about the ultimate humility. And He *exalted them at the proper time* (see 1 Pet. 5:6) with a taste of His dominion.

The Sermon on the Mount is a treatise on the Kingdom. In it Jesus reveals the attitudes that help His followers to access His unseen world. As citizens of heaven, these attitudes are formed in us that we might fully apprehend all that His Kingdom has available. The Beatitudes are actually the "lenses" that the Kingdom is seen through. Repentance involves taking on the mind of Christ revealed in these verses. He could have put it this way: *This is how the repentant mind looks.*

Please take note of the joyful condition of the citizens of His world who are not yet in heaven! *Blessed* means *happy!* The following is a personal paraphrase of Matthew 5:3-12.

3. You are happy if you are poor in spirit, for yours is the Kingdom of Heaven.
4. You are happy if you mourn, for you shall be comforted.
5. You are happy if you are meek, for you shall inherit the earth.
6. You are happy if you hunger and thirst for righteousness, for you shall be filled.
7. You are happy if you are merciful, for you shall obtain mercy.
8. You are happy if you are pure in heart, for you shall see God.
9. You are happy if you are peacemakers, for you shall be called sons of God.
10. You are happy if you are persecuted for righteousness' sake, for yours is the Kingdom of Heaven.
11. You are happy if they revile and persecute you, and say all kinds of evil against you falsely for My sake.
12. Rejoice and be exceedingly glad, for great is your reward in heaven, for so they persecuted the prophets who were before you.

Examine the promised result of each new attitude—*receiving the Kingdom, being comforted, obtaining mercy, seeing God,* etc. Why is this important to recognize? Because many approach the teachings of Jesus as *just another form of the Law.* To most He just brought a new set of rules. *Grace* is different from the *Law* in that the favor comes *before* the obedience. Under grace the commandments of the Lord come fully equipped with the ability to perform them… to those who hear from the heart (see James 1:21-25). *Grace enables what it commands.*

DOMINION REALIZED

The unseen world has influence over the visible. If the people of God will not reach for the Kingdom at hand, the realm of darkness is ready to display its ability to influence. The good news is that *"His* [the Lord's] *kingdom rules over all"* (Ps. 103:19).

Jesus illustrated this reality in Matthew 12:28, saying, "If I cast out demons by the Spirit of God, surely the kingdom of God has come upon you." There are two things to notice that will be covered more thoroughly elsewhere in this book. First, Jesus worked only through the Spirit of God; and second, the Kingdom of God came upon someone in his deliverance. Jesus caused the collision between two worlds: the world of darkness and the world of light. Darkness *always* gives way to light! And in the same way, when the dominion of God was released through Jesus to that man, he became free.

MOVING OUT OF CONVICTION

That same collision between light and darkness happens when the sick are healed. Walter had experienced two strokes in the previous year, which left him without feeling on the entire right side of his body. He showed me a horrible burn on his arm that he had suffered, not knowing he was being burned. Conviction, one of the words used to detect faith (see Heb. 11:1

KJV), began to burn in my heart. While he was still talking, I began to pray for him with my hand on his shoulder. I had to do so quickly. I had become aware of the Kingdom where no numbness existed. I didn't want to become more aware of how severe his problem was. My prayer went something like this: *Father, this was Your idea. You commanded us to pray for things to be here as they are in heaven, and I know there is no numbness there, so there shouldn't be any here. So I command, in the name of Jesus, the nerve endings to come to life. I command full restoration of feeling in this body.*

Soon after I started to pray, he told me that he felt my hand on his shoulder and could even feel the fabric of my shirt with his right hand. That world began to collide with the world of numbness. Numbness lost.

Faith is the key to discovering the superior nature of the invisible realm. It is the "gift of God" within to uncover. In the next chapter we'll learn how faith deals with the unseen and makes room for heaven's invasion.

Chapter 4

FAITH—ANCHORED
IN THE UNSEEN

Now faith is the substance of things hoped for, the evidence of things not seen
(Hebrews 11:1).

FAITH IS THE MIRROR OF THE HEART that reflects the realities of an unseen world—the actual substance of His Kingdom. Through the prayer of faith we are able to pull the reality of His world into this one. That is the function of faith.

Faith has its anchor in the unseen realm. It lives *from* the invisible *toward* the visible. Faith actualizes what it realizes. The Scriptures contrast the life of faith with the limitations of natural sight (see 2 Cor. 5:7). Faith provides eyes for the heart.

Jesus expects people to see from the heart. He once called a group of religious leaders *hypocrites* because they could discern the weather but couldn't discern the times. It's obvious why Jesus would prefer people to recognize the *times* (spiritual climate and seasons) over natural weather conditions, but it's not quite so apparent why He would consider them hypocrites if they didn't.

Many of us have thought that the ability to see into the spiritual realm is more the result of a special gift than an unused potential of everyone. I remind you that Jesus addresses this charge to the Pharisees and Sadducees. The very fact that they, of all people, were required to see is evidence that everyone has been given this ability. They became blind to His dominion because of their own corrupted hearts and were judged for their unfulfilled potential.

We are born again by grace through faith (see Eph. 2:8). The born-again experience enables us to see from the heart (see John 3:3). A heart that doesn't see is a hard heart (see Mark 8:17-18). Faith was never intended only to get us *into* the family. Rather, it is the nature of life in this family. Faith sees. It brings His Kingdom into focus. All of the Father's resources, all of His benefits, are accessible through faith.

To encourage us in our capacity to see, Jesus gave specific instruction, "Seek first the kingdom of God..." (Matt. 6:33). Paul taught us, "Set your mind on things above, not on things on the earth" (Col. 3:2). He also stated, "For the things which are seen are temporary, but the things which are not seen are eternal" (2 Cor. 4:18). The Bible instructs us to turn our attention toward the invisible. This theme is repeated enough in Scripture to make those of us bound by the logic of this Western culture quite nervous.

Herein lies the secret to the supernatural realm that we want restored to the Church. Jesus told us that He only did what He *saw* His Father do. Such an insight is vital for those who want more. The power of His actions—for instance, the mud in the eye of the blind—is rooted in His ability to see.

WORSHIP AND THE
SCHOOL OF FAITH

God is very committed to teaching us how to see. To make this possible He gave us the Holy Spirit as a tutor. The curriculum that He uses is quite varied. But the one class we all qualify for is the greatest of all Christian privileges—worship. Learning *how to see* is not the purpose for our worship, but it is a wonderful by-product.

Those who worship in spirit and truth, as mentioned in John 4:23-24, learn to follow the Holy Spirit's lead. His realm is called the Kingdom of God. The throne of God, which becomes established upon the *praises of His people* (see Ps. 22:3), is the center of that Kingdom. It's in the environment of worship that we learn things that go way beyond what our intellect can grasp (see Eph. 3:20)—and the greatest of these lessons is the value of His presence. David was so affected by this that all his other exploits pale in comparison to his abandoned heart for God. We know that he learned to see into God's realm because of statements like, "I have set the Lord always before me; because He is at my right hand I shall not be moved" (Ps. 16:8). The presence of God affected his seeing. He would constantly practice recognizing the presence of God. He saw God daily, not with the natural eyes, but with the eyes of faith. That priceless revelation was given to a worshiper.

The privilege of worship is a good beginning place for those unaccustomed to addressing some of these kinds of themes found in Scripture. It's in that wonderful ministry that we can learn to pay attention to this God-given gift: the ability to see with the heart. As we learn to worship with purity of heart, our eyes will continue to open. And we can expect to see what He wants us to see.

SEEING THE INVISIBLE

The invisible realm is superior to the natural. The reality of that invisible world dominates the natural world we live in...both positively and negatively. Because the invisible is superior to the natural, faith is anchored in the unseen.

Faith lives within the revealed will of God. When I have misconceptions of who He is and what He is like, my faith is restricted by those misconceptions. For example, if I believe that God allows sickness in order to build character, I'll not have confidence praying in most situations where healing is needed. But if I believe that sickness is to the body what sin is to the soul, then no disease will intimidate me. Faith is much more free to develop when we truly see the heart of God as good.

The same misconceptions of God affect those who need to have faith for their own miracle. A woman who needed a miracle once told me that she felt God had allowed her sickness for a purpose. I told her that if I treated my children that way I'd be arrested for child abuse. She agreed and eventually allowed me to pray for her. After truth came into her heart, her healing came minutes later.

Unbelief is anchored in what is visible or reasonable apart from God. It honors the natural realm as superior to the invisible. The apostle Paul states that what you can see is temporal, and what you can't see is eternal (see 2 Cor. 4:18). Unbelief is faith in the inferior.

The natural realm is the anchor of unbelief. But that realm is not to be considered as evil. Rather, the humble of heart recognize the hand of God through what is seen. God has created all things to speak of Him—whether it is rivers and trees, or angels and heaven. The natural realm carries the witness of His greatness...for those with eyes to see and ears to hear (see Rom. 1:20-21).

REALIST/MATERIALIST

Most all of the people that I've known who are filled with unbelief have called themselves *realists*. This is an honest evaluation, but not one to be proud of. Those kinds of realists believe more in what is visible than they do in what they can't see. Put another way, they believe the material world rules over the spiritual world.

Materialism has been thought simply to be the accumulation of goods. Although it includes that, it is much more. I can own nothing and still be materialistic. I can want nothing and be materialistic because materialism is faith in the natural as the superior reality.

We are a sensual society with a culture shaped by what is picked up through the senses. We're trained to believe only in what we see. Real faith is not living in denial of the natural realm. If the doctor says you have a tumor, it's silly to pretend that it's not there. That's not faith. However, faith is founded on a reality that is superior to that tumor. I can acknowledge the existence of a tumor and still have faith in the provision of His stripes for my healing…I was provisionally healed 2,000 years ago. It is the product of the Kingdom of Heaven—a superior reality. There are no tumors in heaven, and faith brings that reality into this one.

Would satan like to inflict heaven with cancer? Of course he would. But he has no dominion there. He only has dominion here when and where man has come into agreement.

LIVING IN DENIAL

Fear of appearing to live in denial is what keeps many from faith. Why is what anyone thinks so important to you that you'd not be willing to risk all to trust God? The fear of man is very strongly associated with unbelief. Conversely, the fear of God and faith are very closely related.

People of faith are also realists. They just have their foundation in a superior reality.

Unbelief is actually faith in something other than God. He is jealous over our hearts. The one whose primary trust is in another grieves the Holy Spirit.

IT'S NOT IN THE HEAD

Faith is born of the Spirit in the hearts of mankind. Faith is neither intellectual nor anti-intellectual. It is superior to the intellect. The Bible does not say, *With the mind man believes!* Through faith, man is able to come into agreement with the mind of God.

When we submit the things of God to the mind of man, unbelief and religion[1] are the results. When we submit the mind of man to the things of God, we end up with faith and a renewed mind. The mind makes a wonderful servant, but a terrible master.

Much of the opposition to revival comes from soul-driven Christians.[2] The apostle Paul calls them *carnal.* They have not learned how to be led by the Spirit. Anything that doesn't make sense to their rational mind is automatically in conflict with Scripture. This way of thinking is accepted all throughout the Church in Western civilization, which should explain why our God so often looks just like us.

Most of the goals of the modern Church can be accomplished without God. All we need is people, money, and a common objective. Determination can achieve great things. But success is not necessarily a sign that the goal was from God. Little exists in church life to ensure that we are being directed and empowered by the Holy Spirit. Returning to the ministry of Jesus is the only insurance we have of accomplishing such a goal.

FAITH FROM A RELATIONSHIP

The Holy Spirit lives in my spirit. That is the *place* of communion with God. As we learn to receive from our spirits, we learn how to be Spirit led.

"By faith, we understand" (Heb. 11:3). Faith is the foundation for all true intellectualism. When we *learn to learn* that way, we open ourselves up to grow in true faith because faith does not require understanding to function.

I'm sure that most of you have had this experience—you've been reading the Bible, and a verse *jumps out at you.* There is great excitement over this verse that seems to give so much life and encouragement to you. Yet, initially you couldn't teach or explain that verse if your life depended on it. What happened is this: Your spirit received the life-giving power of the Word from the Holy Spirit.[3] When we learn to receive from our spirit, our mind becomes the student and is therefore subject to the Holy Spirit. Through the process of revelation and experience, our mind eventually obtains under-standing. That is biblical learning—the spirit giving influence to the mind.

FAITH IS BOTH SUBSTANCE AND EVIDENCE

Now faith is the substance of things hoped for, the evidence of things not seen (Hebrews 11:1).

Faith is the mirror of the heart that reflects the realities of His world into ours. It is the substance of the unseen realm. This wonderful gift from God is the initial earthly manifestation of what exists in His Kingdom. It is a testimony of an invisible realm called the Kingdom of God. Through prayer we are able to pull that reality into this one—that is how faith functions.

If I go into the local pizza parlor and order a pizza, they will give me a number and a receipt. I am to place that number in a conspicuous place on the table. Someone may walk in off the street and come to my table and announce that they won't give me any pizza. I'll just point to the number and tell him, *When pizza number 52 is done, it's mine!* That number is the *substance* of the pizza hoped for. If that guy tells me that my number isn't any good, I'll point to my receipt. It verifies the value of the number. When my pizza is done, the waiter will walk around looking for my number. How does the product of heaven know where to land? He looks for the substance...the number. If a question comes up over the validity of my number, my receipt, which is contained in the Bible, verifies my right to both the number and the pizza.

Heaven is not moved simply by the needs of man. It's not that God doesn't care. It was out of His great compassion that He sent Jesus. When God is moved by human need, He seldom fixes the problem outright; instead, He provides Kingdom principles that when embraced correct the problems. If God was moved solely by human need then countries like India and Haiti would become the wealthiest nations in the world. It doesn't work like that. Heaven is moved by faith. Faith is the currency of heaven.

A FAITH SUMMARY

The following is a summary of the affects of faith found in Hebrews 11:2-30:

By faith —the elders obtained a testimony,

—we understand,

—Enoch was taken away having pleased God,

—Noah became an heir,

—Abraham obeyed, and dwelled in a land of promise,

—Sarah received strength to conceive, and judged God as faithful who gave her the promise.

By faith —Abraham received promises,

—Isaac blessed his son,

—Joseph gave a prophecy of what would follow his death.

By faith —Moses' parents preserved him, seeing he was special,

—Moses refused to be aligned with the whole Egyptian system and chose instead to be rejected by people.

By faith —the walls of Jericho fell,

—Rahab did not perish.

By faith —they subdued kingdoms,

—worked righteousness,

—obtained promises,

—shut the mouths of lions,

—quenched the violence of fire,

—escaped the edge of the sword,

—were made strong,

—were made valiant in battle,

—turned to flight the enemies.

THE SOURCE OF FAITH

"Faith comes by hearing..." (Rom. 10:17). It does not say that it comes from *having heard*. It is the listening heart, in the present tense, that is ready for heaven's deposit of faith.

The apostle Paul was driven by the command, "Go into all the world and preach the gospel..." (Mark 16:15). However, when he was ready to preach the gospel in Asia, God said no (see Acts 16). What God *had said* appeared to be in conflict with what God *was saying.*[4] Paul then prepared to go to Bithynia. Again, God said no. Following this Paul had a dream of a man calling out to him from Macedonia. This was recognized as the will of God, and they went.

Even though we may know the will of God from Scripture, we still need the Holy Spirit to help us with the interpretation, application, and empowerment to perform His will.

FEARFULNESS

The biblical command repeated most often is: *Do not fear.* Why? Fear attacks the foundation of our relationship with God...our faith. Fear is faith in the devil; it is also called unbelief. Jesus would ask His fearful disciples, *"Why are you so faithless?"* because fearfulness is the same as faithlessness. Fear and faith cannot coexist—they work against each other.

The devil is called Beelzebub, which means, *lord of the flies*. He and his hosts are attracted to decay. We once had a freezer in a building detached from our house. One Sunday we came home from church only to be hit with a wall of smell that is unfortunately hard to forget. I realized in an instant what had happened. Our freezer had died. I thought the stench I had smelled for days was because my boys forgot to take *all* of the trash to the dump. Instead, it was the ever-rotting meat and bear hide in the freezer.

From the front seat of my car, I looked at the window of the shop about 40 feet away. It was black with flies...a number that is still hard to imagine these many years later. The freezer was filled with all sorts of meat. Flies found a happy breeding ground in spoiled flesh and were multiplying in unbelievable numbers. Both the meat and the freezer were taken to the dump.

Issues such as bitterness, jealousy, and hatred qualify as the decay of the heart that invites the devil to come and give influence (see James 3:15-16)—yes, even to Christians. Remember Paul's admonition to the church of Ephesus, "Neither give place to the devil" (Eph. 4:27 KJV). Fear is also a decay of the heart. It attracts the demonic in the same way as bitterness and hatred. How did the flies know where my freezer was? Through the scent of decaying meat. Fear gives off a similar scent. Like faith, fear is *substance* in the spiritual realm. Satan has no power except through our agreement. Fear becomes our heart's response when we come into agreement with his intimidating suggestions.

REACT OR RESPOND

Many who have feared the excesses made by others in the name of faith have ironically embraced unbelief. Reaction to error usually produces error. Response to truth always wins out over those who react to error. Some people would have no belief system were it not for the error of others. Their thoughts and teachings are the antithesis of what others believe and practice. As a result, those who strive for balance become anemic. The word *balance* has come to mean *middle of the road*—of no threat to people or the devil, with little risk, and above all…the best way to keep our nice image intact.

The Church warns its members about the great sin of presumption. God warns us of the sin of unbelief. Jesus didn't say, *When I return will I find people who are excessive and presumptuous?* He was concerned about finding people with faith, the kind He displayed. While we often huddle in groups of like-minded people, those with faith blaze a trail that threatens all of our comfort zones. Faith offends the stationary.

People of great faith are hard to live with. Their reasoning is *otherworldly*. My grandfather, a pastor, sat under the ministry of several great men and women of God of the early 1900s. He used to tell me how not everyone liked Smith Wigglesworth. His faith made other people feel uncomfortable. We either become like them or we avoid them. We find their lifestyle either contagious or offensive with little neutral ground. Smith is well loved today…but it's only because he's dead. Israel loved their dead prophets too.

There's something amazing about unbelief—it is able to fulfill its own expectations. Unbelief is safe because it takes no risk and almost always gets what it expects. Then, after a person gets the answer for their unbelief, they can say, *I told you so.*

A SUPERIOR REALITY

My faith is not just an abiding faith; it is active. It is aggressive by nature. It has focus and purpose. Faith grabs hold of the reality of the Kingdom and forcefully and violently brings it into a collision with this natural one. An inferior kingdom cannot stand.

One of the more common things people tell me when I'm about to pray for their healing is, *I know God can do it.* So does the devil. At best, that is hope…not faith. Faith knows He will.

For one who has faith, there is nothing impossible. There are no impossibilities when there is faith…and there are no exceptions.

Sheri, for instance, came forward for prayer after a wonderful meeting just outside of Nashville, Tennessee. She had suffered with lupus for 24 years, the last four of which had gone into pulmonary hypertension. It had gotten so bad that she had to have an aluminum shunt placed into her heart. To this a pump was attached, which supplied the needed medication to keep her alive. Her doctor told her that without this medication she could live for only three minutes.

When she walked up to me, I actually felt a presence of something I had never felt in that measure before. It was faith. I actually stood back and stared at her for a few moments realizing that I was seeing something completely new for me. As she received prayer, she fell to the ground under the power of God. When she got up, I asked her how she was doing. She described a heat that was on her chest. (Heat often accompanies God's healing touch.) As she left, I told her, *Your faith got you this one!*

That was Saturday night. At 7 a.m. that following morning, the Lord spoke to her saying she didn't need the medication any more.[5] So she removed it. She showed up 14 hours later giving testimony of God's wonderful healing power.

She has since had the aluminum shunt removed—she doesn't need it anymore!

EARS TO HEAR

"So then faith comes by hearing, and hearing by the word of God" (Rom. 10:17). Notice it does not say, *faith comes from having heard.* The whole nature of faith implies a relationship with God that is current. The emphasis is on hearing…in the now! In Genesis, God told Abraham to sacrifice Isaac. As Abraham raised the knife to slay his son, God spoke again. This time He told him not to slay his son, as he had passed the test of being willing to do anything for God. It's a good thing that Abraham's only con-nection with God was not just over what *was said*, but was based upon what He *was saying!*

ANSWERS FOR LIFE'S IMPOSSIBILITIES

What this world needs is for the Church to return to a *show and tell* message of the Kingdom of God. They need an anchor that is greater than everything they can see. The world system has no answers to the world's increasing problems—every solution is only temporary.

Dale came to my office to confess sin. He lived quite some distance from my city, but because he had deceived us out of some money, he felt the need to come and confess in person. After I expressed both God's and my forgiveness, I asked him about his back. He had walked into my office with difficulty and was obviously in great pain. He lifted his shirt to show me two scars that ran on each side of the spine—the full length. He had broken his back some years earlier and had recently been in a car accident that fur-ther aggravated his injury. He then told me that God would probably like to heal him, but that he just got in His way. I told him he wasn't big enough. All I could picture was the greatness of God and the puny condition of man. He looked at me with a stunned look on his face. I went on to explain that God was really big and could pretty much do as He pleased. Although Dale didn't move into great faith, he did begin to doubt his doubt. That was all it took. I laid hands on his back and invited the Holy Spirit to come and give His gift of healing. I then commanded it to be healed. He bent over, placing his hands flat on the floor, saying, *I can't do that!* He proceeded to do it over and over again, each time declaring, *I can't do that!* He left pain-free with full movement and a heart full of praise. This was a man who could barely walk only moments before.

Faith is not the absence of doubt; it's the presence of belief. I may not always feel that I have great faith. But I can always obey, laying my hands on someone and praying. It's a mistake for me to ever examine my faith. I seldom find it. It's better for me to obey *quickly*. After it's over I can look back and see that my obedience came from faith.

THE CLUSTER BOMB EFFECT

When the corporate level of faith grows, it has what I call a *cluster bomb effect*, where innocent bystanders get touched by the miracle-working power of God.

Francis is a woman who had esophagus cancer. One Sunday morning during worship she leaned over to her husband and said, "I was just healed!" She felt the *fire* of God touch her hands and concluded that it represented God's healing touch. When she went to the doctor, she told him of her experience. His response was, "This kind does not go away." After examining her, he stated, "Not only do you not have cancer, you have a new esophagus!"

Corporate faith pulls on heaven in marvelous ways. His world becomes manifest all around us.

Sharon had suffered an accident many years ago in which she had destroyed a tendon that ran down her leg. It left her with restricted movement and partial numbness in her foot. I was giving an altar call for people to get right with God during one of our Saturday night meetings. She began to make all kinds of noise. I stopped the altar call and asked her what happened. She told us of the tingling feeling that ran down her leg and the subsequent restoration of all movement and feeling to her foot. A creative miracle happened without anyone praying.

The crowd at this particular meeting was quite small. But power is not in the number of people in attendance. It's in the number of people in agreement. Exponential power (see Deut. 32:30) is the product of the *unity of faith*.

In some meetings it's easy to mistake enthusiasm for faith. In that setting I emphasize the use of testimonies to stir peoples' hearts to believe for the impossible so He might invade.

MORE THAN BEING LOUD

Just as fear is a tangible element in the spirit world, so faith is tangible there. In the natural a loud voice may intimidate another man. But devils know the difference between the one who is truly bold and aggressive *because of* their faith, and the one who is simply covering his fears with aggressive behavior. Christians often use this tactic when casting out devils. Many of us have yelled threats, called on angels for help, promised to make it harder on the demons on Judgment Day, and other foolish things only to try and cover immaturity and fear. Real faith is anchored in the invisible realm and is connected to the authority given in the name of the Lord Jesus Christ.

The authority to cast out demons is found in rest. Rest is the climate that faith grows in (see Heb. 3:11–4:11). It comes out of the peace of God. And it is the Prince of Peace who will soon crush satan underneath our feet (see Rom. 16:20)! What is restful for us is violent to the powers of hell. That is the violent nature of faith.

This is not to be a soulish attempt at self-confidence or self-determination. Instead, it is a moving of the heart into a place of surrender...a place of rest. A surrendered heart is a heart of faith. And faith must be present to please God.

VIOLENCE AND FAITH

Until now the kingdom of heaven suffers violence, and the violent take it by force (Matthew 11:12).

Two blind men (see Matt. 9:27) who sat by the road called out to Jesus. People told them to be quiet. That only hardened their determination. They became more desperate and cried out all the louder. He called them forth and healed them, saying, "The kingdom has come near you." He attributed their miracle to their faith.

A woman (see Matt. 9:20-22) who had hemorrhaged for 12 years pressed through a crowd. When she was finally able to touch the garment of Jesus, she was healed. He attributed it to her faith.

The stories of this kind are many, all with similar endings—they were healed or delivered because of their faith. Faith may quietly press in, or it may cry out very loudly, but it is always violent in the spirit world. It grabs hold of an invisible reality and won't let go. Taking the Kingdom by faith is the violent act that is necessary to come into what God has made available.

FAITH EMPOWERS

An automobile may have several hundred horsepower. But the car will go nowhere until the clutch is released, connecting the power contained in the running motor and transferring that power to the wheels. So it is with faith. We have all the power of heaven behind us. But it is our faith that connects what is available to the circumstances at hand. Faith takes what is available and makes it actual.

It's not illegal to try to grow in faith. It's not wrong to seek for signs and the increase of miracles. Those are all within the rights of the believer. But learning how to pray is the task at hand. It is the only thing the disciples asked Jesus to teach them. And so we will examine Jesus' Model Prayer for insights on His view of prayer and the release of His dominion.

ENDNOTES

1.   I interpret religion as form without power.

2. The soul is the mind, will, and emotions.

3. "The letter kills, but the Spirit gives life" (2 Cor. 3:6).

4. God never contradicts His Word. But He is willing to contradict our understanding of His Word. The principle of the Great Commission (in Mark 16:15) was not nullified by the Acts 16 situation. Their application of the principle was God's target.

5. When I'm asked what to do regarding medication, I tell people to do what's in their heart. It wouldn't do them any good to do what I had faith for, or to keep them from doing what could be infected by my unbelief.

Chapter 5

PRAYING
HEAVEN DOWN

*If you want anything from God, you will have to pray into heaven. That is where
it all is. If you live in the earth realm and expect to receive from God,
you will never get anything.*[1]

*The Church has been negligent in one thing...
she has not prayed the power of God out of heaven.*[2]

THE FOURTH OF JULY CELEBRATION was the biggest event of the year
for our wonderful community. The parade, rodeo, and demolition derby
were just a few of the activities that took place during the festival that lasted
nearly a week.

Carnivals would also make their way to us, with rides, games, and special foods that are common at those events. One year a fortune-teller tried
to get in on the celebration. She pitched her tent with the others and laid
out her tarot cards, crystal ball, and other psychic paraphernalia. The devil
sent her to impart the gift of *demon possession* to the citizens of my city. The
folks in our church began to pray.

As I walked around her tent I began to declare, *You don't exist in heaven; you are not to exist here. This is my town. You are here illegally. I forbid you to establish roots here! God has declared that wherever the soles of my feet tread, God has given it to me. I bind you to the Word of God that declares that I have authority over you. Be gone!* I continued to walk around the tent like Israel walked around Jericho. Nothing fell in the natural.

I did not speak these things to the woman. I didn't even do it loud enough to draw her attention. She was not my enemy, nor was she my problem. The kingdom of darkness that empowered her was my target.

While she was doing her *sorcery* to a couple seated at her table, I stood on the other side of the tent wall, only a few feet away from the unsuspecting couple. I held my hands toward them, binding the power of hell that was intent on their destruction. I left when I felt I was done. (The hands that are surrendered to God can release the power of heaven into a situation. In the spirit world it is released like lightning. See Habakkuk 3:2-4.)

Even though the fair went on for many more days, she left town the next morning. The power that influenced her had been broken. She couldn't leave fast enough. It was as though the *hornets of Exodus* drove her out of town (see Exod. 23:28).

JESUS GAVE THE MODEL
TO FOLLOW

The Lord's Model Prayer provides the clearest instruction on how we bring the reality of His world into this one. The generals of revival speak to us from ages past, saying, *If you pray, He will come!*

Biblical prayer is always accompanied by radical obedience. God's response to prayer with obedience always releases the nature of heaven into our impaired circumstances.

Jesus' model reveals the only two real priorities of prayer: First, intimacy with God that is expressed in worship—*holy is Your name.* And second, to bring His Kingdom to earth, establishing His dominion over the needs of mankind—*Your Kingdom come.*

As we prepare to examine this prayer, let me highlight one more thought that will help us to better understand the purpose behind prayer. As disciples, we are both citizens and ambassadors of another world. This world is our assignment, but not our home. Our purpose is eternal. The resources needed to complete the assignment are unlimited. The only restrictions are those between our ears.

Let's examine the prayer from Matthew 6:9-13, starting with the first phrase:

"Our Father in heaven, hallowed be Your name."

The title *Father* is a title of honor and a call to relationship. What He did to make it possible for us to call Him "our Father" is all one needs to see to begin to become a true worshiper. *Hallowed* means respected or revered. This too is an expression of praise. In the Book of Revelation, which is actually entitled *The Revelation of Jesus Christ* (not the antichrist!) (see Rev. 1:1), it is obvious that praise and worship are the primary activities of heaven. And so it is to be for the believer here on earth. The more we live as citizens of heaven, the more heaven's activities infect our lifestyles.

Worship is our number one priority in ministry. Everything else we do is to be affected by our devotion to this call. He inhabits our praise. One translation puts it this way, *But You are holy, enthroned in the praises of Israel.* God responds with a literal invasion of heaven to earth through the worship of the believer (see Ps. 22:3).

One of my sons is a worship leader. He took a friend along with his guitar to the mall to worship God. They stopped after three hours of singing and dancing before the Lord. An unsuspecting man walked through the same area where they had been worshiping God. He stopped, reached into his pocket, pulled out illegal drugs, and dropped them onto the ground. No one said anything to him about his sin. How did it happen? Heaven touched earth, and there are no illegal drugs in heaven.

We see this on a regular basis as our ministry teams go to the streets of San Francisco. We work in compassion ministries as well as overt efforts to bring the supernatural power of God into broken lives. Healing and deliverance is the norm. Sometimes this happens in the worship environment.

As His presence becomes manifest upon a worshiping people, even unbelievers are brought into an encounter with God. My son and daughter have ministered to the Lord on troubled streets in San Francisco. As people walked by we saw many who manifested demons while others broke out in joyful laughter as they came into the presence of the Lord.

These things shouldn't surprise us. Look at how God responds to the praises of His people as mentioned in Isaiah 42:13: "The Lord shall go forth like a mighty man; He shall stir up His zeal like a man of war. He shall cry out, yes, shout aloud; He shall prevail against His enemies."

"Your kingdom come. Your will be done on earth as it is in heaven."

This is the primary focus for all prayer—if it exists in heaven, it is to be loosed on earth. It's the praying Christian who *looses* heaven's expression here. When the believer prays according to the revealed will of God, faith is specific and focused. Faith grabs hold of *that reality*. Enduring faith doesn't let go. Such an invasion causes the circumstances here to line up with heaven. The critics of this view sarcastically say, *So I guess we're supposed to pray for streets of gold*. No! But our streets should be known for the same purity and blessing as heaven—"Let our cattle bear without mishap and without loss, let there be no outcry in our streets!" (Ps. 144:14 NASB). Everything that happens here is supposed to be a shadow of heaven. In turn, every revelation that God gives us of heaven is to equip us with a prayer focus.

How much of heaven has God purposed to become manifest here on earth? No one knows for sure. But we do know through Church history that it's more than we have now. And we know through the Scripture that it's even more than has ever entered our minds (see I Cor. 2:9-10; Eph. 3:20-21).

The will of God is seen in the ruling presence of God, *for "where the Spirit of the Lord is, there is liberty"* (2 Cor. 3:17). Wherever the Spirit of the Lord is demonstrating the lordship of Jesus, liberty is the result. Yet another way to say it is that *when the King of kings manifests His dominion, the fruit of that dominion is LIBERTY.* That is the realm called *the Kingdom of God.* God, in response to our cries, brings His world into ours.

Conversely, if it is not free to exist in heaven, it must be bound here. Again, through prayer we are to exercise the authority given to us. "I will give you the keys of the kingdom of heaven; and whatever you bind on earth *shall have been* bound in heaven, and whatever you loose on earth *shall have been* loosed in heaven" (Matt. 16:19 NASB). Notice the phrase *"shall have been."* The implication is that we can only bind or loose here what has already been bound or loosed there. Once again, heaven is our model.

"Give us this day our daily bread."

Is anyone starving in heaven? Of course not. This request is a practical application of how His dominion should be seen here on earth—abundant supply. The abuses of a few in the area of prosperity does not excuse the abandonment of the promises of God to provide abundantly for His children. It is His good pleasure to do so. Because there is complete and perfect provision in heaven, there must be the same here. Heaven sets the standard for a Christian's material world—enough to satisfy the desires born of God and *enough "for every good work"* (2 Cor. 9:8). Our legal basis for provision comes from the heavenly model given to us in Christ Jesus: "And my God shall supply all your need according to His riches in glory by Christ Jesus" (Phil. 4:19). According to what? *His riches.* Where? *In glory.* Heaven's resources are to affect us here and now.

"And forgive us our debts, as we forgive our debtors."

Is there any unforgiveness in heaven? No! Heaven provides the model for our relationships here on earth. "And be kind to one another, tender-hearted, forgiving one another, even as God in Christ forgave you. Therefore be imitators of God as dear children" (Eph. 4:32–5:1). These verses make it quite clear that our model is Jesus Christ...the One ascended to the right hand of the Father...the One whose Kingdom we seek. Once again this prayer illustrates a practical way to pray for heaven's reality to bring an effect on planet earth.

"And do not lead us into temptation, but deliver us from the evil one."

There is no temptation or sin in heaven. Neither is there any presence of evil. Keeping separate from evil is a practical evidence of our coming under our King's rule. This prayer does not imply that God wants to tempt us. We know from James 1:13 that it is impossible for God to entice us to sin. This kind of praying is important because it requires us to face our need for grace. It helps us to align our heart with heaven—one of absolute dependency on God. God's Kingdom gives us the model for the issues of the heart. This prayer is actually a request for God not to promote us beyond what our character can handle. Sometimes, our anointing and gift are ready for increase of responsibility, but our character isn't. When promotion comes too soon the impact of our gift brings a notoriety that becomes the catalyst of our downfall.

The phrase *"deliver us from evil,"* as it is traditionally rendered, actually means, *deliver us from the evil one.* A heart modeled after heaven has great success in spiritual warfare. That's why it says, "Submit to God. Resist the devil and he will flee from you" (James 4:7).

Jesus was able to say, *Satan has nothing in Me.* The believer is to be completely free from all satanic influence and attachments. That is the cry voiced in this prayer.

"For Yours is the kingdom and the power and the glory forever. Amen."

The Kingdom of God is His possession, which is why He alone can give it to us (see Luke 12:32). When we declare that reality, we move into declarations of praise! All through the Scriptures we hear the declarations of praise similar to this one contained in His Model Prayer declaring that *all glory and power* belong to Him.

One of the most important teachings that I have ever received came from Derek Prince about 30 years ago. It was a wonderful message on praise. In it he suggested that if we only have ten minutes to pray we should spend about eight praising God. It's amazing how much we can pray for with the two minutes we have left. That illustration helped me to reinforce the priority of worship that I was learning from my pastor...my dad.

Once again, this prayer has two main objectives: (1) Minister to God out of an intimate personal relationship; and (2) bring the reality of His rulership (the Kingdom) to earth.

An outline of Matthew 6:9-13 gives us the Kingdom approach to prayer:

1. Praise and worship

2. Praying for heaven on earth

    a. Heaven's effect on material needs

    b. Heaven's effect on personal relationships

    c. Heaven's effect on our relationship to evil

3. Praise and worship

> ### "Seek first the kingdom of God and His righteousness, and all these things shall be added to you" (Matthew 6:33).

Granted, this verse is not in the prayer model that Jesus gave in verses 9-13. But it is in the context of His overall message of the Kingdom in the Sermon on the Mount. In it He establishes the priority that encompasses all Christian values and objectives. *Seek His Kingdom first!*

Understanding this prayer helps us to realize the intended goal of all prayer—that the lordship of Jesus would be seen in all circumstances of life. As the Kingdom of God confronts sin, forgiveness is given and change comes to the nature that had only known how to sin. When His rule collides with disease, people are healed. When it runs into the demonized, they are set free. The Kingdom message's nature provides salvation for the whole man—spirit, soul, and body. That is the gospel of Jesus Christ.

It has always seemed to me that the phrase "and all these things shall be added to you" meant that if my priorities were correct He'd make sure I got what I needed. After understanding the Model Prayer better, I'm not so sure that was His intent. He was saying that, if we seek His Kingdom first, we'll find His Kingdom comes fully equipped. It brings with it His answer to our material and relational needs, and our fight against evil.

SETTING UP A NEW FRANCHISE

Suppose I owned a very successful restaurant and you wanted to purchase the right to a franchise. By purchasing a franchise of my restaurant, you would be investing your money to obtain its name and all that goes with it—menus, unique design, management program, and the quality of training for workers. You would be required to follow the prescribed standards established at the flagship restaurant. The color scheme would be the same, as would be the type of furnishings and menu items. The policy manual for employees and the management style would be copied from the main campus. In essence, I would superimpose the main restaurant over each new location until all the locations looked alike.

When we pray for His Kingdom to come, we are asking Him to superimpose the rules, order, and benefits of His world over this one until this one looks like His. That's what happens when the sick are healed or the demonized are set free. His world collides with the world of darkness, and His world always wins. Our battle is always a battle for dominion—a conflict of kingdoms.

CREATED FOR RULERSHIP

We were created for intimacy. From that intimacy comes our commission to rule. Keep in mind that He views ruling differently than most of us. We rule through service. Many have made the mistake of thinking that Christians are to be the heads of all corporations, governments, and departments. As good as that may sound, it's actually a *fruit* of the true goal. Christlikeness—*excellence with humility*—is the real goal. Promotion comes from the Lord. If we spent more time developing a *Kingdom heart*, we'd have more people in key places of leadership.

Prayer is the simplest activity of the believer. Child to Father…lover to lover…conversation…sometimes spoken. Prayer is also one of the more complicated issues for us. Formulas don't work in this Kingdom relationship.

The honor that we have in being able to pray is beyond all comprehension. We are His representation on earth—ambassadors of His world. Our cries, all of them, touch His heart.

PRAYER, THE CHIEF ESSENTIAL

Intimacy is the main purpose of prayer. And it's through relationship that God entrusts to us the secrets of His heart, that we might express them in prayer. That's what He did with Simeon and Anna as He stirred their hearts to pray for the coming of the Messiah long before He was born (see Luke 2:25-38). Even the return of the Lord will be preceded by the declaration of the bride: "The Spirit and the bride say, 'Come'" (Rev. 22:17 NASB).

If these things were going to happen anyway, what would be the purpose of prayer? God has apparently given Himself a self-imposed restriction—to act in the affairs of man in response to prayer.

God has chosen to work through us. We are His delegated authority on planet earth, and prayer is the vehicle that gives occasion for His invasion. Those who don't pray allow darkness to continue ruling. The enemy's greatest efforts at deceiving the Church are centered on the purpose and effect of prayer.

REPRESENTING ANOTHER WORLD

"For our citizenship is in heaven, from which we also eagerly wait for the Savior, the Lord Jesus Christ" (Phil. 3:20). Paul spoke these words to the church at Philippi, a Roman city in the country of Macedonia. It enjoyed a Roman culture and the rule and protection of Roman government, all while living in Macedonia. Philippians understood very well Paul's charge about being citizens of another world. Paul spoke, not about going to heaven some day, but about living as citizens of heaven today...specifically *from heaven toward earth.*[3]

We have the privilege of representing heaven *in* this world, so that we might bring a manifestation of heaven *to* this world.

EMBASSY LIFESTYLE

As ambassadors, we live in one world while representing another. An embassy is the headquarters of an ambassador and his or her staff. It is actually considered a part of the nation it represents. So it is with the believer/

ambassador. The Bible promises: *"Every place that the sole of your foot will tread upon I have given you"* (Josh. 1:3).

Just as ambassadors of the United States have an income based on the standard of living of this nation regardless of what nation they serve in, so also ambassadors of the Kingdom of God live according to the economy of heaven, though they are still on earth. All of our King's resources are at our disposal to carry out His will. That is how Jesus could speak of the carefree life—*consider the sparrow* (see Matt. 6:26).

As an ambassador, the military of the Kingdom I represent is at my disposal to help me carry out the King's orders. If as a representative of a nation my life is threatened, all of my government's military might is prepared to do whatever necessary to protect and deliver me. So it is with heaven's angelic host. They *render service for those who would inherit salvation* (see Heb. 1:14).

This *ambassador mentality* is one I first picked up from Winkey Pratney. When he boards a plane, he reminds himself that while others may represent IBM and XEROX, he is there representing another world. I have followed his example and practiced this principle for close to 30 years. It has helped me to keep a clear perspective on the eternal purpose of every outing.

INTERCESSION OR COMPLAINT SESSION

One of the best reasons to not pray comes from watching some who do. Many who call themselves intercessors live depressed lives. I don't want to minimize the genuine effect of the burden of the Lord that comes upon us when we are praying effectively. It is real and necessary. But an unstable lifestyle has been promoted by those who claim to be intercessors, but have not learned to *release things* in prayer. The burden of the Lord takes us somewhere! I learned this the hard way.

I was taught early in life about the importance of prayer. My youth pastor, Chip Worthington, kept me on track with his teachings, as well as the many books he gave me to read.

I spent a great deal of time praying, and I carried that priority into early adulthood. But my focus in prayer often turned to my own spirituality...or should I say, the lack of it. I would rise early and pray late into the night. God honored the sacrifice I made, but my personal victories did not coincide with my elaborate prayer times. Instead, they seemed more linked to my acts of faith. Because my focus was still on me, there was little victory I actually could trace back to my prayers.

Travailing in prayer is not always a sign of true intercession. Many are not yet able to distinguish the difference between *the burden of their own unbelief and the burden of the Lord.* I now pray until I come into a place of faith for that situation.[4] When that happens, my perspective on the problem changes. I begin to see it from heaven's view. My role also changes. Instead of asking God to invade my circumstances, I begin to command the *mountains to be removed* in His name. It is from this place of faith (or rest) that I discover my role as the pray-er.

Pray until there's a breakthrough. Then exercise the authority given to execute His will over the circumstances at hand.

THE PERFECT STORM

Jesus was sleeping in the middle of a life-threatening storm. The disciples woke Him because they were afraid of dying. He exercised authority and released peace over the storm. It was the peace of heaven that enabled Him to sleep. And it was that same peace that subdued the storm. *You only have authority over the storm you can sleep in.*

If I am filled with anxiety in any given situation, it becomes hard for me to release peace—because I can only give what I have. Authority functions from heaven's peace.

Even after the disciples got their answer to prayer, a stilled storm, Jesus asked them about their unbelief. For most of us an answer to prayer is the reward for our great faith. In this case they got their answer but were said to be *small in faith*. He expected them to exercise the authority He had given them to quiet the seas themselves. Instead, they asked Him to do it. We often pray in the place of risky obedience.

IN ADDITION

Correct theology alone has not enabled us to complete the assignment Jesus gave us 2,000 years ago. The Great Commission hasn't been accomplished through our vast resources of money or personnel. To see the kinds of breakthroughs that Jesus had we must embrace what Jesus embraced: the Holy Spirit. This special gift is the subject of the next chapter. There we will see how the realm of the Spirit is the realm of His Kingdom.

ENDNOTES

1. Albert Hibbert, Smith Wigglesworth: *The Secret of His Power*, (Tulsa, OK: Harrison House, Inc. 1982), 47.

2. John G. Lake, *His Sermons, His Boldness of Faith*, (Ft. Worth, TX: Kenneth Copeland Publications, 1994), 313.

3. More on this later in the book.

4. Sometimes the situation is bigger than we can handle in one prayer session. Obviously, we are to continue sowing into that prayer need. But it does no one any good to do it under the "cloud" of our unbelief.

Chapter 6

THE KINGDOM
AND THE SPIRIT

Assuredly, I say to you, among those born of women there has not risen one greater than John the Baptist; but he who is least in the kingdom of heaven is greater than he (Matthew 11:11).

JOHN THE BAPTIST was the *high-water mark* for all under the Old Covenant. But the least in this new era were born to surpass Him through their relationship with the Holy Spirit.

The members of our church and the students of the Bethel School of Supernatural Ministry often embrace this privilege.

One student named Jason was ordering a meal inside a fast-food restaurant. Not content to share Christ only with those behind the counter, he began to speak past the cashier to three men in a car at the drive-up window! After receiving his food, Jason left noticing they had parked to eat. He renewed his conversation with them and saw that the man in the back seat had a broken leg. So he climbed into the car with them and invited the Holy Spirit to come...and He came. The man began to curse. He had no understanding about the holy *fire* on his leg. They all jumped out of the car, and the injured man removed his brace and stomped his leg. He was completely healed! The three were so moved by God's goodness that they opened the trunk of their car, which was filled with illegal drugs. They dumped the narcotics onto the pavement, dancing on them and destroying them! Jason brought the three men to the Alabaster House, our 24-hour prayer house, and led them to Christ. The kindness of God led them to repentance. This is the normal Christian life.

The Holy Spirit is the agent of heaven who makes these kinds of encounters possible. Not only that, He makes them the norm for those who would follow.

THE NEW STANDARD

Jesus sets a standard with this statement—*John the Baptist was the greatest of all Old Testament prophets.* He didn't do any miracles that we know of. His ministry was gloriously necessary, but not one we'd normally compare to some of the more spectacular prophets like Elijah or Daniel. Yet the One who knows all says he's the greatest. There is a truth contained in this passage that helps us to see our potential from heaven's perspective. It is such a wonderful truth that all of hell has made a priority of trying to keep us from its simplicity.

With that in mind, a more startling bit of news comes next—*He who is least in the Kingdom of Heaven is greater than he.* He wasn't saying that the people in heaven were greater than John. There's no purpose for such a statement. He was talking about a realm of living that was soon to become available to every believer. John prophesied of Christ's coming, and went so far as to confess his personal need of it.

> *He who is coming after me is mightier than I. . .He will baptize you with the Holy Spirit and fire* (Matthew 3:11).

Jesus came to be baptized...John tried to prevent Him, saying, "I need to be baptized by You..." (Matthew 3:14).

John confessed his personal need of Jesus' baptism. Not one of the Old Testament prophets, not even John, had what was about to be offered to the *least of all saints*. It is the baptism in the Holy Spirit that became God's goal for mankind.

The baptism in the Holy Spirit makes a lifestyle available to us to which not even John had access. Jesus whetted our appetite for this lifestyle through His example, then He gave us the promise of its availability.

AN ULTIMATE GOAL

There is a difference between immediate and ultimate goals. Success with an immediate goal makes it possible to reach an ultimate goal. But failure in the immediate prevents us from reaching our final goal.

Bowlers know this. Each lane not only has ten pins at the far end, it also has markers on the lane itself. A good bowler knows how his or her ball rotates as it is released from a hand. Bowlers will aim at a marker in the lane as an initial target. Yet they receive no points for hitting it. Points are only given when the ultimate target is hit—the pins at the end of the lane.

Likewise, salvation was not the ultimate goal of Christ's coming. It was the immediate target...the marker in the lane. Without accomplishing redemption, there was no hope for the ultimate goal—which was to fill each born-again person with the Holy Spirit. God's desire is for the believer to overflow with Himself, that we might *"be filled with all the fullness of God."* (Eph. 3:19). The resulting fullness of the Spirit was different than anyone had ever before experienced. For that reason, the greatest of all Old Testament prophets could confess: "I need to be baptized by You," meaning, "I need Your baptism...the one I was assigned to announce!"

The baptism in the Holy Spirit makes a lifestyle available to us that not even John had access to. Consider this: We could travel off of this planet in any direction at the speed of light, 186,000 miles a second, for billions of years, and never begin to exhaust what we already know to exist. All of that rests in the palm of His hand. And it's *this* God who wants to fill us with His fullness. That ought to make a difference!

AN OLD TESTAMENT PICTURE

Israel left Egypt when the blood of a lamb was shed and applied to the doorposts of their homes. In the same way, we were set free from sin when the blood of Jesus was applied to our lives. The Israelites soon arrived at the Red Sea. Going through that body of water is referred to as *the baptism of Moses* (see I Cor. 10:2). Similarly, we face the waters of baptism after our conversion. When the Jews finally entered the Promised Land, they entered through a river—another baptism.

This baptism was not a departure from sin. Such was illustrated when they left Egypt. This new baptism would take them into a different way of life. For example: they fought wars on the wilderness side of the river and won. But once they crossed the Jordan River, wars would be fought differently. Now they would march around a city in silence for days, finally raising up a shout and watching the walls fall (see Josh. 6). Later, they would experience the challenge of sending a choir into battle first (see 2 Chron. 20:21). And then there was the time God intentionally sent over 30,000 soldiers back home so He could fight a war with 300 torch-wielding trumpet blowers.

He makes the Promised Land possible, and we pay the price to live there. He'll give us His baptism of fire if we'll give Him something worth burning.

This baptism in the Holy Spirit is the fulfillment of the Old Testament picture of entering the Promised Land. Suppose the children of Israel had chosen to cross the Jordan but became content to live on the banks of the river. They would have missed the purpose for crossing the river in the first place. There were nations to destroy and cities to possess. Contentment short of God's purposes would mean having to learn to live with the enemy. That is what it is like when a believer is baptized in the Holy Spirit but never goes beyond speaking in tongues. When we become satisfied apart from God's ultimate purpose of dominion, we learn to tolerate the devil in some area of our life. As glorious as the gift of tongues is, it is an entrance point to a lifestyle of power. That power has been given to us that we might dispossess the strongholds of hell and take possession for the glory of God.

THE KINGDOM COMES IN POWER

I tell you the truth, some who are standing here will not taste death before they see the kingdom of God come with power (Mark 9:1 NIV).

Each time this is mentioned in the Gospels, it is followed by the incident on the Mount of Transfiguration. Some have considered this to mean that what happened to Jesus on that mountain was the Kingdom coming in power. However, if that were so, then why would Jesus need to emphasize that some there would not die until they saw the Kingdom come with power? Jesus was speaking of a much grander event. He spoke of the coming *promise of the Father*...the event that would clothe us with power from on high—the baptism in the Holy Spirit.

Somehow, I always thought that the baptism in the Holy Spirit was a one-time event; I received my prayer language and that was it. The Bible teaches differently. In Acts 2 we find 120 being baptized in the Spirit in the upper room. Yet, in Acts 4 we find some of the same crowd being *refilled*. Some have put it this way: one baptism, many fillings. Why? We leak.

Over the past decade, revival fire has been carried by Rodney Howard-Browne, and it has found a home in Toronto and Pensacola. People travel from around the world to these different *watering holes* because of an instinctive hunger for more. In some places they stand in lines, waiting for prayer.

In others they crowd around the front of a sanctuary waiting for someone to be used by God to lay hands on them and bless them. Critics have called this activity a "bless me club." Personally, because of my passion for the blessing of God, I have little problem with those who return time after time to receive another blessing. I *need* His blessing. The problem is not in receiving more of the blessing of God. It's the refusal to give it away to others once we have received it ourselves.

The time spent receiving prayer has become a tool God has used to fill His people with more of Himself. It has become a method for this wonderful time of impartation.

THE KINGDOM, THE SPIRIT REALM

But if I cast out demons by the Spirit of God, surely the kingdom of God has come upon you (Matthew 12:28).

Look at this phrase, "by the Spirit of God...the kingdom." The Holy Spirit encompasses the Kingdom. While they are not the same, they are inseparable. The Holy Spirit enforces the lordship of Jesus, marking His territory with liberty (see 2 Cor. 3:17). The *King's domain* becomes evident through His work.

The second part of this verse reveals the nature of ministry. Anointed ministry causes the collision of two worlds—the world of darkness with the world of light. This passage shows the nature of deliverance. When the Kingdom of God comes upon someone, powers of darkness are forced to leave.

When a light is turned on, darkness doesn't resist. There is no debate. It doesn't stay dark for a few minutes until light finally wins. On the contrary, light is so superior to darkness that its triumph is immediate.

The Holy Spirit has no battle wounds. He bears no teeth marks from the demonic realm fighting for preeminence. Jesus is Lord, period. Those who learn how to work with the Holy Spirit actually cause the reality of His world (His dominion) to collide with the powers of darkness that have influence over a person or situation. The greater the manifestation of His presence, the quicker the victory.

THE VALUE OF HIS PRESENCE

By far the greatest gift ever received by us is the Holy Spirit Himself. Those who discover the value of His presence enter realms of intimacy with God never previously considered possible. Out of this vital relationship arises a ministry of power that formerly was only a dream. The incomprehensible becomes possible because He is with us.

I will be with you is a promise made by God to all His servants. Moses heard it when he faced the challenge of delivering Israel from Egypt (see Exod. 3:12). Joshua received this promise when he led Israel into the Promised Land (see Josh. 1:9). When Gideon received the call of God to be a deliverer for Israel, God sealed it with the same promise (see Judg. 6:16). In the New Testament, this promise came to all believers through the Great Commission (see Matt. 28:19). It comes when God has required something of us that is humanly impossible. It's important to see this. It's the presence of God that links us to the impossible. I tell our folks, *He is in me for my sake, but He's upon me for yours.* His presence makes anything possible!

God doesn't have to try to do supernatural things. He is supernatural. He would have to try to not be. If He is invited to a situation, we should expect nothing but supernatural invasion.

HIS PRESENCE IN OUR SHADOWS

Part of the privilege of ministry is learning how to release the Holy Spirit in a location. When I pastored in Weaverville, California, our church offices were downtown, located directly across from one bar and right next to another. This downtown area was the commercial center for the entire county—a perfect place for a church office!

It's not good when Christians try to do business only with other Christians. We are salt and light. We shine best in dark places! I love business and business people and have genuine interest in their success. Before entering a store, I often pray for the Holy Spirit to be released through me. If I need something on one side of the store, I'll enter on the opposite end in order to walk through the entire store. Many opportunities for ministry have developed as I've learned how to release His presence in the marketplace.

People laid the sick in the streets hoping that Peter's shadow would fall on them and they'd be healed (see Acts 5:15). Nevertheless, it wasn't Peter's shadow that brought healing. There is no substance to a shadow. Peter was *overshadowed* by the Holy Spirit, and it was that presence that brought the miracles. The anointing is an expression of the person of the Holy Spirit. He is tangible. There were times in Jesus' ministry when everyone who touched Christ's clothing was healed or delivered (see Mark 6:56). The anointing is substance. It is the actual presence of the Holy Spirit, and He can be released into our surroundings.

RESURRECTION IN AFRICA

Pastor Surprise is an apostolic leader working with Rolland and Heidi Baker of Iris Ministries in Mozambique. During an evangelistic crusade in which he was preaching, a 9-year-old girl died, which threatened to end the series of meetings. The entire village was stricken with grief. The next day Pastor Surprise went to visit the family, and the child's body was still in the hut where she had died the night before. As he was praying for the family, he happened to be holding the little girl's hand. He was not praying for her to rise from the dead, yet after a few minutes the young girl squeezed his hand. She was raised up about 12 hours after her death because someone was full of the Holy Spirit. He overflowed with the resurrection power of Jesus that filled him while he was trying to comfort the family!

A bottle is not completely full until it overflows. So it is with the Holy Spirit. Fullness is measured in overflow. When we get introspective, we restrict the flow of the Holy Spirit. We become like the Dead Sea; water flows in, but nothing flows out, and nothing can live in its stagnant waters. The Holy Spirit is released through faith and compassion, and faith and compassion are never self-centered.

FOLLOWING YOUR LEADER OFF THE MAP

History provides us with a lesson from a great military leader. Alexander the Great led his armies in victory after victory, and his desire for ever greater conquest finally brought him to the foot of the Himalayas. He wanted to go beyond these intimidating mountains. Yet, no one knew what was on the other side. Senior officers were troubled by his new vision. Why? They had gone to the edge of their map—there was no map for the new territory that Alexander wanted to possess. These officers had a decision to make: would they be willing to follow their leader off the map, or would they be content to live within its boundaries? They chose to follow Alexander.

Following the leading of the Holy Spirit can present us with the same dilemma. While he never contradicts His Word, He is very comfortable contradicting our understanding of it. Those who feel safe because of their intellectual grasp of Scriptures enjoy a false sense of security. None of us has a full grasp of Scripture, but we all have the Holy Spirit. He is our common denominator who will always lead us into truth. But to follow Him, we must be willing to follow off the map—to go beyond what we know. To do so successfully we must recognize His presence above all.

There is a great difference between the way Jesus did ministry and the way it typically is done today. He was completely dependent on what the Father was doing and saying. He illustrated this lifestyle after His Holy

Spirit baptism. He followed the Holy Spirit's leading, even when it seemed unreasonable, which it often did.

The Church has all too often lived according to an intellectual approach to the Scriptures, void of the Holy Spirit's influence. We have programs and institutions that in no way require the Spirit of God to survive. In fact, much of what we call ministry has no safeguard in it to ensure that He is even present. When our focus is not the presence of God, we end up doing the best we can for God. Our intentions may be noble, but they are powerless in effect.

When Jason began sharing the gospel through the drive-through window of a fast-food restaurant, his actions were *off the map.* Yet they bore fruit for the King.

COMPASSION AND THE RELEASE OF HIS PRESENCE

Jesus often healed after being moved with compassion. I frequently detect the leading of the Holy Spirit by recognizing His affection for someone else. Being drawn to a person through compassion usually means that there will be some realm of supernatural ministry to them—either with a word of encouragement, or a miracle of healing or deliverance. Loving people is Christ's agenda, and surrender of my own agenda makes me available for His.

The Holy Spirit is the invading agent of heaven. In the next chapter we'll see why His presence terrifies all the powers of hell.

Chapter 7

THE ANOINTING AND THE ANTICHRIST SPIRIT

———————— ⁘ ————————

Christ is not Jesus' last name. The word Christ means "Anointed One" or "Messiah." It is a title that points to an experience. It was not sufficient that Jesus be sent from heaven to earth with a title. He had to receive the anointing in an experience to accomplish what the Father desired.

THE WORD *anointing* means "to smear." The Holy Spirit is the oil of God that was smeared all over Jesus at His water baptism (see Luke 3:21-22). The name Jesus Christ implies that Jesus is the One smeared with the Holy Spirit.

But there is another spirit that works to ambush the Church in every age. This power was identified by the apostle John when he said, "Even now many antichrists have come" (I John 2:18). The nature of the antichrist spirit is found in its name: *anti*, "against"; *Christ*, "Anointed One."

Jesus lived His earthly life with human limitations. He laid His divinity aside (see Phil. 2:5-7) as He sought to fulfill the assignment given to Him by the Father: to live life as a man without sin, and then die in the place of mankind for sin. This would be essential in His plan to redeem mankind. The sacrifice that could atone for sin had to be a lamb (powerless), and had to be spotless (without sin).

The anointing Jesus received was the equipment necessary, given by the Father, to make it possible for Him to live beyond human limitations. For He was not only to redeem man, He was to reveal the Father. In doing so, He was to unveil the Father's realm called heaven. That would include doing supernatural things. The anointing is what linked Jesus, the man, to the divine, enabling Him to destroy the works of the devil. These miraculous ways helped to set something in motion that mankind could inherit once we were redeemed. Heaven—that supernatural realm—was to become mankind's daily bread.

Its "present tense" existence was explained in Jesus' statement, "The Kingdom of Heaven is at hand." That means heaven is not just our eternal destination, but also is a present reality, and it's within arm's reach.

QUALIFYING ANOINTING

To fulfill His mission, Jesus needed the Holy Spirit; and that mission, with all its objectives, was to finish the Father's work (see John 4:34). If the Son of God was that reliant upon the anointing, His behavior should clarify our need for the Holy Spirit's presence upon us to do what the Father has assigned. We'll discuss more about this matter in a later chapter. For now, it's vital to understand that we must be clothed with the Holy Spirit for supernatural ministry. In the Old Testament, it was the anointing that qualified a priest for ministry (see Exod. 40:15). According to Jesus' example, New Testament ministry is the same—anointing brings supernatural results.

This anointing is what enabled Jesus to *do only what He saw His Father do*, and to *say only what He heard His Father say*. It was the Holy Spirit that revealed the Father to Jesus.

It would seem that with all the significance attached to the name "Jesus," anyone desiring to undermine His work of redemption might be referred to as "Anti-Jesus," not "Anti-Christ." Even religious cults recognize and value Jesus, the man. At the very least, cults consider Him to be a teacher or a prophet and possibly "a" son of God. This horrendous error provides us with an understanding of why *antichrist* was the name given to this spirit of opposition. The spirits of hell are at war against the anointing, for without the anointing mankind is no threat to their dominion.

Jesus' concern for mankind was applauded. His humility was revered, but it was the anointing that released the supernatural. And it was the supernatural invasion of God Himself that was rejected by the religious leaders. This anointing is actually the person of the Holy Spirit upon someone to equip them for supernatural endeavors. So revered is the Holy Spirit in the Godhead, that Jesus said, "Anyone who speaks a word against the Son of Man, it will be forgiven him; but whoever speaks against the Holy Spirit, it will not be forgiven him, either in this age or in the age to come" (Matt. 12:32).

EMPOWERED MINISTRY

It was Holy Spirit-empowered ministry that caused people to forsake all to follow Jesus. They were drawn by the supernatural in word and in deed. His words cut deep into the heart of mankind, while His deeds revealed the heart of the Father. The anointing of the Holy Spirit forever changed the lives of the humble. But it was also Holy Spirit empowered ministry that caused great offense to the proud and brought about His crucifixion. The same sun that melts the ice hardens the clay. Similarly, a work of God can bring about two completely different responses, depending on the condition of the hearts of people.

God is our Father, and we inherit His genetic code. Every believer has written into his or her spiritual DNA the desire for the supernatural. It is our predetermined sense of destiny. This God-born passion dissipates when it has been taught and reasoned away, when it's not been exercised, or when it's been buried under disappointment (see Prov. 13:12).

The spirit of the antichrist is at work today, attempting to influence believers to reject everything that has to do with the Holy Spirit's anointing. This rejection takes on many religious forms, but basically it boils down to this: we reject what we can't control. That spirit has worked to reduce the gospel to a mere intellectual message, rather than a supernatural God encounter. It tolerates the mention of power if it's in the past. Occasionally, it considers that power is appropriate for people in faraway places. But, never does this spirit expect the anointing of God's power to be available in the here and now. The spirit of control works against one of God's favorite elements in man: faith. Trust is misplaced as it becomes anchored in man's ability to reason.

It is the antichrist spirit that has given rise to religious spirits. A religious spirit is a demonic presence that works to get us to substitute being led by our intellect instead of the Spirit of God. Being led by the Holy Spirit is an ongoing God encounter. Religion idolizes concepts and avoids personal experience. It works to get us to worship past accomplishments at the expense of any present activity of God in our life. That spirit often feeds on the residue of past revivals. Its favorite tactic is to cast in stone an ideology learned from previous moves of the Holy Spirit. For example: it values tears and despises laughter. Sounds like idolatry, doesn't it? Anything that will take the place of dependence upon the Holy Spirit and His empowering work can be traced back to this spirit of opposition.

THE REALM BEYOND REASON

Following the anointing (the Holy Spirit) is very similar to Israel following the cloud of the Lord's presence in the wilderness. The Israelites had no control over Him. He led, and the people followed. Wherever He went, supernatural activities took place. If they departed from the cloud, the miracles that sustained them would be gone. Can you imagine what would have happened if our fear-oriented theologians had been there? They would have created new doctrines explaining why the supernatural ministry that brought them out of Egypt was no longer necessary to bring them into the Promised Land. After all, now they had the tablets of stone. Then, as today, the real issue is the priority we place upon His presence. When that's intact, the supernatural abounds, but without it we have to make up new doctrines for why we're OK as we are.

In New Testament terms, being a people focused on His presence means that we are willing to live beyond reason. Not impulsively or foolishly, for these are poor imitations for real faith. The realm beyond reason is the world of obedience to God. Obedience is the expression of faith, and faith is our claim ticket to the God realm. Strangely, this focus on His presence causes us to become like wind, which is also the nature of the Holy Spirit (see John 3:8). His nature is powerful and righteous, but His ways cannot be controlled. He is unpredictable.

As church leaders, this hits us at our weakest point. For most churches, very little of what we do is dependent upon the Holy Spirit. If He were not to show up, most churches would never miss Him. Billy Graham is credited with saying, "Ninety-five percent of today's church activities would continue if the Holy Spirit were removed from us. In the early Church, ninety-five percent of all her activities would have stopped if the Holy Spirit were removed." I agree. We plan our services, and call it diligence. We plan our year, and call it vision. I'll never forget the Sunday that the Lord informed me that it wasn't my service, and I couldn't do as I pleased. (Planning is biblical. But our diligence and vision must never include usurping the authority of the Holy Spirit. The lordship of Jesus is seen in our willingness to follow the Holy Spirit's leading. He wants His Church back!) But how can we follow Him if we don't recognize His presence?

The more pronounced His presence, the more unique the manifestations of our God encounters become. Although the manifestations we experience while encountering Him are important, it's God Himself we long for.

HE KNEW HE'D MAKE US UNCOMFORTABLE

It's difficult for most to follow the leading of the Holy Spirit because we are so limited in our experience with Him. Most know Him only as the One who convicts of sin or gives comfort when we're troubled. The bottom line is we are not accustomed to recognizing the Holy Spirit's actual presence. We are acquainted with a small list of acceptable manifestations that sometimes happen when He shows up, such as tears, or perhaps a sense of peace when our favorite song is sung. But few recognize just Him alone. To make matters worse, many unknowingly reject Him because He either shows up in a way that they are unaccustomed to, or He failed to come as He has in the past. (Consider the arrogance of automatically rejecting everything that we don't understand, or have never recognized the Scriptures to say. It implies that if God hasn't done it or shown it to us first, He wouldn't possibly do it to someone else.)

While few would admit it, the attitude of the Church in recent days has been, "If I'm uncomfortable with something, it must not be from God." This attitude has given rise to many self-appointed watchdogs who poison the Church with their own fears. Hunger for God then gives way to fear of deception. What do I trust most: my ability to be deceived or His ability to keep me? And why do you think He gave us the Comforter? He knew His ways would make us uncomfortable first.

HOW DO YOU PICTURE "BALANCE?"

Fear of deception has opened the door for a tragic movement among believers. It states that because we have the Bible we are emotionally unbalanced and in danger of deception if we seek for an actual "felt" experience with God. Such fears cause believers to become polarized—fear separates and alienates. This is the picture that many paint: in one corner we have balanced looking people who value the Bible as the Word of God, and in the other we have emotionally unbalanced people who seek after esoteric, spiritual experiences with God. Is that an accurate biblical picture? Jesus made a frightening statement regarding those who hold to Bible study vs. experience, "You search the Scriptures, for in them you think you have eternal life; and these are they which testify of Me" (John 5:39).

If our study of the Bible doesn't lead us to a deeper relationship (an encounter) with God, then it simply is adding to our tendency toward spiritual pride. We increase our knowledge of the Bible to feel good about our standing with God, and to better equip us to argue with those who disagree with us. Any group wanting to defend a doctrine is prone to this temptation without a God encounter. Consider the potential implications of this thought: those who first appear to be under control may, in fact, be out of control—His control! And many of those accused of being members of an emotional "bless me club" can give actual testimony of God's touch that has changed their lives forever. They become the more biblical picture of balance.

Jesus did not say, "My sheep will know My book." It is His *voice* that we are to know. Why the distinction? Because anyone can know the Bible as a book—the devil himself knows and quotes the Scriptures. But only those whose lives are dependent on the person of the Holy Spirit will consistently recognize His voice. This is not to say that the Bible has little or no importance. Quite the opposite is true. The Bible is the Word of God, and His voice will *always* be confirmed by Scripture. That voice gives impact to what is in print. We must diligently study the Scriptures, remembering that it is in knowing Him that the greatest truths of Scripture will be understood.

In this present outpouring, God is dealing with this specific need. We are being saturated with His presence in order that we might learn His voice. As He opens up His Word to us, we become more dependent upon Him. People are once again turning their focus on the greatest gift ever received—God Himself. While the anointing is often referred to as an *it*, it is more accurately *Him*.

As the Holy Spirit receives back the reins over His people, He works to reset a more biblical parameter for the Christian life. This frightening change is for the better. We can and must know the God of the Bible by experience. The apostle Paul put it this way, "To know the love of Christ which passes knowledge; that you may be filled with all the fullness of God" (Eph. 3:19). Do you *know* what *surpasses knowledge*? It is His promise. Consider the result: "That you may be filled with all the fullness of God." What a reward! Jesus puts it this way, "And he who loves Me will be loved by My Father, and I will love him and manifest Myself to him" (John 14:21).

THE GOAL OF THE ANTICHRIST SPIRIT

The antichrist spirit has a goal for the Church—embrace Jesus apart from the anointing. Without the anointing, He becomes a safe religious figure who is sure not to challenge or offend us. Paul described this deceptive possibility as "having a form of godliness but denying its power. And from such people turn away!" (2 Tim. 3:5).

How can people who love God be offended by the anointing of the Holy Spirit?

1. He moves like wind—apart from our control (see John 3:8).

2. His thoughts are very different from ours. The Scripture states that our logic and His are not just different, they are opposed to each other (see Rom. 8:7; Isa. 55:8-9). Let's be honest…they are worlds apart!

3. He refuses to be restricted by our understanding of His Word.

Every time we follow the leading of the Holy Spirit, we fly in the face of the antichrist spirit. While the foolishness of some who claim to be Spirit-led have made this adventure more difficult, we nevertheless are assured of succeeding if it is truly our passionate desire. He'll not give a stone to anyone who asks for bread.

ANOINTED TO TEACH

If the Holy Spirit is the power behind the teaching gift, what should it look like? What kind of model did Jesus provide for this particular ministry? In the next chapter we will examine the role of the teacher and his or her partnership with the Holy Spirit.

Chapter 8

TEACHING INTO
AN ENCOUNTER

*Any revelation from God's Word that does not lead us to an encounter with
God only serves to make us more religious. The Church cannot afford
"form without power," for it creates Christians without purpose.*

JESUS, THE MODEL TEACHER, never separated teaching from doing. He is
the pattern for this gift. God's revealed Word, declared through the lips of
an anointed teacher, ought to lead to demonstrations of power.

Nicodemus said to Jesus, "Rabbi, we know that You are a teacher come
from God; for no one can do these signs that You do unless God is with
him" (John 3:2). It was understood that God's kind of teachers don't just
talk—they do. And the *doing* that is referred to in John's Gospel is the per-
forming of signs and wonders.

Jesus established the ultimate example in ministry by combining the
proclamation of the gospel with signs and wonders. Matthew records this
phenomenon this way: "And Jesus went about all Galilee, teaching in their
synagogues, preaching the gospel of the kingdom, and healing all kinds
of sickness and all kinds of disease among the people" (Matt. 4:23). And

again, "Then Jesus went about all the cities and villages, teaching in their synagogues, preaching the gospel of the kingdom, and healing every sickness and every disease among the people" (Matt. 9:35).

He then commanded His disciples to minister with the same focus—the 12 were sent out with, "And as you go, preach, saying, 'The kingdom of heaven is at hand.' Heal the sick, cleanse the lepers, raise the dead, cast out demons. Freely you have received, freely give" (Matt. 10:7-8). He commissioned the seventy by saying, "And heal the sick there, and say to them, 'The kingdom of God has come near to you'" (Luke 10:9).

The Gospel of John records how this combination of words and supernatural works takes place, "The words that I speak to you I do not speak on My own authority; but the Father who dwells in Me does the works" (John 14:10). It's apparent that we speak the *word*, and the Father *does the works*—miracles!

As men and women of God who teach, we must require from ourselves *doing, with power!* And this *doing* must include a breaking into the impossible—through signs and wonders.

Bible teachers are to instruct in order to explain *what they just did*, or *are about to do*. Those who restrict themselves to mere words limit their gift, and may unintentionally lead believers to pride by increasing knowledge without an increased awareness of God's presence and power. It's in the trenches of Christlike ministry that we learn to become totally dependent upon God. Moving in the impossible through relying on God short-circuits the development of pride.

PERSONAL EXPERIENCE

In 1987 I attended one of John Wimber's conferences on signs and wonders in Anaheim, California. I left discouraged. Everything that was taught, including many of the illustrations, I had taught. The reason for my discouragement was the fact that they had fruit for what they believed. All I had was good doctrine.

There comes a time when simply knowing truth will no longer satisfy. If it does not change circumstances for good, what good is it? A serious reexamination of personal priorities began. It was apparent that I could no longer expect good things to happen simply because I believed they could... or even should. There was a risk factor I had failed to enter into—Wimber called it *faith*. Teaching MUST be followed with *action* that makes room for God to move.[1]

Things changed immediately. We prayed for people and saw miracles. It was glorious, but it didn't take long to discover that there were many also that weren't healed. Discouragement set in, and the pursuit with risks decreased.

On my first trip to Toronto in March of 1995, I promised God if He would touch me again, I would never back off. I would never again *change the subject*. My promise meant that I would make the outpouring of the Holy Spirit—with the full manifestations of His gifts—the sole purpose for my existence. And I would never stray from that call—no matter what! He touched me, and I have pursued without fail.

RESISTING THE INFLUENCE OF OUR OWN CULTURE

Our culture has castrated the role of the teacher. It is possible to attend college, get a business degree, and never have received any teaching by someone who ever owned a business. We value concepts and ideas above experience with results. I wish that pertained only to secular schools—but the culture, which values ideas above experience, has shaped most of our Bible schools, seminaries, and denominations. Many present-day movements have made a virtue out of *staying the course* without a God experience.

To make matters worse, those who speak subjectively of an experience are often considered suspect, and even dangerous. But God cannot be known apart from experience. Randy Clark, the man God used to initiate the fires of revival in Toronto in 1994, puts it this way: "Anyone who doesn't have an experience with God, doesn't know God." He is a person, not a philosophy or a concept. It's time for those who have encountered God to stop pandering to fear by watering down their story. We must whet the appetites of the people of God for more of the supernatural. Testimony has the ability to stir up that kind of hunger.

KINGDOM REALIZED

As our ministry teams travel around the world, we have come to expect certain things. Healing, deliverance, and conversions are the fruits of our labors. While healing is seldom the subject we teach on, it is one of the most common results. As we proclaim the message of the Kingdom of God, people get well. The Father seems to say *Amen!* to His own message by confirming the Word with power (see Mark 16:20). Peter knew this when he prayed for boldness in his preaching, expecting that God would respond by "extending His hand to heal, and signs and wonders would be done in the name of His holy servant Jesus" (Acts 4:29-30 NASB). God has promised to back up our message with power if our message is the gospel of His Kingdom.

POWER VS. PRIDE

The problems we face today are not new. The apostle Paul had great concern for the Corinthian church, for they were being enticed by a gospel without power.

> *I do not write these things to shame you, but as my beloved children I warn you. For though you might have ten thousand instructors in Christ,*

yet you do not have many fathers; for in Christ Jesus I have begotten you through the gospel. Therefore I urge you, imitate me.

For this reason I have sent Timothy to you, who is my beloved and faithful son in the Lord, who will remind you of my ways in Christ, as I teach everywhere in every church.

Now some are puffed up, as though I were not coming to you. But I will come to you shortly, if the Lord wills, and I will know, not the word of those who are puffed up, but the power.

For the kingdom of God is not in word but in power (I Corinthians 4:14-20).

Paul begins by contrasting teachers and fathers. The teachers mentioned were different from the kind that Jesus intended the Church to have. Paul concedes they may be believers, saying these instructors are "in Christ." But note that he later refers to them as being "puffed up."

In this post-denominational era we are seeing an unprecedented movement of believers gathering around spiritual fathers (not gender specific). In times past we gathered around certain truths, which led to the formation of denominations. The strength of such a gathering is the obvious agreement in doctrine, and usually practice. The weakness is it doesn't allow for much variety or change. At the turn of the twentieth century, the people who received the baptism in the Holy Spirit with speaking in tongues were no longer welcome in many of these churches, because most denominations held statements of faith cast in stone.

But now this gravitational pull toward fathers is happening even within denominations. Such a gathering of believers allows for differences in non-essential doctrines without causing division. Many consider this movement to be a restoration of the apostolic order of God.

Paul's second concern is about the puffed-up condition of his spiritual children. He makes his point by contrasting faithfulness and pride, which he defined as *being puffed up*. Paul was very concerned that they would be tricked by the theories of good public speakers. Personal charisma is often valued more by the church than either anointing or truth. People of little character can often have positions of leadership in the church if they have personality. Paul found this particularly troubling. He had worked hard to bring the Corinthians into the faith. He had chosen not to *wow* them with what he knew. In fact, he led them to an encounter with the God of all power who would become the anchor of their faith (see I Cor. 2:1-5). But now the sermonizers had come on the scene. Paul's answer was to send them someone just like himself—Timothy. They needed a reminder of what their spiritual father was like. This would help them to recalibrate their value system to imitate people of substance, who are also people of power!

Paul makes a stunning statement clarifying the right choice. He said, "The kingdom of God is not in word but in power" (I Cor. 4:20). The original language puts it like this—"The Kingdom of God is not in *logos* but in *dunamis*." Apparently they had a lot of teachers who were good at speaking many words, but displayed little power. They did not follow the pattern that Jesus set for them. *Dunamis* is "the power of God displayed and imparted in a Holy Spirit outpouring." That is the Kingdom!

Two chapters earlier Paul lays out his ministry priority as *bringing the people of Corinth to a place of faith in God's power* (*dunamis*) (see I Cor. 2:5). Here he addresses how they were set up to fail if things didn't change. Any time the people of God become preoccupied with concepts and ideologies instead of a Christlike expression of life and power, they are set up to fail, no matter how good those ideas are. Christianity is not a philosophy; it is a relationship. It's the *God encounter* that makes the concepts powerful. We must require this of ourselves.[2] How? We must seek until we find (see Luke 11:10).

FATHERS WITH POWER VS.
TEACHERS WITH ONLY WORDS

	Fathers	Teachers (not after Jesus' example)
Lifestyle	Imitate fathers	Gather around ideas (divisive)
Attitude	Humility	Pride (puffed up)
Ministry	Power	Many words
Focus	The Kingdom	Teachings

GOD IS BIGGER THAN HIS BOOK

You are wrong because you know neither the Scriptures nor God's power (Matthew 22:29 AMP).

In this passage Jesus rebukes the Pharisees for their ignorance of the Scriptures *and* God's power. His rebuke comes within the context of *marriage* and *resurrection*, but is aimed at the ignorance infecting every area of their lives.

What was the cause? They didn't allow the Scriptures to lead them to God. They didn't understand...not really understand. The word *know* in this passage speaks of "personal experience." They tried to learn apart from such an experience. They were the champions of those who spent time studying God's Word. But their study didn't lead them to an encounter with God. It became an end in itself.

The Holy Spirit is the *dunamis* of heaven. An encounter with God is often a power encounter. Such encounters vary from person to person according to God's design. And it's the lack of power encounters that lead to a misunderstanding of God and His Word. Experience is necessary in building a true knowledge of the Word. Many fear experience because it *might* lead away from Scripture. The mistakes of some have led many to fear experiential pursuit.[3] But it is illegitimate to allow fear to keep us from pursuing a deeper experience with God! Embracing such fear causes a failure to the other extreme, which is culturally more acceptable, but significantly worse in eternity.

God does as He pleases. While true to His Word, He does not avoid acting outside of our understanding of it. For example, He's a loving God who hates Esau (see Mal. 1:2-3). He's the One who has been respectfully called a gentleman, yet who knocked Saul off of his donkey (see Acts 9:4) and picked Ezekiel up off the ground by his hair (see Ezek. 8:3). He's the bright and morning star (see Rev. 22:16) who veils Himself in darkness (see Ps. 97:2). He hates divorce (see Mal. 2:16), yet is Himself divorced (see Jer. 3:8). This list of seemingly conflicting ideas could go on for much longer than any of us could bear. Yet this uncomfortable tension is designed to keep us honest and truly dependent on the Holy Spirit for understanding who God is and what He is saying to us through His book. God is so foreign to our natural ways of thinking that we only truly see what He shows us—and we can only understand Him through relationship.

The Bible is the absolute Word of God. It reveals God; the obvious, the unexplainable, the mysterious, and sometimes offensive. It all reveals the greatness of our God. Yet it does not contain Him. God is bigger than His book.

Revival is mixed with many such dilemmas—God doing what we've never seen Him do before—all to confirm that He is whom He said in His Word. We have the inward conflict of following the One who changes not, yet promises to do a new thing in us. This becomes even more confusing when we try to fit that new thing into the mold made by our past successful experiences.

Not everyone handles this challenge well. Many hide their need to be in control behind the banner of "staying anchored to the Word of God." By rejecting those who differ from them, they successfully protect themselves from discomfort, and from the change for which they've been praying.

ROAD MAP OR TOUR GUIDE

The acceptable way of studying Scripture puts the power of revelation into the hands of anyone who can afford a *Strong's Concordance* and a few other miscellaneous study materials. Put in the time, and you can learn some wonderful things. I don't want to discount a regular disciplined approach to study, or certainly those wonderful study tools, as it is God who gives us the hunger to learn. But in reality, the Bible is a closed book. Anything I can get from the Word without God will not change my life. It is closed to insure that I remain dependent on the Holy Spirit. It is that desperate approach to Scripture that delights the heart of God. *"It is the glory of God to conceal a matter, but the glory of kings is to search out a matter"* (Prov. 25:2). He loves to feed those who are truly hungry.

Bible study is often promoted so that we will get formulas for living. Certainly there are principles that can be laid in an A to Z fashion. But too often that approach makes the Bible a *road map*. When I treat the Bible as a road map, I live as though I can find my way through my own understanding of His book. I believe this perspective of Scriptures actually describes living under the Law, not living under grace. Living under the Law is the tendency to desire a list of preset boundaries, and not a relationship. While both the Law and grace have commandments, grace comes with an inbuilt ability to obey what was commanded. Under grace I don't get a road map...I get a tour guide—the Holy Spirit. He directs, reveals, and empowers me to *be* and *do* what the Word says.

There are many concepts that the Church has held dear desiring to maintain a devotion to Scripture. But some of these actually work against the true value of God's Word. For example: many who reject the move of the Holy Spirit have claimed that the Church doesn't need signs and wonders because we have the Bible. Yet, that teaching contradicts the very Word it tries to exalt. If you assign ten new believers the task of studying the Bible to find God's heart for this generation, not one of them would conclude that spiritual gifts are not for today. You have to be taught that stuff! The doctrine stating *signs and wonders are no longer needed because we have the Bible* was created by people who hadn't seen God's power and needed an explanation to justify their own powerless churches.

Revelation that doesn't lead to a God encounter only serves to make me more religious. Unless Scripture leads me to Him, I only become better equipped to debate with those who disagree with my way of thinking.

"Knowledge puffs up..." (1 Cor. 8:1). Notice Paul didn't say *unbiblical* knowledge, or *carnal* knowledge. Knowledge, including that which comes from Scripture, has the potential to make me proud. So how can I protect myself from the pride that comes from knowledge, even when it's from the Bible? I must be certain that it takes me to Jesus!

The pride that comes from mere Bible knowledge is divisive. It creates an appetite for one's own opinion. "He who speaks from himself seeks his own glory; but He who seeks the glory of the One who sent Him is true, and no unrighteousness is in Him" (John 7:18). Those trained without a revelation that takes us to Him are trained to speak from themselves, for their own glory. This drive for knowledge without an encounter with God wars against true righteousness.

Not only does righteousness suffer, so does our faith. "How can you believe, who receive honor from one another, and do not seek the honor that comes from the only God?" (John 5:44). That desire for glory from man somehow displaces faith. The heart that fears God only—the one that seeks first His Kingdom and desires God to receive all honor and glory—that heart is the heart where faith is born.

The mission of heaven is to infiltrate earth with its realities. All teaching is to lead us to that end, for training in the Kingdom is not without purpose. We are being trained to run the family business. This is the discovery of the next chapter.

ENDNOTES

1. Making room for God doesn't mean He can't move without our approval. It simply means He delights in our invitation.

2. It would be easy at this point to think that I'm only addressing power as that which changes a physical condition in the body, or some problem in nature. It certainly includes these kinds of situations. We must remember that the love of God is the greatest power in the universe. It can transform a life as nothing else. We just cannot use this fact as an excuse to avoid the obvious needs of the sick and tormented all around us. We must be moved with the love of God to the point that we seek His face until we are *clothed with power from on high!*

3. Being deceived didn't start with believing something unscriptural. It started with a heart full of compromise. For no one is ever deceived except they first compromise (see I Tim. 1:18-19).

Chapter 9

THE WORKS OF
THE FATHER

Don't believe Me unless I carry out My Father's work (John 10:37 NLT).

*For this purpose the Son of God was manifested, that He might
destroy the works of the devil* (1 John 3:8).

FOR HUNDREDS OF YEARS the prophets spoke of the Messiah's coming.
They gave over 300 specific details describing Him. Jesus fulfilled them all!
The angels also gave witness to His divinity when they came with a mes-
sage for the shepherds: "For there is born to you this day...a Savior, who
is Christ the Lord" (Luke 2:11). Nature itself testified to the arrival of the
Messiah with the star that led the wise men (see Matt. 2:1). Yet with this
one statement, "Unless I do the works of the Father, do not believe Me"
(John 10:37), Jesus put the credibility of all these *messengers* on the line.
Their ministries would have been in vain without one more ingredient to
confirm who He really was. That ingredient was *miracles*.

Jesus gave people the right to disbelieve it all if there was no demonstration of power upon His ministry. I hunger for the day when the Church will

make the same statement to the world. *If we're not doing the miracles that Jesus did, you don't have to believe us.*

EVEN AS A CHILD, JESUS KNEW HIS ASSIGNMENT

The verses mentioned at the beginning of this chapter deal with two subjects—*doing the works of the Father,* and *destroying the works of the devil.* These two things are inseparable. They help to clarify the purpose for Christ's coming. He was driven by one overwhelming passion: pleasing His heavenly Father.

The unveiling of His priorities started long before His ministry began. He was only 12. The realization that Jesus was missing came after Mary and Joseph had traveled several days from Jerusalem. They returned to search for their 12-year-old son.

We can only imagine what might have been going through their minds during their three days of separation. He was their miracle child…the promised One. Did they lose Him through carelessness? Was their job of raising Him finished? Had they failed?

They finally found Him in the temple discussing the Scriptures with adults! There's no doubt they were very happy and relieved. But realistically, they were probably also a bit upset. To make matters worse, Jesus didn't seem the least bit concerned about their anxiety. In fact, He seems a little surprised that they didn't know where He'd be. We hear no apology; we find no explanations, just a statement about His priorities: "Did you not know that I must be about My Father's business?" (Luke 2:49). Here the revelation of purpose began. Even at a young age, He seemed to show no concern for the probability that He caused an offense in His attempt to obey His heavenly Father. Think about it: any fear of what people might think of Him was nonexistent at the age of 12. He refused to allow the possibility of misunderstanding and conflict to keep Him from the Father's purposes.

The first and only recorded words of Jesus in His youth were all about His purpose. Obeying the Father was His whole ambition. Those words were sufficient. Later in adulthood He confessed that obeying the Father remained His priority. It actually brought Him *nourishment*—"My food is to do the will of Him who sent Me" (John 4:34).

A RISKY BUSINESS

Did Jesus forget to tell Mary and Joseph where He would be? Or, did He do what He did realizing that it would affect others the way it did? I believe the latter: He was willing to risk being misunderstood. The Father's business often requires such a risk. Remember, He had not yet gained the credibility He had later in life; as yet there hadn't been any moving sermons, healings, water turned into wine, raising of the dead, or casting out of demons. He was simply a 12-year-old with priorities that were different from everyone else.

Eighteen years later, at the beginning of His ministry, Jesus is found teaching His disciples what He tried to teach Mom and Dad: the priority of the Father's business. Statements such as, "I can of Myself do nothing" (John 5:19), "I do not seek My own will but the will of the Father" (John 5:30), and "I always do those things that please Him" (John 8:29), all testify of His utter dependence on the Father, and His one passion to please Him alone.

A JEWISH CUSTOM

It was the custom of a Jewish father to take his son to the city square when he had reached manhood. He would announce to the city that his son was equal to himself in all business affairs, meaning when they dealt with the son they were dealing with the father. In doing so, he would anounce to the whole city, "This is my much loved son, in whom I am well pleased."

At the water baptism of Jesus, when He was 30 years old, the prophet John the Baptist pronounced that Jesus was "the Lamb of God who takes away the sin of the world" (John 1:29). The Holy Spirit came upon Him, clothing Him in power, enabling Him to carry out His purpose. Then the Father spoke from heaven, "This is My much loved Son, in whom I am well pleased" (Matt. 3:17).

In that moment, both the Father and the Holy Spirit affirmed the primary purpose embraced by the Son of God was to reveal and carry on the Father's business. Jesus declared the specifics of that role in His first sermon: "The Spirit of the Lord is upon Me, because He has anointed Me to preach the gospel to the poor; He has sent Me to heal the brokenhearted, to proclaim liberty to the captives and recovery of sight to the blind, to set at liberty those who are oppressed; to proclaim the acceptable year of the Lord" (Luke 4:18-19). Jesus' life illustrated what that pronouncement was all about—bringing salvation to the spirit, soul, and body of man, thus destroying the works of the devil (see I John 3:8). This was an expression of a Kingdom that is ever increasing and continually unfolding (see Isa. 9:7).

THE MISSING LINK

The secret of His ministry is seen in His statements: "The Son can do nothing of Himself, but what He sees the Father do...the Son also does in like manner" (John 5:19), and "I speak to the world those things which I heard from Him" (John 8:26). His obedience put the bounty of heaven on a collision course with the desperate condition of mankind on earth. It was His dependence on the Father that brought forth the reality of the Kingdom into this world. It's what enabled Him to say, "The Kingdom of Heaven is at hand!"

Jesus displayed the Father's heart. All His actions were earthly expressions of His Father in heaven. The Book of Hebrews calls Jesus the exact representation of His Father's nature (see Heb. 1:3 NASB). Jesus said, "If you've seen Me you've seen My Father" (see John 14:9). The life of Jesus is a revelation of the Father and His business. It is the heart of that business to give life to mankind (see John 10:10), and destroy all the works of the destroyer (see I John 3:8).

Jesus continues to point the way to the Father. It has now become our job, by means of the Holy Spirit, to discover and display the Father's heart: giving life, and destroying the works of the devil.

ABOUT THE FATHER

Most of the Pharisees spent their lives serving God without ever discovering the Father's heart! Jesus offended these religious leaders most because He demonstrated what the Father wanted. While the Pharisees thought God was concerned about the Sabbath, Jesus worked to help the ones the Sabbath was created for. These leaders were accustomed to the miracles of the Scriptures remaining in the past. But Jesus broke into their comfort zones by ushering the supernatural into their cities. With every miracle He showed the entire religious community the *Father's business.* For them to adapt, everything would have to be overhauled. It was easier to brand Him a liar, declaring His works to be of the devil and eventually killing this One who reminded them of what had to be changed.

Understanding that the Father's business has to do with signs and wonders is no guarantee that we will truly fulfill God's purpose for our lives. It is much more than doing miracles, or even getting conversions. The supernatural interventions of God were done to reveal the extravagant heart of the Father for people. Every miracle is a revelation of His nature. And in that revelation is embedded an invitation for relationship.

The Pharisees' error is a very easy one for us to repeat. They had no understanding of the Father's heart. And much Christian activity exists that has no relationship to that supreme value. In this present hour we need much more than to learn how to identify our personal gifts or discover ways to be more successful in ministry. We need the Father Himself. We need His presence—His alone. The gospel is the story of the Father wooing the hearts of mankind through His love. All the other stuff we do overflows from that discovery.

THE JOY AND POWER OF ALL MINISTRY

We can travel the globe and preach the gospel, but without a personal revelation of the Father's heart we're carrying around secondhand news—a story without a relationship. It might save people because it is truth, but there is so much more. Jesus, at the age of 12, taught us that lesson: we must be about our Father's business. And the Father's business flows from His heart. When we discover this, we find both the joy and the power of all ministry—we will find His presence.

The renewal that started in Toronto in 1994 has since spread around the world. It has both the Father's heart and the presence of the Holy Spirit as major focal points. In a sense, they are the same, or should we say they are *different sides of the same coin*. His presence always reveals His heart.

In the same way that Jesus revealed the Father's heart to Israel, so the Church is to *be a manifestation* of the Father's heart to the world. We are the carriers of His presence, doers of His will. Giving what we have received releases Him into situations previously held in the grip of darkness. That is our responsibility and privilege.

EVERYONE IS A CANDIDATE

Everyone in our community is a target for God's love. There are no exceptions. The testimonies of radical transformation come from every sector of society and every conceivable place—school, work, home, the malls and stores, and even the parks, streets, and homeless camps. Why? There is a growing company of people who have the Father's business in mind. They consciously take Him wherever they go.

When Jason, one of our students, was asked to come to the courthouse to serve on a jury, he went with the Father's business in mind. As he walked from the parking lot to the jurors' building, he saw two young men who looked troubled. The Lord began to talk to Jason about the older of the two. As Jason ministered to him, he addressed specific problems he had with his father. He realized that Jason couldn't have known this information without God showing it to him.[1] Therefore, the young man received Christ.

Jason finally made it to the jury selection building. During a long break he began to pray for God's leading. He noticed a man on the other side of the room seated in a wheelchair. It was the electric type that moved by a toggle switch on the armrest. After a brief conversation with him, he found out he, too, was a believer. Jason encouraged him with God's promises and then asked him to look at him. They held hands and prayed. Strength came into the man's body as the pain left. Jason told him to stand.

The gentleman asked, "What if I fall?"

To which Jason responded, "What if you don't?"

It was enough to bring the courage needed, and in plain sight of all the others in the room, this man stood to his feet, waving his arms about. It had been years since he was able to stand. Jason turned to the crowd and declared, "God is here to heal!"

Before the day was over, two others had received the healing touch of Jesus. That is the Father's business, and every believer has a part to play in carrying out this privileged assignment.

REDISCOVERING PURPOSE

We have the privilege of rediscovering God's original purpose for His people. We who long for this must pursue Him with reckless abandon. The following is a list of things to do to help make your pursuit practical:

1. Prayer—be specific, and be relentless in praying for miracles in every part of your life. Bring the promises of God before Him in your pursuit. He hasn't forgotten what He has said and does not need our reminder. However, He enjoys seeing us standing on His covenant when we pray. Prayer with fasting is to be an integral part of this quest, as He revealed this to be an important way to get a breakthrough (see Mark 9:29). I even pray for specific diseases for which I'm not seeing a breakthrough.

2. Study—the most obvious place for study is in the Scriptures. Spend months reading and rereading the Gospels. Look for models to follow. Look especially at all references to the Kingdom, and ask God to open the mysteries of the Kingdom to you (see Matt. 13:11). The right to understand such things belongs to the saints who are willing to obey. Another great place for study is to find all references to "reformation," those periods of transformation that Israel went through under different leaders (revivalist)[2] in the Scriptures. Good places to begin are with David, Hezekiah, Ezra, and Nehemiah. Their lives become prophetic messages for us. All true study is driven by hunger. If you don't have questions, you won't recognize the answers.

3. Read—find the books that have been written by the generals of God's army—those who truly do the stuff. There is a great storehouse of information for those willing to pursue. Don't forget the leaders of the great healing revival of the 1950s. *God's Generals*, by Roberts Liardon, is a great place to start.

If you're afraid of reading about those who later fell into sin and deception (some of these people ended in disaster), stay away from Gideon, Samson, Solomon's Proverbs, and the Song of Solomon. The author of those books also ended in tragedy. We must learn to eat the meat and throw out the bones.

4. Laying on of hands—pursue the men and women of God who carry an anointing in their lives for the miraculous. Such an anointing can be transferred to others through the laying on of hands (see 2 Tim. 1:6). Occasionally there are ministry times when such an individual is willing to pray for those who desire an increase of anointing. I have traveled extensively in pursuit of MORE.

5. Associations—King David was known for killing Goliath in his youth. Yet there are at least four other giants killed in Scripture—all killed by the men who followed David, the giant killer. If you want to kill giants, hang around a giant killer. It rubs off.

Grace is that which enables us to live in the Kingdom, and in part it is received by how we respond to the gifts of Christ: apostles, prophets, evangelists, pastors, and teachers. We actually receive the *grace to function* from these gifts. If you hang around an evangelist, you will think evangelistically. The same happens when we associate with those who regularly experience signs and wonders in their lives.

6. Obedience—no matter how much preparation is done to increase the anointing for miracles in a life, it never comes to fruition without radical obedience. I must look for the sick and tormented in order to pray for them. And if they are healed, I give God the praise. If they aren't, I still give God the praise, and *continue* to look for people to pray for. I learned a long time ago that more people are healed when you pray for more people! Until we act on what we know, our knowledge is nothing more than a theory. Real learning comes through doing.

POWER IS NOT OPTIONAL

Jesus said, "As the Father sent me, I also send you." He did the works of the Father, and then passed the baton on to us. In the next chapter we'll discover which is more important, character or power. The answer may surprise you.

ENDNOTES

1. That is what we call a *word of knowledge*. A believer knows something about another that they could not know apart from God revealing it to them. God often uses this gift to let that person know that He cares. It stirs their faith to be able to receive the miracle that is to follow.

2. One likely will not find the word *reformation* in Scripture. Find passages that deal with the lives of these individuals and look for descriptions of spiritual renewal or reformation in Israel's history.

Chapter 10

POWERLESSNESS: UNNECESSARY AND UNBALANCED

I'm not impressed with anyone's life unless they have integrity. But I'm not happy with their life until they are dangerous.[1] As much as I have the ability to do so, I'll not let those around me get away with just being nice people!

MANY BELIEVERS HAVE MADE IT their primary goal in life to be well-respected citizens of their communities. Good character enables us to be solid contributors to society, but most of what is recognized as a Christian lifestyle can be accomplished by people who don't even know God. Every believer should be highly respected *and more*. It's the *and more* part that we're often lacking.

While character must be at the heart of our ministries, power revolutionizes the world around us. Until the Church returns to Jesus' model for true revolutionaries, we will continue to be recognized by the world merely as nice people—while it is overcome with disease and torment, on its way to hell.

Some Christians actually have considered it to be more noble to choose *character* over *power*. But we must not separate the two. It is an unjustifiable, illegitimate choice. Together they bring us to the only real issue—obedience.

Once, while teaching a group of students about the importance of signs and wonders in the ministry of the gospel, a young man spoke up, saying, "I'll pursue signs and wonders when I know I have more of the character of Christ in me." As good as that may sound, it comes from a religious mind-set, not a heart abandoned to the gospel of Jesus Christ. In response to this student's comment, I opened to the Gospel of Matthew and read the Lord's charge: "Go therefore and make disciples of all nations...teaching them to observe all things that I have commanded you" (Matt. 28:19). I then asked him, "Who gave you the right to determine when you are ready to obey His command?"

IMPRESSING GOD

Does anyone think that God is impressed with us when we tell Him, "I'll obey You when I have more character"? Character is shaped through obedience. Jesus commanded His disciples to go, and in going they were to teach all that they had been taught. And part of what they were taught was specific training on how to live and operate in the miraculous (see Matt. 10:1;5-8;17; Luke 9:1-6). They were commanded to "heal the sick, cleanse the lepers, raise the dead, and cast out demons" (Matt. 10:8). And now they were responsible to teach this requirement as the lifestyle for all who were to become followers of Jesus Christ. In this way, *His* standard could remain *the* standard—the norm for all who call upon the name of the Lord for salvation.

Many consider themselves unworthy of God using them in the miraculous, and therefore never pursue that realm. Isn't it ironic that Christians will disobey God by not diligently seeking after spiritual gifts—they won't lay hands on the sick or seek to deliver the demonized—because they realize their need for more character? In none of the commissions of Jesus to His disciples did He deal specifically with character.

Is it possible the reason there are so few miracles in North America is because too many before us thought they had to become better Christians before God could use them? Yes! That single lie has kept us in perpetual immaturity because it protects us from the power encounter that transforms us. The result is we have converts trained and over trained until they have no life, vision, or ingenuity left. This next generation of converts must be handled differently. We must help them by giving them their identity as world changers, provide them with a model for character, passion, and power, and open up opportunities to serve.

Mario Murillo puts it this way, "When he picks up a Bible, his focus will not be on emotional healing or self-esteem. He'll ask you where the trigger is and how you fire it. When he reads the Word, he will want to apply it to the taking over of neighborhoods for God!"[2]

THE ANOINTING, A KEY TO PERSONAL GROWTH

Christlike character can never be fully developed without serving under the anointing. Anointed ministry brings us into contact with the power needed for personal transformation.

Both the Old and New Testaments are filled with great examples of *empowering for supernatural endeavors*. An important principle is found in the story of King Saul. God spoke, saying that the Spirit of the Lord would come upon him and turn him into another man (see I Sam. 10:6). The anointing transforms the vessel it flows through. Two key phrases follow this promise:

1. "God gave him another heart."

2. "Then the Spirit of the Lord came upon him, and He prophesied among them [the prophets]" (I Sam. 10:9-10).

Saul was given an opportunity to become all that Israel needed him to be (a king with a new heart), and learn to do all he needed to do (hear from God and declare His words—prophesy).

I have a dear friend who had a huge character flaw that spiritually crippled him and his family for a season. Yet during this time, he still had a very strong prophetic anointing. He was not the first person to think that his successful ministry was a sign of God's approval of his private life. Many have fallen victim to that error through the years. When I confronted him about his secret sin, he wept with deep sorrow.

Because of his place of influence in the church, I felt a keen responsibility to bring him under discipline.³ No organization is any stronger than its ability to discipline its members, whether it is a business, government, church, or family. Part of my restriction for him was to keep him from giving prophetic words for a season. He accepted this direction as necessary.

After several months of this restriction, I became increasingly troubled over the statement regarding King Saul and its relationship to my friend. I realized if I didn't allow him to minister (under the anointing) I'd be limiting his exposure to the very thing that would seal and establish his victory. When I released him to prophesy again, there was a new purity and power in his voice. It was his personal encounter with the anointing in ministry that "turned him into another man."⁴

COUNTERFEITS EXIST

A counterfeit hundred dollar bill does not nullify the value of the real thing. Likewise, a counterfeit, abused, or abandoned gift does not invalidate our need for the Holy Spirit's power to live as Jesus did.

Pennies are not counterfeited because they're not worth the effort. In the same way, the devil only works to copy or distort those things in the Christian life that have the greatest potential effect. When I see others who have pursued great things in God but have failed, I get motivated to *pick up where they left off*. It tells me there's a treasure in that field, and I'm ready to look for it with reckless abandon.[5] The abuses of one person never justify the neglect of another.

Many of those who are embarrassed over the abuses of power, and the subsequent blemishes upon the Church, are seldom offended over the absence of signs and wonders. The eyes of the critics quickly move to the ones who tried and failed, overlooking the countless millions who confess salvation in Jesus, but never *pursue the gifts* as commanded. But the eyes of Jesus quickly look to see if there is faith on the earth—"When I return will I find faith on earth?" (see Luke 18:8). For every charlatan there are a thousand good citizens who accomplish little or nothing for the Kingdom.

THE PURPOSE OF THE POWER

Many believe His power exists only to help us overcome sin. This understanding stops very short of the Father's intent for us to *become witnesses* of another world. Doesn't it seem strange that our whole Christian life should be focused on overcoming something that has already been defeated? Sin and its nature have been yanked out by the roots. Many constantly call out to God for more power to live in victory. What more can He do for us? If His death wasn't enough, what else is there? That battle has already been fought and won! Is it possible that the process of constantly bringing up issues dealt with by the blood is what has actually given life to those issues?

Many in the Church are camped on the wrong side of the Cross. The apostle Paul spoke to this issue when he said, "Likewise you also, reckon yourselves to be dead indeed to sin, but alive to God in Christ Jesus our Lord" (Rom. 6:11). The word *reckon* points to our need to change our minds. I don't need power to overcome something if I'm dead to it. But I do need power for boldness (see Acts 4:28-29) for the miraculous and for the impossible.

Part of our problem is this: we are accustomed only to doing things for God that are not impossible. If God doesn't show up and help us, we can still succeed. There must be an aspect of the Christian life that is impossible without divine intervention. That keeps us on the edge and puts us in contact with our true calling.

Make no mistake, character is a supreme issue with God. But His approach is much different than ours. His righteousness/character is not built into us by our own efforts. It is developed when we quit striving and learn to abandon ourselves completely to His will.

CLOTHED WITH POWER

So great was the discipless' need for power to become witnesses that they were not to leave Jerusalem until they had it. That word *power* (*dunamis*) speaks of the miracle realm. It comes from *dunamai*, which means "ability." Think about it—we get to be clothed with *God's ability!*

The remaining 11 disciples were already the most trained people in signs and wonders in all of history. No one had seen or done more, except Jesus. And it was those 11 who had to stay until they were clothed with *power from on high.* When they got it they knew it. This power came through an encounter with God.

Some, because of their fear of error, have said it's improper to seek for an experience with God. After all, many deceived groups have come from those who based their beliefs on experiences in conflict with Scripture. Under the guidance of such attitudes, fear becomes our teacher. But why aren't those same individuals afraid of belonging to the doctrinally stable camps that are powerless? Is this deception any less dangerous than that of the power abuser? Will you bury your gifts and tell the Master when He comes that you were afraid of being wrong? Power and character are so closely aligned in Scripture that you cannot be weak in one without undermining the other.

OUR RELATIONSHIP WITH THE HOLY SPIRIT

Around 25 years ago I heard someone mention that if we would learn what it meant to "not grieve" and "not quench" the Holy Spirit, we would know the secret to being full of the Spirit. While that may be overly simplistic, this individual tapped into two very important truths that deal directly with the "character vs. power" trap.

The command, "Do not grieve the Holy Spirit" (Eph. 4:30), explains how our sin affects God. It causes Him grief. This command is character centered. Sin is defined in two ways: doing wrong things, and a failure to do right things: "To him who knows to do good and does not do it, to him it is sin" (James 4:17). Departing from the character of Christ in either of these ways brings grief to the Holy Spirit.

Continuing with this theme, we have the command, "Do not quench the Spirit" (1 Thess. 5:19). This mandate is focused on our need to follow His leading. To *quench* means to "stop the flow" of something. As the Holy Spirit is ready to bring salvation, healing, and deliverance, we are to *flow* with Him. Failure to do so hinders His efforts to bring us into the supernatural.

If He is to be free to move in our lives, we will constantly be involved in impossibilities. The supernatural is His natural realm. The more important the Holy Spirit becomes to us, the more these issues will be paramount in our hearts.

PURSUE AN ENCOUNTER

At some point we must believe in a God who is big enough to keep us safe in our quest for more of Him. Practically speaking, many Christian's devil is bigger than their God. How could a created, fallen being ever be compared with the infinite Lord of glory? It's an issue of trust. If I focus on my need to protect myself from deception, I will always be overwhelmingly aware of the power of the devil. If my heart is completely turned to the One who is "able to keep me from falling" (see Jude 24-25), He is the only One I become impressed with. My life reflects what I see with my heart.

So how do we walk in the power of God? First, we must pursue Him. The life of power is a life of abiding in Christ (staying plugged into our power source). The hunger for the demonstration of power must not be separated from our passion for Him. But realize this, our hunger for Him in part must be seen in our lustful pursuit of spiritual gifts (see I Cor. 14:1). That is His command!

In this endeavor I must passionately desire life-changing encounters with God, over and over again. I must cry out day and night for them...and be specific. I must be willing to travel to get what I need. If God is moving somewhere else more than where I live, I must *go!* If He is using someone more than He is using me, I must humbly go to them and ask them to pray for me with the laying on of hands.

Some may ask, "Why can't God touch me where I am?" He can. But He usually moves in ways that emphasize our need for others, rather than adding to our independence. Wise men have always been willing to travel.

MY STORY—GLORIOUS, BUT NOT PLEASANT

In my personal quest for increased power and anointing in my ministry, I have traveled to many cities, including Toronto. God has used my experiences in such places to set me up for life-changing encounters at home.

Once, in the middle of the night, God came in answer to my prayer for more of Him, yet not in a way I had expected. I went from a dead sleep to being wide-awake in a moment. Unexplainable power began to pulsate through my body, seemingly just shy of electrocution. It was as though I had been plugged into a wall socket with a thousand volts of electricity flowing through my body. My arms and legs shot out in silent explosions as if something was released through my hands and feet. The more I tried to stop it, the worse it got.

I soon discovered that this was not a wrestling match I was going to win. I heard no voice, nor did I have any visions. This was simply the most overwhelming experience of my life. It was raw power...*it* was God. He came in response to a prayer I had been praying for months—*God, I must have more of You at any cost!*

The evening before was glorious. We were having meetings with a good friend and prophet, Dick Joyce. The year was 1995. At the end of the meeting, I prayed for a friend who was having difficulty experiencing God's presence. I told him that I felt God was going to surprise him with an encounter that could come in the middle of the day, or even at 3 a.m. When the power fell on me that night, I looked at the clock. It was 3 a.m., exactly. I knew I had been set up.

For months I had been asking God to give me more of Him. I wasn't sure of the correct way to pray, nor did I understand the doctrine behind my request. All I knew was that I was hungry for God. It had been my constant cry day and night.

This divine moment was glorious, but not pleasant. At first I was embarrassed, even though I was the only one who knew I was in that condition. As I lay there, I had a mental picture of me standing before my congregation, preaching the Word as I loved to do. But I saw myself with my arms and legs flailing about as though I had serious physical problems. The scene changed—I was walking down the main street of our town, in front of my favorite restaurant, again arms and legs moving about without control.

I didn't know of anyone who would believe that this was from God. I recalled Jacob and his encounter with the angel of the Lord. He limped for the rest of His life. And then there was Mary, the mother of Jesus. She had an experience with God that not even her fiancée believed, although a visit from an angel helped to change his mind. As a result, she bore the Christ-child...and then bore a stigma for the remainder of her days as *the mother of the illegitimate child.* It was becoming clear; the favor of God sometimes looks different from the perspective of earth than from heaven. My request for more of God carried a price.

Tears began to soak my pillowcase as I remembered the prayers of the previous months and contrasted them with the scenes that just passed through my mind. At the forefront was the realization that God wanted to make an exchange—His increased presence for my dignity. It's difficult to explain how you know the purpose of such an encounter. All I can say is you just *know.* You know His purpose so clearly that every other reality fades into the shadows, as God puts His finger on the one thing that matters to Him.

In the midst of the tears came a point of no return. I gladly yielded, crying, *More, God. More! I must have more of You at any cost! If I lose respectability and get You in the exchange, I'll gladly make that trade. Just give me more of You!*

The power surges didn't stop. They continued throughout the night, with me weeping and praying, *More Lord, more; please give me more of You.* It all stopped at 6:38 a.m., at which time I got out of bed completely refreshed. This experience continued the following two nights, beginning moments after getting into bed.

PURSUE AGAINST THE GRAIN

Biblical passion is a mysterious mixture of humility, supernatural hunger, and faith. I pursue because I have been pursued. Lethargy must not be found in me. And if the average Christian life around me falls short of the biblical standard, I must pursue against the grain. If people are not being healed, I will not supply a rationale so that all those around me remain comfortable with the void. Instead, I will pursue the healing until it comes or the individual goes to be with the Lord.[6] I will not lower the standard of the Bible to my level of experience.

Jesus healed everyone who came to Him. To accept any other standard is to *bring the Bible down to our level of experience*, and deny the nature of the One who changes not.

As for the ministry of power, whatever I receive from God I must give away. You only get to keep what you give away. If you want to see people healed, look for those who are sick and offer to pray for them. While I am not the healer, I do have control over my willingness to serve those in need. If I minister to the needy, I give Him an opportunity to show His extravagant love for people. The ministry of signs and wonders will go nowhere if we are afraid of failure. As Randy Clark puts it, "I must be willing to fail to succeed."

LOOK FOR FRUIT

Jesus said that we must receive the Kingdom like a child. The life of power is at home in the heart of a child. A child has an insatiable appetite to learn. Be childlike and read the works of those who have succeeded in the healing ministry. Stay away from the books and tapes of those who say it shouldn't or can't be done. If the author doesn't walk in power, don't listen, no matter how proficient they may be in another field. An expert in biblical finances is not necessarily proficient in signs and wonders. Maintain respect for that individual's place in God and his or her area of expertise, but never waste precious time reading the stuff of those who do not do what they teach. We have grown fat on the theories of classroom Christians. We must learn from those who *just do it!*

Someone once brought a book to my office that was critical of the revival that started in Toronto in January of 1994. I refused to read it and threw it away. You might say, "You're not very open-minded." You're right. I am responsible to protect what God has given me. No one else has that assignment. Burning within my soul is a piece of the original flame from the day of Pentecost. It's been handed down generation after generation. That fire burns deep inside, and because of it I'll never be the same again.

My passion for Jesus is growing continually. And the signs and wonders He promised are happening as a regular part of life.

For me to consider the criticisms of this revival would be the same as giving audience to someone trying to prove I should have married another woman. First of all, I love my wife and have no interest in anyone else. Second, I refuse to entertain the thoughts of any person who desires to undermine my love for her. Only those who will add to my commitment to her are allowed such an audience with me. Anything less would be foolishness on my part.

The critics of this revival are unknowingly attempting to separate me from my first love. I will not give them place. I have many friends who are able to read the books of the critics with no ill effect. I respect them for their ability to stick their hands in the mire without getting their hearts dirty. I don't care to do it. It's just not my gift. Learn how you function best, then function!

While I have no time for critics, I do welcome the "wounds of a friend" (see Prov. 27:6). The corrections offered through meaningful relationships keep us from deception.

WHAT IF NOTHING HAPPENS

If we teach, preach, or witness and nothing happens, we must go back to the drawing board—our knees. Do not make excuses for powerlessness. For decades the Church has been guilty of creating doctrine to justify their lack of power, instead of crying out to God until He changed them. The lie they came to believe has given rise to an entire branch of theology that has infected the Body of Christ with a fear of the Holy Spirit. It deceives under the guise of staying undeceived. The Word must go forth with power. Power is the realm of the Spirit. A powerless Word is *the letter* not *the Spirit*. And we all know, "The letter kills, but the Spirit gives life" (2 Cor. 3:6). Lives must be changed in our ministry of the Word. Keep in mind that conversion is the greatest and most precious miracle of all.

"Christ did not send me to baptize, but to preach the gospel—not with words of human wisdom, lest the cross of Christ be emptied of its power" (I Cor. 1:17 NIV). If the gospel is powerless, it is because human wisdom has had its influence.

PRAYER, THE GATEWAY TO POWER

Whenever I have taken time to seek God about the need for power to back up His message, He always comes through with an increase. Miracles increase. I learned something very helpful along these lines from Randy Clark. When he notices there are certain kinds of healings that are not taking place in his meetings, he cries out to God mentioning specific diseases in his prayers. He was having very few miracles having to do with the brain— such as dyslexia. After crying out for these kinds of miracle manifestations, he started to experience a breakthrough. I have followed his lead and have never seen God fail. Specific requests are good because they are measurable. Some of our prayers are too general. God could answer them and we would never know it.

After learning this principle from Randy's example, I began to pray for disorders in the brain. One such miracle came to a woman named Cindy. She was told that a third of her brain was shut down. As a result, she had 23 learning disorders. She could do nothing with memorization, numbers, or maps. On one of our Friday night services, she stood in line for prayer for the blessing of God. When she was prayed for, she fell under the weight of His glory. During the time in which she lay there, overcome by God's power, she had a vision in which Jesus asked her if she would like for Him to heal her. She of course said yes. At His command, she jumped up off of the floor and ran to get her Bible. For the first time in her life everything was where it was supposed to be on the page. When she testified of the miracle a couple of weeks later, she quoted many verses she had put to memory in such a short time.

PAY ME NOW, OR PAY ME LATER

We hear a lot about what the anointing costs. Without question, walking with God in power will cost all who give themselves to this mandate. But the absence of power is even more costly. In the next chapter we'll discover how eternity is affected by our powerlessness.

ENDNOTES

1. Dangerous to the powers of hell, and the works of darkness.

2. Mario Murillo, *Fresh Fire*, (Anthony Douglas Publishing, 1991), 85.

3. Discipline can bring an individual into personal victory, but punishment bridles with shame.

4. This illustration is not to take away from the importance of discipline. Biblical discipline is not punishment. It is choosing, in love, restrictions that are best for that person and the entire church family. The length of his discipline was nearing the point at which it would have become punishment and would have kept him from the very thing he needed.

5. Reckless abandon is not the same as spiritual carelessness. Most of the failures in the past have come because leaders became too detached from the people that God put in their lives. I pursue dangerous things, but I keep accountable, and I work to protect my relationships on all levels. I believe this is the realm of safety that many have abandoned in their pursuit of their "treasure in the field."

6. At this point the prayer for resurrection is appropriate!

THE HIGH
COST OF
LOW POWER

Win for the Lamb that was slain the reward for His suffering.
—the Moravians

REVIVAL IS THE ATMOSPHERE in which Christ's power is most likely to be manifested. It touches every part of human life, breaking into society with sparks of revolution. Such glory is costly, and it is not to be taken lightly. Nevertheless, a powerless Church is far more costly in terms of human suffering and lost souls. During revival, hell is plundered and heaven is populated. Without revival, hell is populated...period.

Let me illustrate the necessity of signs and wonders in our quest to see our cities transformed and the glory of God fill the earth. Without the following, the world suffers, God is grieved, and we are the most to be pitied:

1. SIGNS AND WONDERS REVEAL THE NATURE OF GOD...

A primary purpose of the miracle realm is to reveal the nature of God. The lack of miracles works like a thief, stealing precious revelation that is within the grasp of every man, woman, and child. Our debt to mankind is to give them answers for the impossible, and a personal encounter with God. And that encounter must include great power.[1]

We are to be a witness for God. To give *witness* is to "represent." This actually means to *re-present* Him. Therefore, to re-present Him without power is a major shortcoming. It is impossible to give an adequate witness of God without demonstrating His supernatural power. The supernatural is His natural realm. Jesus was an exact representation of the Father's nature (see Heb. 1:3 NASB). His re-presentation of the Father is to be a model for us as we learn how to re-present Him.

The miracle realm of God is always with purpose. He doesn't come upon people with power to show off or entertain. Demonstrations of power are redemptive in nature. Even the cataclysmic activities of the Old Testament were designed to bring people to repentance.

Healing is never only one-dimensional. While a miracle may change one's physical health, it also sparks a revolution deep within the human heart. Both reveal the nature of God, which must never be compromised through powerless Christianity.

2. SIGNS AND WONDERS EXPOSE SIN AND BRING PEOPLE TO A DECISION...

When Simon Peter saw it [the miraculous catch of fish], *he fell down at Jesus' knees, saying, "Depart from me, for I am a sinful man, O Lord!"* (Luke 5:8).

Peter had been fishing all night with no success. Jesus told him to cast nets to the other side of the boat, which doubtless he had already done many times. When he did it at the bidding of the Master, the catch of fish was so great it nearly sank the boat. Peter called for help from the other boats. His response to this miracle was, "I am a sinful man."

Who told him that he was a sinner? There is no record of sermons, rebukes, or any such thing in the boat that day—just good fishing. So how did he come under such conviction for sin? It was in the miracle. Power exposes. It draws a line in the sand and forces people to a decision.

Demonstrations of power are no guarantee that people will repent. One only needs to look at Moses to realize that sometimes the miraculous only causes our Pharaohs to become more resolved to destroy us when they see power. Without acts of power, the Pharisees might have forgotten about the Church that was born from the blood of Jesus poured out at the cross. Power stirred up the zeal of opposition in them. We must be sober minded about this: power often causes people to decide what they're for or against. Power removes the middle ground.

Mercy ministries are absolutely essential in the ministry of the gospel. They are one of the ways the love of God can and must be seen. Yet they are not complete without demonstrations of power. Why? The reality is this: the world will usually applaud such efforts because they know we should be doing them. We must realize the sad truth—it is common for people to acknowledge the kindness of the Church and still not be brought to repentance. But power forces the issue because of its inherent ability to humble mankind.

Jesus said, "If I had not done among them the works which no one else did, they would have no sin" (John 15:24).

Is He saying that sin didn't exist in the hearts of the Jews until He performed miracles? I doubt it very much. He is explaining the principle revealed in Peter's repentance. Power exposes sin and brings people to a decision. When power is missing, we are not using the weapons that were in

Jesus' arsenal when He ministered to the lost. The outcome? Most remain lost. Power forces people to be aware of God on a personal level, and it is demanding in nature.

3. SIGNS AND WONDERS BRING COURAGE...

The children of Ephraim, being armed and carrying bows, turned back in the day of battle. They did not keep the covenant of God; they refused to walk in His law, and forgot His works and His wonders that He had shown them (Psalm 78:9-11).

A very profound part of the Jewish culture was shaped by the command to *keep the testimonies of the Lord.* The family itself was driven by the ongoing revelation of God contained in His commandments and testimonies. They were to talk about the Law of God and what God had done when they went to bed at night, rose up in the morning, walked along, etc. Just about any time of the day was a perfect time to talk about God's wondrous works.

To insure they didn't forget, they were to build monuments that would help them to remember the invasion of God into their lives. For example: they piled stones to mark the place where Israel crossed the Jordan River (see Josh. 3:1-17). That was so that when their young ones would ask, *Hey Dad...why is that pile of stones there?* They could respond with the story of how God worked among them.

The testimony of God creates an appetite for more of the activities of God. Expectation grows wherever people are mindful of His supernatural nature and covenant. When the expectation grows, miracles increase. When the miracles increase, testimonies increase as well. You can see the cycle. The simple act of sharing a testimony about God can stir up others until they expect and see God work in their day.

The reverse is also true. Where they decrease, miracles are expected less. If there is less expectation for miracles, they happen even less. As you can see, there is also a possible downward spiral. Forgetting what God has done by removing the testimony from our lips ultimately causes us to become fearful in the day of battle. The story of the children of Ephraim is tragic because they were thoroughly equipped to win. They just lacked courage. Their courage was to come from their memory of who God had been to them.

4. THE SUPERNATURAL IS THE KEY TO THE SIN CITIES OF THE WORLD...

Then He began to rebuke the cities in which most of His mighty works had been done, because they did not repent:

"Woe to you, Chorazin! Woe to you Bethsaida! For if the mighty works which were done in you had been done in Tyre and Sidon, they would have repented long ago in sackcloth and ashes.

"But I say to you, it will be more tolerable for Tyre and Sidon in the day of judgment than for you. And you Capernaum, who are exalted to heaven, will be brought down to Hades; for if the mighty works which were done in you had been done in Sodom, it would have remained until this day.

"But I say to you that it shall be more tolerable for the land of Sodom in the day of judgment than for you" (Matthew 11:20-24).

This passage of Scripture makes a distinction between religious cities and those known for sin. The religious city had a numbed awareness of its need for God, while the sinful city was conscious that something was missing.[2] Religion is even more cruel than sin.

The cities that Jesus addresses here saw more signs and wonders than all the rest combined. The miracles Jesus performed were so great in number that the apostle John said recording them could fill up all of the books in the world (see John 21:25). This gives us perspective on the rebuke of Jesus upon the hard-hearted cities.

Jesus was limited in what He could do in Nazareth because of their unbelief (see Mark 6:1-6). Yet in Chorazin and Bethsaida, His miracles appear to be limitless, which suggests these cities had a measure of faith. His stern rebuke didn't appear to come because they didn't appreciate His working of miracles. They must have. Their problem was that they added such a move to what they were already doing, instead of making Him the focal point of their lives. That's what religion does. Like Jesus said, they failed to repent and change their way of thinking (alter their perspective on life itself).

Many enjoy the move of God, but don't genuinely repent (change their life's perspective, making His activities the focus and ambition of their lives). The revelation that came to them through the miraculous increased their responsibility, thus requiring change. It never came.

The anointing in Capernaum was so great that some translations say they were *exalted to heaven*. Could He be saying that the miracle realm around them was so great that it made their city the most like heaven of any city on earth? If so, Capernaum became, for a brief season, the example of *on earth as it is in heaven*. They made room for His great work, but never made the adjustment in their lives to make it their main focus.

But there is another message contained in this story. Tyre, Sidon, and Sodom would have repented had they been exposed to the same dimension of *outpouring!* Did you hear it? *They would have repented!* It's a prophetic promise for today. Miracles on the streets of the "sin cities" of the world *will cause them to repent!* It is this secret that gives us access to the heart of these great cities! The San Franciscos and the Amsterdams, the New Orleneses and the Rio de Janeiros of this world *will* repent...if there is an army of saints, full of the Holy Ghost, walking their streets, caring for the broken, bringing the God of power into their impossible circumstances. They will repent! That's a promise. They simply await those with the message of the Kingdom to come.

Powerlessness cancels that possibility, and in its place comes God's judgment.

5. MIRACLES REVEAL HIS GLORY...

This beginning of signs Jesus did in Cana of Galilee, and manifested His glory; and His disciples believed in Him (John 2:11).

Jesus attended a wedding where they ran out of wine. As yet He hadn't performed any of the wonders for which He would later become known. Mary knew who her son was and what was possible. So in this time of need His mother, Mary, turned to Him and said, "They have no wine." Jesus responded to her saying, "Woman, what does your concern have to do with Me? My hour has not yet come." But then Mary did something amazing—she turned to the servants and said, "Whatever He says to you, do it!" (John 2:4-5). Her faith just made room for the extravagance of God! Jesus followed this with the miracle of turning the water into wine.

Now, what really happened? It's important to remember that Jesus only did what He saw His Father do, and He only said what He heard His Father say. When Mary first mentioned the need for wine to Jesus, it is safe to say He noticed that the Father was not involved in doing any miracles for that wedding. Besides, He knew that this wasn't *His hour*...the time to be revealed as the *miracle worker*. That's what brought the response, "Woman, what does your concern have to do with Me. My hour has not yet come." Mary, however, responded with *faith* and had the servants ready to do "...whatever He says to you."

Jesus again looked to see what the Father was doing and now noticed that He was turning water into wine. So Jesus followed His lead and did the miracle. Her faith so touched the heart of the Father that He apparently changed the chosen time to unveil Jesus as the miracle worker. Faith moves heaven, so that heaven will move earth.

According to John 2:11, this demonstration of God's power released the glory of God into that location. Signs and wonders do that. They release the glory of God into our cities. The need—be it physical sickness, poverty, oppression, etc.—represents the impact of darkness. The miracle displaces darkness and replaces it with light—glory. When miracles are absent, so is the glory of God, which is the manifested presence of Jesus.

As glory is released, it displaces the powers of darkness and replaces it with the actually ruling presence of God. The house is *clean and swept* and becomes filled with the furnishings of heaven (see Luke 11:25). As the powers of darkness are removed, they must be replaced with right things, or the enemy has legal access to return, making the last state of the man worse than the first. Miracles do both—they remove the ruling influence of hell while establishing the ruling presence of God.

How will the glory of God cover the earth? I believe that, at least in part, it will be through a people who walk in power, bringing the testimony of Jesus to the nations of the world. There will be a generation that will catch this and will invade the world system with this living testimony of who Jesus is!

6. SIGNS DIRECT PEOPLE TO GIVE GLORY TO GOD...

Now when the multitudes saw it, they marveled and glorified God, who had given such power to men (Matthew 9:8).

I talk about the miracle working power of God in almost every meeting I lead, whether it be a traditional church service, a conference, even a board or staff meeting. When I'm speaking away from home, I will often do this to stir up faith and help listeners to direct their hearts to God. When I'm through, I ask them this question: *How many of you gave praise and glory to God when I shared those testimonies?* Most every hand goes up. Then I remind them of this one important thing—*If there were no power and corresponding testimony, God would have never received that glory. Without power, we rob God of the glory He is due!*

7. SIGNS THEMSELVES GIVE HIM GLORY!

Bless the Lord, all His works, in all places of His dominion. Bless the Lord, O my soul! (Psalm 103:22)

All Your works shall praise You, O Lord, and Your saints shall bless You (Psalm 145:10).

Not only do miracles stir the hearts of men to give glory to God, miracles give Him glory on their own. I'm not sure how this works, but somehow an act of God has a life of its own and contains the ability to actually give God glory without the assistance of mankind. The absence of miracles robs God of the glory that He is to receive from the life released in His own works.

8. MIRACLES ARE A UNIFYING FORCE FOR THE GENERATIONS...

One generation shall praise Your works to another, and shall declare Your mighty acts (Psalm 145:4).

We will not hide them from their children, telling to the generation to come the praises of the Lord, and His strength and His wonderful works that He has done. For He established a testimony in Jacob, and appointed a law in Israel, which He commanded our fathers, that they should make them known to their children; that the generation to come might know them, the children who would be born, that they may arise and declare them to their children, that they may set their hope in God... (Psalm 78:4-8).

Israel was to build monuments in memory of the activities of God. The reason? So that in their everyday existence there would be a reminder to coming generations of who God is, and what His covenant with His people looks like.

The testimony was to be both a record of God's activity with His people and an invitation for others to know Him in that way. One generation would speak of God's testimony to another. It doesn't say that the older generation would speak to the younger. While that is what is most often thought of in this verse, it is equally true that a younger generation would experience God, and the older could benefit. Encounters with the almighty God become a unifying factor for generations!

9. SIGNS AND WONDERS AFFIRM WHO JESUS IS...

If I do not do the works of My Father, do not believe Me; but if I do, though you do not believe Me, believe the works, that you may know and believe that the Father is in Me, and I in Him (John 10:37-38).

If the Jews struggled with believing in Jesus as their Messiah, He simply told them to look at the miracles and believe them. Why? A sign always leads you somewhere. He was not afraid of where His signs would lead them. Somehow that simple step of believing in what they saw eventually could enable them to believe in Jesus Himself (see John 10:36)—as in the case of Nicodemus. Every miracle testified of Jesus' identity. Without miracles, there can never be a full revelation of Jesus.

10. MIRACLES HELP PEOPLE HEAR FROM GOD...

And the multitudes with one accord heeded the things spoken by Philip, hearing and seeing the miracles which he did (Acts 8:6).

Philip was the messenger of God for the city of Samaria. They were able to hear his words as being from God, because of the miracles. Acts of power help people to tune their hearts to the things of God. It helps to break them loose from the rationale that this material world is the ultimate reality. Such a shift in perspective is essential to the most basic response to God. In essence, that is what the word *repentance* means. Miracles provide the grace for repentance.

The desperation that miracles cause is in part responsible for this phenomenon. As our interests turn from all that is natural, we direct our attention to Him. This change of heart opens both the eyes and ears of the hearts. As a result, we see what has been right in front of us all this time, and we hear what God has been saying throughout our lives.

Miracles cause a shift in priorities. They are an important aid in helping us to hear more clearly. Without them we are more inclined to be directed by our own minds and call it spirituality.

11. MIRACLES HELP PEOPLE OBEY GOD...

For I will not dare to speak of any of those things which Christ has not accomplished through me, in word and deed, to make the Gentiles obedient—in mighty signs and wonders, by the power of the Spirit of God, so that from Jerusalem and round about to Illyricum I have fully preached the gospel of Christ (Romans 15:18-19).

Here the apostle Paul demonstrates how the Gentiles were brought into obedience through the power of the Spirit of God, expressed in signs and wonders. This was what he considered as *fully* preaching the gospel. It wasn't a complete message without a demonstration of the power of God. It's how God says *Amen* to His own declared Word!

The Bible is filled with the stories of heroes who gained the courage to obey God in the most difficult of circumstances through a personal encounter with the miraculous. Nothing thrills the heart more than knowing God. He is limitless in power. He is for us and not against us, and is big enough to make up for our smallness. Conversely, being raised in a home where there is little or no evidence of the things in which we believe disillusions a generation created for great exploits.

12. MIRACLES VALIDATE THE IDENTITY OF BOTH THE SON OF GOD AND HIS CHURCH...

This man came to Jesus by night and said to Him, "Rabbi, we know that You are a teacher come from God; for no one can do these signs that You do unless God is with him" (John 3:2).

The promise, "I will be with you," was given many times throughout the Scriptures. It was always given to one who would be brought into impossible circumstances—circumstances that would need a miracle.[3] While His presence is comforting, while His sweet fellowship is what draws me into an intimate relationship with Him, His presence also is a provision from heaven designed to bring me into a place of great courage for signs and wonders.

It was understood by the Jews that if God is with you there should be miracles—"...for no one can do these signs that You do unless God is with him." In the Great Commission of Matthew 28:18-20, we find this phrase—"I am with you always, even to the end of the age." His presence is the assurance of His intent to use us in the miraculous. His moving into the life of all believers is a prophetic act that declares His supernatural purpose for His people.

HOW DO WE GET THE POWER?

Jesus commanded the most highly trained individuals in the supernatural to ever walk the earth to "wait in Jerusalem for what the Father has promised" (see Acts 1:4). Luke states it this way, "Tarry in the city of Jerusalem until you are endued with power from on high" (Luke 24:49). Even though they had been with Him, even though they had experienced His power through their own ministry, they were to wait for *dunamis*—the ability to perform miracles.

It is as if they had been working under the umbrella of His anointing. The time had come for them to get an anointing of their own through an encounter with God. The baptism of fire would give them their own ongoing encounter that would help to keep them at the center of God's will *when* persecution came.

The baptism of the Holy Spirit is an immersion into the *dunamis* of heaven. The ability to pray in tongues is a wonderful gift given through this baptism. I pray in tongues constantly, and am grateful for such a gift from God. But to think that speaking in tongues is *the* purpose for such a holy invasion is embarrassingly simplistic. It would be the same as saying that when Israel crossed the Jordan River it was the same as possessing the Promised Land. Yes, they were in it, they could see it, but they did not possess it! Their river crossing gave them the legal access to the possession. This wonderful Spirit baptism has given us such an access. But to stand on the banks proclaiming *it's all mine,* is foolishness at best. Such ignorance has caused great numbers of people to halt their pursuit once they've received their spiritual language. They have been taught they are now full of the Holy Spirit. A glass is only full when it overflows. Fullness can only be measured by overflow.

The fullness of God ought to do more for me than give me a supernatural language. If that's all there was, I'd have no complaint. It's a glorious gift from God. But His purposes bring us into more, to a divine partnership in which we become co-laborers with Christ. Power came to make us witnesses. When the Spirit of God came upon the people in the Scriptures, all of nature bowed before them. Power was displayed, and impossibilities gave way to the full expression of God's presence.

READING THE SIGNS

Many fear signs and wonders because of the possibility of deception. So, in order to prevent any opportunity of being deceived, they replace displays of power with religious traditions, Christian activities, or even Bible study. They often become satisfied with knowledge. But, when this happens, who is deceived?

Signs have a purpose. They are not an end in themselves. They point to a greater reality. When we exit a building, we don't go out through the exit sign. When we need to put out a fire, we don't beat it out with the sign pointing to the fire hose. The sign is real. But it points to a reality greater than itself.

A sign along a highway can confirm we are on the right road. Without signs we have no way of knowing we are where we think we are. Signs aren't needed when I travel familiar roads. But I do need them when I'm going where I've never been. So it is in this present move of God. We've gone as far as we can with our present understanding of Scripture. It's time to let signs have their place. They illustrate Scripture, all the while pointing to Jesus, the Son of God. Yet they also confirm to a people who have embraced an authentic gospel that they are going in the right direction.

Not one of us understood salvation until we were saved. It was the miracle—an experience—which gave us understanding. So it is with signs. They point us to the person. In this hour, the *experience* will help to open up those portions of Scripture that have been closed to us.[4]

No one in their right mind would claim to understand all that is contained in the Bible for us today. Yet to suggest that more is coming causes many to fear. Get over it, so you don't miss it!

HOW WE RELATE TO THE WORLD

The next chapter shows us what we actually owe the world, and how to give it to them.

ENDNOTES

1. That encounter is to include other things too. For example: the love of God must be evident through us, as should character, etc. The purpose of this book, however, is to fill a literary gap to help in our much-needed return to a gospel of power, as well as one of love and character.

2. This principle is dealt with further in Chapter 15 "How to Miss a Revival."

3. Look at Moses (see Exod. 3:12), Joshua (see Josh. 1:9), and Gideon (see Judg. 6:12) for further study on this subject.

4. Strong relationships and accountability are what helps us stay safe and undeceived.

Chapter 12

OUR DEBT TO THE WORLD: AN ENCOUNTER WITH GOD

The anointing of the Holy Spirit is His actual presence upon us for ministry.
The purpose of the anointing is to make the supernatural natural.

GOD'S COVENANT PROMISE, "I will be with you," has always been linked to mankind's need for courage to face the impossible. There is no question that the presence of God is what brings us great comfort and peace. But the presence of God was always promised to His chosen ones to give them assurance in the face of less than favorable circumstances.

He is the great treasure of mankind. He always will be. It is this revelation that enabled the revolutionary exploits of the apostle Paul. It's what strengthened a king named David to risk his life in order to transform the system of sacrifice and worship. Moses needed this assurance as the man who was sent to face Pharaoh and his demon-possessed magicians. They all needed incredible confidence to fulfill their callings.

Joshua was faced with filling the big shoes of Moses, who was the man with whom God talked face-to-face. And now, Joshua was to lead Israel to where Moses was unable to go himself. God's word to him was one of great encouragement and exhortation. It ends with the ultimate promise, "I will be with you" (see Josh. 1:5-9).

Gideon was also given an impossible task. He was the least of his family, which was the least of his tribe, which was the least in Israel. Yet God had chosen him to lead Israel into victory against the Midianites. His encounter is one of the most interesting recorded in Scripture. Many a fearful person has taken comfort in Gideon's *turn around experience*. God initiated his transformation with the promise, "I will be with you."

The Great Commission provides more interesting reading for those who remember what kind of men God was giving His charge to—greedy, prideful, angry, and self-centered. Yet Jesus called them to change the world. What was the one word of assurance that He gave them before departing from sight? "I will be with you always..." (see Matt. 28:19-21).

We know that such a promise is given to everyone who calls on the name of the Lord for salvation. But why do some walk with a greater sense of God's presence than others? Some people place high value on the presence of God, and others don't. The ones who do enjoy fellowship throughout their day with the Holy Spirit are extremely conscious of how He feels about their words, attitudes, and activities. The thought of grieving Him brings great sorrow. It's their passion to give Him preeminence in everything. That passion brings that believer into a supernatural life—one with the constant activity of the Holy Spirit working through them.

SMEARED WITH GOD

The presence of God is to be realized in the anointing. Remember, anointing means *smeared*—it is God covering us with His power-filled presence. Supernatural things happen when we walk in the anointing!

For the most part, the anointing has been hoarded by the Church for the Church. Many have misunderstood why God has covered us with Himself, thinking it is for our enjoyment only. But we must remember, in the Kingdom of God we only get to keep what we give away. This wonderful presence of God is to be taken to the world. If it isn't, our effectiveness decreases. Does He leave us? No. But perhaps this phrase will help to clarify this point: *He is in me for my sake, but He's upon me for yours!*

Not only is all ministry to be Spirit empowered, it is to have a *gathering element* to it. Jesus said, "He who does not gather with Me scatters" (Luke 11:23). If our ministries do not gather, they will divide. Either we take what God has given us and give it to the world, or what we have received will bring division. It's our perspective on the world that keeps us in the center of His purposes.

The anointing equips us to bring the world into an encounter with God. That encounter is what we owe them. For that reason, every caring evangelist should cry out for a greater anointing; every believer should cry for the same. When we are smeared with God, it rubs off on all we come into contact with—and it's that anointing that breaks the yokes of darkness (see Isa. 10:27).

The most common understanding of our need for the anointing is in the preaching of the Word or praying for the sick. These are just two of the very common ways of bringing this encounter to people. While these are true, it's the person with the continual anointing that opens up many more opportunities for ministry.

I used to frequent a local health food store. It was the kind that had strange music and many books by various gurus and cultic spiritual guides.

I did business there because of a commitment I made to bring the light of God to the darkest places in town. I wanted them to see a contrast between what they thought was light and what is actually light. Before entering, I would pray specifically that the anointing of God would rest upon me and flow through me. I would walk up and down the aisles praying quietly in the Spirit, wanting God to fill the store. One day the owner came to me and said, "Something is different when you come into the store." A door opened that day that gave me many opportunities for future ministry. The anointing upon me equipped me for service.

DON'T UNDERESTIMATE THIS TOOL

Jesus was walking down a crowded road with people from all sides trying to get close to Him. A woman reached out and touched His garment. He stopped and asked, "Who touched Me?" The disciples were startled by such a question, because to them it had such an obvious answer—everyone! But Jesus went on to say that He felt virtue (*dunamis*) flow from Him. He was anointed by the Holy Spirit. The actual power of the Spirit of God left His being and flowed into that woman and healed her. The anointing was resident in Jesus' physical body—the same as with every believer. The faith of that woman put a demand on that anointing in Jesus. She was healed, because *the anointing breaks the yoke* (see Isa. 10:27).

A very popular verse for receiving an offering is, "Freely you have received, freely give" (Matt. 10:8). But the context of the verse is often forgotten. Jesus was referring to the ministry of the supernatural. Listen to the implication: "I have received something that I am to give away!" What? The Holy Spirit. He is the greatest gift anyone could ever receive. And He is living in me.

When we minister in the anointing, we actually give away the presence of God—we impart Him to others. Jesus went on to teach His disciples what it meant to *give it away*. It included the obvious things, such as: healing the sick, casting out demons, etc. But it also included one often forgotten aspect: "When you go into a house...let your peace come upon it." There is an actual impartation of His presence that we are able to make in these situations. This is how we bring the lost into an encounter with God. We learn to recognize His presence, cooperate with His passion for people, and invite them to receive *salvation*.[1]

He has made us stewards of the presence of God. It is not as though we can manipulate and use His presence for our own religious purposes. We are moved upon by the Holy Spirit, thereby becoming co-laborers with Christ. In that position we invite Him to invade the circumstances that arise before us.

The more obvious ways are in preaching or praying for people's specific needs. Don't underestimate this important tool. By looking for chances to serve, we give the Holy Spirit the opportunity to do what only He can do—miracles. I don't see everyone I pray for healed. I'm not batting even close to a thousand. But there are many more healed than would be had I not prayed for anyone!

Give God a chance to do what only He can do. He looks for those who are willing to be *smeared* with Him, allowing His presence to affect others for good. A visiting minister recently told us, "The difference between you and me is this: if I pray for a dead person and they are not raised from the dead, I pray for the next dead person too. I don't quit!"

Jesus said, "If I do not do the works of My Father, do not believe Me" (John 10:37). The works of the Father are miracles. Even the Son of God stated it was the miraculous that validated His ministry on earth. In that context He said, "...he who believes in Me...greater works than these he will do, because I go to My Father" (John 14:12). The miraculous is a large part of the plan of God for this world. And it is to come through the Church.

I look forward to the day when the Church stands up and says, "Don't believe us unless we are doing the works that Jesus did!" The Bible says that we are to pursue earnestly (lustfully!) spiritual gifts (see 1 Cor. 14:1), and that those gifts make us *established* (see Rom. 1:11). Which ones? All of them.

GETTING HEAVEN INTO US

I owe the world a Spirit-filled life, for I owe them an encounter with God. Without the fullness of the Holy Spirit in and upon me, I do not give God a surrendered vessel to flow through.

The fullness of the Spirit was the goal of God throughout the law and prophets. Salvation was the immediate goal, but the ultimate goal on earth was the fullness of the Spirit in the believer. Getting us to heaven is not near as great a challenge as it is to get heaven into us. This is accomplished through the *fullness of the Spirit* in us.

JACOB'S REVELATION

Jacob, an Old Testament patriarch, was sleeping in the great outdoors when he had a dream that contained one of the more startling revelations ever received by man. He saw an open heaven with a ladder coming down to earth. On the ladder were angels ascending and descending. He was frightened and said, *God is here and I didn't even know it* (see Gen. 28:16). That statement describes much of what we've been witnessing in this revival for the past several years—God is present, yet many remain unaware of His presence.

I have witnessed God's touch upon thousands of people in this present outpouring—conversions, healings, restored marriages, addictions broken, and the demonized set free. The list of *how lives have been changed* is gloriously long, and increasing daily. Yet as these have been changed, there have always been those in the same meeting who can hardly wait for the service to end and get out the door. One person recognizes God's presence and is forever changed, the other never realized what could have been.

JESUS, THE TABERNACLE OF GOD

Jacob's dream provides us with the first mention of *the house of God* in Scripture. This house contained *His presence, a gate into heaven, a ladder, and angels ascending and descending between heaven and earth.*

Jesus affirms Jacob's revelation about the house of God on planet earth, but in a way that is completely unexpected. John 1:14 says, "The Word was made flesh, and dwelt among us." The word *dwelt* means, "tabernacled." Jesus is introduced here as the *Tabernacle of God on earth.* Later, in the same chapter, Jesus says that His followers would see "angels ascending and descending upon the Son of Man" (John 1:51). The details of the Genesis 28 revelation of the house of God are seen in the person of Jesus. He is an illustration of Jacob's revelation.

JESUS PASSED THE BATON

For us to become all that God intended, we must remember that Jesus' life was a model of what mankind could become if it were in right relationship with the Father. Through the shedding of His blood, it would be possible for everyone who believed on His name to do as He did and become as He was. This meant then that every true believer would have access to the realm of life that Jesus lived in.

Jesus came as the light of the world. He then passed the baton to us, announcing that we are the light of the world. Jesus came as the miracle worker. He said that we would do "greater works" than He did (see John 14:12). He then pulled the greatest surprise of all, saying, "Right now the Holy Spirit is with you, but He's going to be in you."[2] Jesus, who illustrates to us what is possible for those who are *right with God*, now says that His people are to be the tabernacle of God on planet earth. Paul affirms this revelation with statements such as, "Do you not know that you are the temple of God?" (1 Cor. 3:16), and "you are a dwelling place of God" (Eph. 2:22).

What was the initial revelation of the house of God? It has the presence of God, a gate to heaven, and a ladder with angels ascending and descending upon it. Why is this important to understand? This revelation shows the resources that are at our disposal to carry out the Master's plan.

Frank Damazio, of City Bible Church in Portland, Oregon, has a great teaching regarding this principle and the local church. He calls them *Gate Churches*. This principle of being the stewards of the heavenly realm then becomes more than the assignment of the individual, and becomes the privilege of an entire Church for the sake of their entire city.

ANGELS ON ASSIGNMENT

Angels are impressive beings. They are glorious and powerful. So much so that when they showed up in Scripture, people often fell to worship them. While it is foolish to worship them, it is equally foolish to ignore them. Angels are assigned to serve wherever we serve, *if the supernatural element is needed.* "Are not all angels ministering spirits sent to serve those who will inherit salvation?" (Heb. 1:14).

I believe angels have been bored because we live the kind of lifestyle that doesn't require much of their help. Their assignment is to assist us in supernatural endeavors. If we are not people of risk, then there is little room for the supernatural. Risks must be taken to pursue solutions to impossible situations. When the Church regains its appetite for the impossible, the angels will increase their activities among men.

As the fires of revival intensify, so do the supernatural activities around us. If angels are assigned to assist us in supernatural endeavors, then there must be need for the supernatural. Risk must be taken to pursue solutions to impossible situations. The gospel of power is the answer to the tragic condition of humankind. John Wimber said, "Faith is spelled R-I-S-K." If we really want more of God then we must change our lifestyle so that His manifested presence will increase upon us. This is not an act on our part to somehow manipulate God. Instead, it is the bold attempt to take Him at

His Word so that as we radically obey His charge, and He says *Amen* with the miraculous (see Mark 16:20). I challenge you to pursue God passionately! And in your pursuit, insist on a supernatural lifestyle—one that keeps the hosts of heaven busy, ushering in the King and His Kingdom!

DON'T BOSS ANGELS

While God has provided angels to assist us in our commission, I don't take the posture that we are to command angels. Some feel they have that liberty. However, I believe it is a dangerous proposition. There is reason to believe that they are to be commissioned by God Himself in response to our prayers.

Daniel needed an answer from God. He prayed for 21 days. An angel finally showed up with his answer. He said to Daniel, "Do not fear, Daniel, for from the first day that you set your heart to understand, and to humble yourself before your God, your words were heard; and I have come because of your words. But the prince of the kingdom of Persia withstood me twenty-one days; and behold, Michael, one of the chief princes, came to help me, for I had been left alone there with the kings of Persia" (Dan. 10:12-13). When Daniel prayed, God responded by sending an angel with the answer. The angel ran into interference. Daniel continued to pray, which appears to have helped to release the archangel Michael to fight and release the first angel to deliver the message.

There are many other times angels came in response to the prayers of the saints. Each time they were sent out for service by the Father. I think it's best to pray much and leave commanding angels to God.

ENTERING THE TWILIGHT ZONE

I travel to many cities that are spiritually very dark. When you enter such cities you can feel the oppression. Considering what I represent to that city, it would be wrong for me to focus on the darkness. I don't ever want to be impressed with the devil's work. I come as a *house of God*. As such I contain a gate to heaven, with a ladder providing angelic activities according to the need of the moment. Simply put, *I am an open heaven!* This does not apply to a select few. On the contrary, this revelation is about the house of God and the principles of the house apply to all believers. But few realize or implement this *potential* blessing. With an open heaven I become a vehicle in the hand of God to release the resources of heaven into the calamities of mankind. Angels are commissioned to carry out the will of God. "Bless the Lord, you His angels, who excel in strength, who do His word, heeding the voice of His word" (Ps. 103:20). He is more eager to invade this world than we are to receive the invasion. And angels play an integral part.

They respond to His command and enforce His Word. But the *voice of His word* is heard when the Father speaks to the hearts of His people. Angels await the people of God speaking His word. I believe angels pick up the fragrance of the throne room through the word spoken by people. They can tell when a word has its origins in the heart of the Father. And, in turn, they recognize that word as their assignment.

I recently saw this happen at a meeting in Germany. Before the meeting, I was praying with some of the leaders that had sponsored the meetings. As we were praying, I saw a woman sitting to my right with an arthritic spine. It was a brief picture of the mind, which is the visual equivalent of the *still small voice*—as easy to miss as it is to get. In this picture I had her stand and declared over her, *The Lord Jesus heals you!*

When it came time for the meeting, I asked if there was anyone there with arthritis in the spine. A woman to my right waved her hand. I had her stand and declared over her, *The Lord Jesus heals you!* I then asked her where was her pain.

She wept saying, "It is impossible, but it is gone!" Angels enforced a word that originated in the heart of the Father. But for that moment, I was the *voice of His word*.

GOD, THE DELEGATOR

When God chose to bring the Messiah through the Virgin Mary, He sent Gabriel the angel to bring the message. When the apostle Paul was about to suffer shipwreck, an angel of the Lord told him what would happen. On numerous occasions throughout Scripture angels did what God could have done easily Himself. But why didn't God do those things Himself? For the same reason He doesn't preach the gospel: He has chosen to let His creation enjoy the privilege of service in His Kingdom. Service with purpose affirms identity. A godly self-esteem is derived from doing "as He pleases." And true service is an overflow of worship.[3]

WHEN GOD COLORS OUTSIDE THE LINES

His world has been breaking into ours with regularity in salvations, healings, and deliverances. The manifestations of that invasion vary. They are quite fascinating and too numerous to catalog. While some are difficult to understand at first glance, we know that God always works redemptively.

On many occasions laughter has filled a room, bringing healing to broken hearts. Gold dust sometimes covers people's faces, hands, or clothing during worship or ministry time. Oil sometimes appears on the hands of His people; and it especially happens among children. A wind has come into a room with no open windows, doors, vents, etc. At some locations, believers have seen an actual cloud of His presence appearing over the heads of worshiping people. We've also had the fragrance of heaven fill a room. In my own experience the fragrance of heaven filled our car while Beni and I were worshiping on a short trip. It lasted for about 30 minutes, and was a smell that I could actually taste, similar to granules of sugar sprinkled on my tongue. I have seen the small gems that suddenly appeared in people's hands as they worshiped God. Since early in 1998 we have had feathers fall in our meetings. At first I thought birds were getting into our air conditioning ducts. But then they started falling in other rooms of the church not connected with the same ductwork. They now fall most anywhere we go—airports, homes, restaurants, offices, and the like.

I mention this phenomenon because it seems to offend many that fully embrace this move of God. Jerrel Miller, editor of *The Remnant*, a newspaper whose purpose is to record the events surrounding this revival, took a lot of heat when he reported this unusual manifestation. Those who criticized his report are participants in this revival. It's easy once we've made some adjustments in our belief system about what God can and will do to think that we have stretched far enough. "Our beliefs now encompass the move of God." Nothing could be further from the truth. Like the generations before us, they are dangerously close to regulating God's work by a *new and revised list of acceptable manifestations*. No longer is it just tears during a special song or a time of repentance following a moving sermon. Our new list includes falling, shaking, laughter, etc. The problem is—it is still a list. And God will violate it. He must. We must learn to recognize His move by recognizing His presence. Our lists are only good for revealing our present understanding or experience. While I don't seek to promote strange manifestations, or go after *novelty*, I do refuse to be embarrassed over what God is doing. The list that keeps us from certain types of errors also keeps us from certain types of victories.

REFUSING TO BE
EMBARRASSED BY GOD

His manifestations, while offensive to the minds of many, are limitless in number, and are simple indicators of God's presence and purpose. Why are they necessary? Because He wants to take us farther, and we can only get there by following signs. Our present understanding of Scripture can only take us so far.

Remember, signs are realities that point to a greater reality. If He is giving us signs, who are we to say they are unimportant? Many react to this position because they fear *sign worship*. While their reasoning may be noble in intent, it is foolish to think I can carry out my assignment from God and ignore God's *personal notes* along the way. In the natural we use signs to help us find a city, a particular restaurant, or a place of business. It's practical. In the same way, signs and wonders are a natural part of the Kingdom of God. They are the normal way to get us from where we are to where we need to be. That is their purpose. Had the wise men not followed the star they would have had to be content reading about the experiences of others. I am not. There's a difference between *worshiping signs* and *following signs*; the first is forbidden, the latter is essential. When we follow His signs to the greater depths in God, His signs follow us in greater measure for the sake of mankind.

KNOWING THE GOD OF POWER

Whenever I teach on pursuing a gospel of power, someone occasionally follows my message with an affirmation of our need for power, but reminds everyone of the priority of knowing *the God of power*. True words indeed. Power has little pleasure if there is no intimate relationship with God. But that comment is often religious in nature. Someone who has a passion for the power and glory of God intimidates those who don't. My hunger for His power is only surpassed by my desire for Him. It's been my pursuit of Him that has led me to this passion for an authentic gospel.

Something happened in me that won't let me accept a gospel that isn't backed with signs and wonders. Is it because I have caught a revelation of miracles on the earth? No! It caught me. I have discovered there isn't any lasting satisfaction in life apart from expressions of faith.

SEEING HIM AS HE IS

The next chapter brings a most startling bit of truth to us about what it means to be like Jesus.

ENDNOTES

1. Salvation—*sozo*—salvation, healing, and deliverance.

2. See John 14:17 (personal paraphrase).

3. Remember, we always become like the one we worship. How could He want anything more for us than that?

Chapter 13

OUR IDENTITY
IN THIS WORLD

———————— ❧ ————————

While most of the Church is still trying to become as Jesus was, the Bible declares,
"As He is, so are we in this world" (1 John 4:17).

JESUS WAS THE SUFFERING SERVANT, headed for the cross. But Jesus is triumphantly resurrected, ascended, and glorified. In the Revelation of Jesus Christ, John described Him in this way: "His head and hair were white like wool, as white as snow, and His eyes like a flame of fire; His feet were like fine brass, as if refined in a furnace, and His voice as the sound of many waters" (Rev. 1:14-15).

The "as He is, so are we" declaration is far beyond what any of us could have imagined; especially in light of the glorified description of Jesus in Revelation 1. Yet, the Holy Spirit was sent specifically for this purpose, that we might attain "to the measure of the stature of the fullness of Christ" (Eph. 4:13).

The Holy Spirit came with the ultimate assignment at the perfect time. During Jesus' ministry, it was said, "The Holy Spirit was not yet given, because Jesus was not yet glorified" (John 7:39). The Holy Spirit comforts us, gives us gifts, reminds us of what Jesus has said, and clothes us with power. But He does all this to *make us like Jesus.* That is His primary mission. So why didn't the Father send Him until Jesus was glorified? Because without Jesus in His glorified state there was no *heavenly model of what we were to become!* As a sculptor looks at a model and fashions the clay into its likeness, so the Holy Spirit looks to the glorified Son and shapes us into His image. *As He is, so are we in this world.*

THE CHRISTIAN LIFE

The Christian life is not found *on* the Cross. It is found *because* of the Cross. It is His resurrection power that energizes the believer. Does this diminish the value of the Cross? No! The shed blood of the spotless Lamb wiped out the power and presence of sin in our lives. *We have nothing without the Cross!* Yet, the Cross is not the end—it is the beginning, the entrance to the Christian Life. Even for Jesus the cross was something to be endured in order to obtain the joy on the other side (see Heb. 12:2)! *The great majority of the Christian world is still weeping at the foot of the cross. The consciousness of mankind remains fixed on the Christ who died, not on the Christ who lives. People are looking back to the Redeemer who was, not the Redeemer who is.*[1]

Suppose I had been forgiven a financial debt. It could be said I have been brought *out of the red.* Yet, after my debts are forgiven, I still am *not in the black.* I have nothing unless the one who forgave my debt gives me money to call my own, and that's what Christ did for you and me. His blood wiped out my debt of sin. But it was His resurrection that brought me *into the black* (see John 10:10).

Why is this important? *Because it profoundly changes our sense of identity and purpose.*

Jesus became poor so that I could become rich. He suffered with stripes to free me from affliction, and He became sin so I might become the righteousness of God (see 2 Cor. 5:21). Why then should I try to become *as He was,* when He suffered so I could become *as He is?* At some point, the reality of the resurrection must come into play in our lives—we must discover the power of the resurrection for all who believe (see Eph. 1:21; 3:20).

COUNTERFEIT CROSS

Jesus said, "If anyone desires to come after Me, let him deny himself, and take up his cross, and follow Me" (Matt. 16:24). A misunderstanding of this call has led many to follow His life of self-denial, but to stop short of His life of power. For them the cross-walk involves trying to crucify their sin nature by embracing joyless brokenness as an evidence of the cross. But, we must *follow Him all the way*—to a lifestyle empowered by the resurrection!

Most every religion has a copy of the *cross-walk*. Self-denial, self-abasement, and the like are all easily copied by the sects of this world. People admire those who have religious disciplines. They applaud fasting and respect those who embrace poverty or endure disease for the sake of personal spirituality. But show them a life filled with joy because of the transforming power of God, and they will not only applaud but will want to be like you. Religion is unable to mimic the life of resurrection with its victory over sin and hell.

One who embraces an inferior cross is constantly filled with introspection and self-induced suffering. But the cross is not self-applied—Jesus did not nail Himself to the cross. Christians who are trapped by this counterfeit are constantly talking about their weaknesses. If the devil finds us uninterested in evil, then he'll try to get us to focus on our unworthiness and inability. This is especially noticeable in prayer meetings where people try to project great brokenness before God, hoping to earn revival. They will often reconfess old sins searching for real humility.

In my own pursuit of God, I often became preoccupied with ME! It was easy to think that being constantly aware of my faults and weaknesses was humility. It's not! If I'm the main subject, talking incessantly about my weaknesses, I have entered into the most subtle form of pride. Repeated phrases such as, "I'm so unworthy," become a nauseating replacement for the declarations of the worthiness of God. By being *sold* on my own unrighteousness, the enemy has disengaged me from effective service. It's a perversion of true holiness when introspection causes my spiritual self-esteem to increase, but my effectiveness in demonstrating the power of the gospel to decrease.

True brokenness causes complete dependency on God, moving us to radical obedience that releases the power of the gospel to the world around us.

IMPURE MOTIVES

I struggled for many years with self-evaluation. The main problem was that I never found anything good in me. It always led to discouragement, which led to doubt, and eventually took me to unbelief. Somehow I had developed the notion that this was how I could become holy—by showing tremendous concern for my own motives.

It may sound strange, but I don't examine my motives anymore. That's not my job. I work hard to obey God in everything that I am and do. If I am *out to lunch* on a matter, it is His job to point that out to me. After many years of trying to do what only He could do, I discovered I was not the Holy Spirit. I cannot convict and deliver myself of sin. Does that mean that I never deal with impure motives? No. He has shown Himself to be very eager to point out my constant need for repentance and change. But He's the one with the spotlight, and He alone can give the grace to change.

There is a major difference between the believer who is being dealt with by God, and the one who has become introspective. When God searches the heart, He finds things in us that He wants to change. He brings conviction because of His commitment to deliver us. Such a revelation brought me to pray in the following manner:

> *Father, You know that I don't do so well when I look inward, so I'm going to stop. I am relying on You to point out to me the things that I need to see.*

I promise to stay in Your Word. You said that Your Word was a sword—
so please use it to cut me deeply. Expose those things in me that are not
pleasing to You. But in doing so, please give me the grace to forsake them.
I also promise to come before You daily. Your presence is like a fire. Please
burn from me those things that are unpleasing to You. Melt my heart until
it becomes like the heart of Jesus. Be merciful to me in these things. I also
promise to stay in fellowship with Your people. You said that iron sharpens
iron. I expect You to anoint the "wounds of a friend" to bring me to my
senses when I'm being resistant toward You. Please use these tools to shape
my life until Jesus alone is seen in me. I believe that You have given me
Your heart and mind. By Your grace I am a new creation. I want that
reality to be seen that the name of Jesus would be held in highest honor.

COUNTERING THE COUNTERFEIT

I believe that for the most part this counterfeit cross-walk is embraced because it requires no faith. It's easy to see my weakness, my propensity toward sin, and my inability to be like Jesus. Confessing this truth requires no faith at all. On the contrary, to do as Paul commanded in Romans 6:13, to consider myself dead to sin, I must believe God!

Therefore, in your weakest state declare, "I AM STRONG!" Agree with God regardless of how you feel and discover the power of resurrection. Without faith it is impossible to please Him. The first place that faith must be exercised is in our own standing with God.

When God gave Moses a noble task, he responded, "Who am I?" God changed the subject saying, "Certainly I will be with you." When we are focused on our lack, the Father tries to change the subject to something that will lead us to the source and foundation of faith: Himself. The *noble call* always reveals the nobility of the *Caller*.

Apart from Christ, we are unworthy. And it's true that without Him we are nothing. But I'm not without Him, and I never will be again! At what point do we start thinking of our worth through His eyes? If it's true that the value of something is measured by what someone else will pay, then we need to rethink our worth. Do we ever acknowledge who we are before Him? Please don't misunderstand, I'm not encouraging arrogance or cockiness. But wouldn't it honor Him more if we believed that He actually did a good enough job in saving us, and that we really are saved? Jesus paid the ultimate price to make it possible for us to have a change in our identity. Isn't it time we believe it and receive the benefits? If we don't, we'll break down in our confidence as we stand before the world in these final days. The boldness we need is not self-confidence, but the confidence that the Father has in the work of His Son in us. It's no longer a question of heaven or hell. It's only a question of how much of hell's thinking I will allow into this heavenly mind of mine.

Doesn't it honor Him more when His children no longer see themselves only as *sinners saved by grace*, but now as *heirs of God*? Isn't it a greater form of humility to believe Him when He says we are precious in His sight when we don't feel very precious? Doesn't it honor Him more when we think of ourselves as free from sin because He said we are? At some point we must rise up to the high call of God and stop saying things about ourselves that are no longer true. If we're going to fully come into what God has for us in this last days' revival, we will have to come to grips with the issue of being more than *sinners saved by grace*. Maturity comes from faith in the sufficiency of God's redemptive work that establishes us as sons and daughters of the Most High.

BECOMING LIKE HIM

As He is, so are we in this world. The revelation of Jesus in His glorified state has at least four overwhelming characteristics that directly affect the coming transformation of the Church; these must be embraced as a part of God's plan in these final hours.

Glory—This is the manifested presence of Jesus. Revival history is filled with stories of His manifest presence resting upon His people. He lives in all believers, but the glory of His presence comes to rest on only a few. It is sometimes seen and frequently felt. He is returning for a glorious Church. It is not an option.

Tongues of fire were seen on the heads of the apostles on the day of Pentecost. In more modern times, fire has been seen blazing from the top of church buildings when the people of God are gathered together in His name. At the Azusa Street revival, the fire department was called to extinguish a blaze, only to discover that the people inside were worshiping Jesus. Water couldn't put it out as it was not a natural fire. All the powers of hell cannot put it out. The only ones capable of such a thing are those to whom that fire has been entrusted. Well-meaning believers will often use control as a means to bring this fire into order, thinking they are serving God. On the other hand, some will turn to hype to fan an emotional flame when the fire is no longer there. Both are expressions of the carnal man—and when the carnal man is in charge, the glory of God must lift.

If the Father filled the Old Testament houses with His glory, though they were built by human hands, how much more will He fill the place that He builds with His own hands! He is building us into His eternal dwelling place.

Power—To be *as He is* involves being a continuous expression of power. The baptism in the Holy Spirit clothes us with this heavenly element. As clothing is on the outside of the body, so that power is to be the most visible part of the believing Church. It is the *power of salvation*—for the body, soul, and spirit.

Many in the world around us seek for help from the psychic and cultist before coming to the Church. They also reach for medical help, legitimate and otherwise, before they ask for our prayers. Why? For the most part we are not clothed with heaven's power. If we had it, they would see it. If they saw it, they would come.

The power vacuum in the Church allows cults and false prophetic gifts to flourish. But there will be no contest when such counterfeits go up against this Elijah generation that becomes clothed with heaven's power on the Mount Carmel of human reasoning.

Triumph—Jesus conquered all things: the power of hell, the grave, sin, and the devil. He was raised from the dead, ascended to the right hand of the Father, and was glorified above all. Every name and power has been placed under His feet. He calls us His body—and this body has feet. Figuratively speaking, He is saying the lowest part of His body has authority over the highest part of everything else. This victory doesn't mean we live without battles; it simply means our victory is secured.

The attitude of those who live *from* the triumph of Christ is different than those who live under the influence of their past. The only part of the past that we have legal access to is the *testimony of the Lord* (see Ps. 119:111). The rest is dead, buried, forgotten, and covered under the blood. The past should have no negative effect on the way we live, as the blood of Jesus is more than sufficient. Living from the victory of Christ is the privilege for every believer. This realization is at the foundation of a Church that will triumph even as He has triumphed.

Holiness—Jesus is perfectly holy—separate *from* all that is evil, *unto* all that is good. Holiness is the language through which the nature of God is revealed. The psalmist penned the phrase, "in the beauty of holiness." Holiness in the Church reveals the beauty of God.

Our understanding of holiness, even in certain seasons of revival, has often been centered around our behavior—what we can and cannot do. However, what in the past incorrectly has been reduced to a list of "dos and don'ts" will soon become the greatest revelation of God the world has ever seen. Whereas power demonstrates the heart of God, holiness reveals the beauty of His nature. This is the hour of the great unveiling of the beauty of holiness.

CONCLUSION

Zacharias was given a promise from God that was beyond his comprehension: he was to have a son in his old age. It was hard to believe, so he asked God to give him confirmation. Apparently an angel speaking to him wasn't a big enough sign! God silenced him for nine months. When God silences the voices of unbelief, it is usually because their words could affect the outcome of a promise. When Zacharias saw God's promise fulfilled and he chose to name his son according to the command, against the wishes of his relatives, God loosed his tongue. Obedience against popular opinion will often reintroduce someone to personal faith. And that's a faith that goes against understanding.

Mary was also given a promise beyond comprehension: she was to give birth to the Son of God. When she couldn't understand, she asked how it was possible since she was a virgin. Understanding a promise from God has never been the prerequisite to its fulfillment. Ignorance asks for understanding; unbelief asks for proof. She stands apart from Zacharias because while being ignorant she surrendered to the promise. Her cry remains one of the most important expressions the Church can learn in this day—*"Be it unto me according to Your word."*

We've discussed an incredible promise of paramount importance for the Church. There are few things further from our grasp than the statement, *As He is, so are we in this world.* And so we have the choice: to stand in the shoes of Zacharias and lose our voice, or walk in the ways of Mary and invite God to restore to us the promises we cannot control.

This identity establishes a security in character as we engage in spiritual warfare. The next chapter provides us with insights necessary to succeed in war!

ENDNOTE

I.   John G. Lake, *His Life, His Sermons, His Boldness of Faith,* (Ft. Worth, TX: Kenneth Copeland Publications, 1994), 57.

Chapter 14

WARRING TO
INVADE!

The real Christian is a royal fighter. He is the one who loves to enter into the contest with his whole soul and take the situation captive for the Lord Jesus Christ.[1]

FOR TOO LONG THE CHURCH has played defense in the battle for souls. We hear of what some cult or political party is planning to do, and we react by creating strategies to counter the enemies' plans. Committees are formed, boards discuss, and pastors preach against whatever it is the devil is doing or about to do. This may come as a surprise, but I don't care what the devil plans to do. The Great Commission puts me on the offensive. I've got the ball. And if I carry the ball effectively, his plans won't matter.

Picture a football team in a huddle on the playing field. The coach sends in the play, and the quarterback communicates with his offensive teammates. On the sidelines is the opposing team's offense. Their quarterback lines up out of bounds with his offensive team, but they don't have the game ball, nor are they on the actual playing field. Now imagine the real offense getting distracted by the intimidating actions of the other offense. Caught up in their antics, the quarterback runs off the field in a panic, informing the coach that they better put the defense on the field because the other team is about to use a surprise play.

As foolish as that may sound, it is the condition of much of the Church in this hour. Satan reveals his plans to put us on the defensive. The devil roars, and we act as if we got bit. Let's stop this foolishness and quit praising the devil with endless discussions of *what's wrong in the world because of him.* We have the ball. The alumni from the ages past watch with excitement as the *two-minute offense* has been put on the field. The superior potential of this generation has nothing to do with our goodness, but it does have everything to do with the Master's plan of placing us at this point in history. We are to be the devil's worst nightmare.

WHY SATAN LEAKS HIS OWN SECRETS

I honestly believe that satan will allow his strategies to become known so that we will react accordingly. Satan likes being in control. And he is whenever we're not. Reactions come from fear.

We are not *holding on till Jesus comes!* We are an overcoming body of people that has been blood bought, is Spirit-filled, and commissioned by God Himself, in order that *all* He has spoken should come to pass. When we plan according to the devil's plans, we automatically clothe ourselves with the wrong mentality. Such incorrect attitudes can become the very *stronghold in our thinking* that invites a legal assault from hell. As such, our fears become self-fulfilling prophecies.

BIBLICAL SECRETS OF WAR

Spiritual warfare is unavoidable, and ignoring this subject won't make it go away. Therefore, we must learn to battle with supernatural authority! The following principles are often overlooked insights:

1. "Then it came to pass, when Pharaoh had let the people go, that God did not lead them by way of the land of the Philistines, although that was near; for God said, 'Lest perhaps the people change their minds when they see war, and return to Egypt'" (Exod. 13:17).

God is mindful of what we can handle in our present state. He leads us away from any war that might cause us to turn and abandon our call. The implication is that He leads us only into a battle we are prepared to win.

The safest place in this war is obedience. In the center of His will, we face only the situations we are equipped to win. Outside of the center is where many Christians fall, facing undue pressures that are self-inflicted. His will is the only safe place to be.

2. "You prepare a table before me in the presence of my enemies" (Ps. 23:5).

God is in no way intimidated by the devil's antics. In fact, God wants fellowship with us right before the devil's eyes. Intimacy with God is our strong suit. Never allow anything to distract you from this point of strength. Many become too "warfare intense" for their own good. Such intensity often involves displays of human strength—not grace. Choosing this *warfare intense* mentality causes us to depart from joy and intimacy with God. It's an indication that we have strayed from our *first love* (see Rev. 2:4). Paul's intimacy with God enabled him to say from a demon infested Roman prison, "Rejoice always; again I say, rejoice!"

3. "...in no way alarmed by your opponents—which is a sign of destruction for them, but of salvation for you, and that too, from God" (Phil. 1:28 NASB).

When we refuse fear, the enemy becomes terrified. A confident heart is a sure sign of his ultimate destruction and our present victory! Do not fear—ever. Return to the promises of God, spend time with people of faith, and encourage one another with the testimonies of the Lord. Praise

God for who He is until fear no longer knocks at the door. This is not an option, for fear actually invites the enemy to come to kill, steal, and destroy.

4. "Therefore submit to God. Resist the devil and he will flee from you" (James 4:7).

Submission is the key to personal triumph. Our main battle in spiritual warfare is not against the devil. It is against the flesh. Coming into subjection puts the resources of heaven at our disposal for enduring victory—enforcing what has already been obtained at Calvary.

5. "… and the gates of hell shall not prevail against it [the Church]" (Matt. 16:18 KJV).

I was not left on planet earth to be in hiding waiting for Jesus' return. I am here as a military representative of heaven. The Church is on the attack. That's why the *gates of hell*, the place of demonic government and strength, *will not prevail* against the Church.

6. "He increased His people greatly, and made them stronger than their enemies. He turned their heart to hate His people, to deal craftily with His servants" (Ps. 105:24-25).

First, God makes us strong, and then He stirs up the devil's hatred toward us. Why? It's not because He wants to create problems for His Church. It's because He likes to see the devil defeated by those who are made in His image, who have a relationship of love with Him by choice. We are His delegated authority. It is His delight to have us enforce the triumph of Jesus. "To execute on them the written judgment—this honor have all His saints" (Ps. 149:9).

7. "…let the inhabitants of Sela sing aloud.…He will arouse His zeal like a man of war. He will shout, yes, He will raise a war cry. He will prevail against His enemies" (Isa. 42:11,13 NASB).

Our ministry to God is one of life's most important privileges. Praise honors God. But it also edifies us and destroys the powers of hell!

It's amazing to think that I can praise Him, have His peace fill my soul, and have Him say that I am a mighty man of valor. All I did was worship Him. He destroyed the powers of hell on my behalf and gave me the 'points' for the victory.

This is by no means a complete list. It's just enough to turn our perspective of spiritual warfare from one that is religious and carnal, to one that has a Kingdom mind-set. Repent, change your way of thinking, and you'll be able to see how 'at hand' His Kingdom really is.

We were born in a war. There are no time-outs, no vacations, no leaves of absence. The safest place is in the center of God's will, which is the place of deep intimacy. There He allows only the battles to come our way that we are equipped to win.

Not only is this the safest place, it is the most joyful place for each believer. Outside of intimacy, we are likely to miss the greatest event on earth. That is the subject of the next chapter.

ENDNOTE

1. John G. Lake, *His Life, His Sermons, His Boldness of Faith*, (Ft. Worth, TX: Kenneth Copeland Publications, 1994), 205.

Chapter 15

HOW TO MISS
A REVIVAL

Revival is central to the message of the Kingdom, for it is in revival that we more clearly see what His dominion looks like and how it is to affect society. Revival, at its best, is, Thy Kingdom come. In a way, revival illustrates the normal Christian life.

BEFORE THE MESSIAH CAME, the religious leaders prayed for and taught about His coming. There was a worldwide stirring, even in a secular society, about something wonderful that was about to happen. And then in a manger in Bethlehem, Jesus was born.

The stargazers knew who He was and traveled a great distance to worship and give Him gifts. The devil also knew, and moved Herod to kill the first-born males in an attempt to stop Jesus' plan to redeem mankind. After he failed, he tried to lure Jesus to sin with temptation in the wilderness. What is even more startling is that this visitation of God did not escape the notice of the demon-possessed. Such was *the man at the Gadarenes*. When he saw Jesus, he fell down before Him in worship and was soon set free from his life of torment. Yet, the religious leaders that prayed for His coming didn't recognize Him when He came.

Paul and Silas preached the gospel throughout Asia Minor. The religious leaders said they were of the devil. But a demon-possessed fortune-teller girl said they were of God. How is it that those who are thought to be spiritually blind are able to see, and those who were known for their insight didn't recognize what God was doing?

History is filled with people who prayed for a visitation of God and missed it when it came. And this happened even though some had a strong relationship with God.

A DIFFERENT KIND OF BLINDNESS

Many believers have a blindness that the world doesn't have. The world knows its need. But for many Christians, once they are born again, they gradually stop recognizing their need. There is something about desperation for God that enables a person to recognize whether or not something is from God. Jesus spoke of this phenomenon, saying, "For judgment I have come into this world, that those who do not see may see, and that those who see may be made blind" (John 9:39).

The testimony of history and the record of Scripture warn us of the possibility of this error. "Therefore let him who thinks he stands take heed lest he fall" (I Cor. 10:12). Matthew says it's the *dull of heart* who can't see (see Matt. 13:15). A dull knife is one that has been used. The implication is that the dull of heart had a history in God, but did not keep current in what God was doing. We maintain our *sharp edge* as we recognize our need and passionately pursue Jesus. This *first love* somehow keeps us safely in the center of God's activities on earth.

The church of Ephesus received a letter from God. In it, Jesus addressed the fact that they had left their first love. First love is passionate by nature and dominates all other issues in one's life. If they didn't correct this problem, God said He would remove their 'lampstand.' While theologians don't all agree on what that lampstand is, one thing is for certain: a lamp enables us to see. Without it the church in Ephesus would lose their perceptive abilities. The above mentioned blindness or dullness is not always the kind that leads to hell. It just doesn't lead us to the fullness of what God has intended for us while here on earth. When passion dies, the lamp of perception is eventually removed.

KEEPING CURRENT

This phenomenon has been seen in Church history. Those who reject a move of God are generally those who were the last to experience one. This is not true of everyone, as there are always those whose hunger for God only increases throughout their years. But many form the attitude that *they have arrived*, not to perfection, but to where God intended. They paid a price to experience *the* move of God.

They wonder, "Why would God do something new, without showing it to us first?" God is a God of new things. Hungering for Him requires us to embrace the change brought on by His *new things*. Passion for God keeps us fresh and equips us to recognize the hand of God, even when others reject it. This present move requires that of us. The fear of deception gets swallowed up by confidence that God is able to keep us from falling (see Jude 24).

I'm thankful for the many seasoned saints who consider this present move a gift from heaven. Many Church historians have declared this revival to be genuine. They have seen that it bears the same fruit, and causes the same stirrings in the Church as previous revivals in history. It's been encouraging to hear various theologians affirming this revival as a true move of God. Yet, it's not their seal of approval I look for.

Whenever the great leaders of the Church stand up and declare that this is a revival, I'm encouraged. It has happened in my own denomination. But even that does not interest me as much as God's true mark of a revival. In His wisdom, He created things in such a way that when He is on the move the world often takes notice first. I look for the response of the demonized. It's the drug addict, the ex-con, and the prostitute that I want to hear from.

When God moves in revival power, these people look on, not as critics, but as people in great need of God. And we are hearing from them in great numbers. They are being transformed, saying, "Only God could make this change in my life. This is God!"

Being in a place of great need enables a person to detect when God is doing something new. That *place of great need* doesn't have to be drug addiction or prostitution. Every Christian is supposed to maintain a desperate heart for God. We are in great need! Jesus addressed that fact with these words: *"Blessed are the poor in spirit, for theirs is the kingdom of heaven"* (Matt. 5:3). Remaining poor in spirit, combined with a *first love passion for Jesus*, are the keys God created to anchor us to the center of His work.

HOW DO THE SAINTS MISS THE MOVE OF GOD?

Andrew Murray is one of the great saints of God from the early part of the twentieth century. He was known as a great teacher with a passion for prayer. His cries for revival are legendary. When he visited Wales to examine the revival of 1904, he was moved by the awesome presence of God. But he left Wales thinking that if he stayed he could unintentionally contaminate the purity of God's work. He didn't press into the revival he had been praying for.

Moves of God usually come with a stigma—something that is unappealing and considered repulsive by some. Tongues became the twentieth-century stigma that many were unwilling to bear. G. Campbell Morgan, the great man of God and Bible expositor, rejected the Pentecostal Revival, calling it *the last vomit of hell!* Bearing reproach is often a requirement to walk in revival.

Once a person is born again, there seems to be little incentive to the natural mind to pursue more of what brings disgrace. It's that absence of desperation that causes believers to miss God.

BEARING HIS REPROACH

Mary received the most shocking announcement ever given to a person. She was to give birth to the Christ child. She was chosen by God, being called "highly favored of the Lord."

This favor started with a visitation from an angel. That experience was quite frightening! Then she was given news that was incomprehensible and impossible to explain. The initial shock was followed by the duty of having to tell Joseph, her husband to be. His response was to "put her away secretly" (see Matt. 1:19). In other words, he didn't believe it was God, and didn't want to go through with their wedding plans. After all, where is the chapter and verse for this manifestation of how God works with His people? It's never happened before. There was no biblical precedent of a virgin giving birth to a child.

On top of this obvious conflict with Joseph, Mary would have to bear the stigma of being the mother of an illegitimate child all the days of her life. Favor from heaven's perspective is not always so pleasant from ours.

Like Mary, those who experience revival have spiritual encounters that are beyond reason. We seldom have immediate understanding of what God is doing and why. Sometimes our dearest friends want to *put us away*, declaring the move to be from the devil. And then there's the fact that we are looked at as a *fringe element* by the rest of the Body of Christ. The willingness to bear reproach from our brothers and sisters is part of the cost we pay for the move of the Spirit.

"Therefore Jesus…suffered outside the gate. Therefore let us go forth to Him, outside the camp, bearing His reproach" (Heb. 13:12-13). Revival usually takes us outside the camp—the religious community. That is often where He is—*outside the camp!*

Stigma by itself is no guarantee what we're experiencing is a true move of God. Some people earn reproach through heresy, impurity, and legalism. The embarrassing tension of being numbered with these is what makes the true stigma that much harder to bear. Daniel knew this inner conflict. He remained true to his call despite being considered *just another magician* by the king and his court.

HEAVEN NOW, OR HEAVEN HERE

As has been stated, quenching the Spirit is probably responsible for the end of more revivals than any other single cause. Even those who have embraced the move of God often come to a place where their comfort zone is stretched about as far as they are willing to go. They then begin to look for a place to settle—a place of understanding and control.

The second greatest reason for a revival's end is when the Church begins to look for the return of the Lord instead of pursuing a greater break-through in the Great Commission. *That kind* of hunger for heaven is not encouraged in Scripture. It turns the blessed hope into the blessed escape. To want Jesus to come back now is to sentence billions of people to hell forever. It's not that we shouldn't long for heaven. Paul said that longing was to be a comfort for the Christian. But to seek for the end of all things is to pronounce judgment on all of mankind outside of Christ. Even Paul didn't want to return to Corinth until their obedience was complete. Is Jesus, the One who paid for all sin, eager to return without that final great harvest? I think not.

I believe the desire for the Church to be in heaven now is actually the counterfeit of *seeking first the Kingdom.* There's a difference between crying for *heaven now* and *heaven here!* If a revival has brought us to the *end* of our dreams, does that mean we have reached the end of His? A revival must go beyond all we could imagine. Anything less falls short.

Many revivalists had such significant breakthroughs that they viewed the Lord's return to be at hand. They failed to equip the Church to do what they were gifted to do. As a result, they touched multitudes instead of nations and generations.

We must plan as though we have a lifetime to live, but work and pray as though we have very little time left.

CLOSE ENCOUNTERS

The disciples, who were accustomed to Jesus surprising them at every turn in the road, found themselves in yet another unusual situation: waiting for the promise of the Father—whatever that was. The ten days spent together no doubt provided opportunity to express sorrow over their stupid conversations about who was the greatest among them and who would never forsake the Lord. Something of that nature must have happened because they were still together without Jesus being there keeping the peace.

They were about to have an encounter that would dwarf every previous experience. God was about to saturate their beings with Himself, taking the power they saw flowing through Jesus and causing it to explode within them. This would be the culmination of God's restorative and commissioning efforts since man abandoned the call to subdue the earth back in Genesis. This would become the high-water mark for all of mankind—ever.

Ten days had passed, Pentecost had come, and they were still praying as they did the other nine days. "And suddenly…"(Acts 2:2). A room with 120 people was now filled with the sound of wind, fire, and ecstatic expressions of praise uttered through known and unknown languages (see Acts 2:4-11).

No matter how people interpret Paul's instruction on the use of spiritual gifts, one thing must be agreed upon: this meeting was entirely directed by the Holy Spirit. This infant Church hadn't learned enough to try and control God. They hadn't developed biases over acceptable and unacceptable practices. They had no biblical or experiential grid for what was happening. Notice the elements of this Spirit-directed service:

1. They were praying.

2. They were in unity.

3. They all spoke in tongues.

4. Unbelievers heard those tongues.

5. People were saved.[1]

Consider the Acts 2 company's predicament: they just had an encounter with God without a chapter and verse to explain what just happened. Peter, under the direction of the Holy Spirit, chose to use Joel 2 as the proof-text to give the needed backbone to their experience. Joel 2 declares there would be an outpouring of the Holy Spirit involving prophecy, dreams, and visions. The outpouring happened as promised in Acts 2, but it had none of the things mentioned by Joel. Instead, it had the sound of wind, fire, and tongues. It was God who used this passage to support this new experience.

The very fact that this seems like an improper interpretation of Scripture should reveal to us that it is we who often approach His book incorrectly. The Bible is not a book of lists that confine or corral God. The Word does not contain God—it reveals Him. Joel 2 revealed the nature of God's work among man. Acts 2 was an illustration of what God intended by that prophecy.

TO BE OR NOT TO BE OFFENSIVE

Many church services are designed to be as unoffensive as possible. The assumption is that any use of the gifts of the Spirit will send people running, turning them off to the gospel. They are already turned off.

For the most part, expressive worship, ministry in spiritual gifts, and the like only turn off Christians who have had the unfortunate experience of being taught against them. And many of these same individuals warm up to such things when they face an impossible situation and need the help of someone experienced in the gospel of power.

The Church has an unhealthy addiction to perfection: the kind that makes no allowances for messes. This standard can only be met by restricting or rejecting the use of the gifts of the Spirit. "Let all things be done decently and in order" (I Cor. 14:40). The "all things" of this verse refer to the manifestations of the Holy Spirit. Therefore, *all things must be done* before we have the right to discuss order.

Keeping things tidy has become our great commission. The gifts of the Spirit interfere with the drive for order, and order becomes valued above increase. So why should we value an occasional mess? "Where no oxen are, the trough is clean; but much increase comes by the strength of an ox" (Prov. 14:4). Messes are necessary for increase.

How important is increase to God? Jesus once cursed a fig tree for not bearing fruit out of season (see Mark 11:13-14)! A man in one of His parables was cast into outer darkness for burying his money and not obtaining an increase for his master (see Matt. 25:24-30).

There is a big difference between graveyards and nurseries. One has perfect order, and the other has life. The childless person may walk into the church nursery with all the joyous activities of the children and mistakenly call the place out of order. Compared to their living room, it is. But when a parent walks in and sees her little one playing with other youngsters, she thinks it is perfect! It's all a matter of perspective. Order is for the purpose of promoting life. Beyond that it works against the things we say we value.

IN WHOSE IMAGE

We miss God when we live as though we have Him figured out. We have the habit of making Him look like us. In fact, if we think we understand Him we have probably conformed Him into our image. There must remain mystery in our relationship with this One who has purposed to work beyond our capacity to imagine (see Eph. 3:20). To endeavor to know Him is to embark on an adventure in which questions increase.

Our God-born desire for revival must keep us desperate enough to recognize Him when He comes. Without such desperation, we get satisfied with our present status and become our own worst enemies at changing history.

History cannot be changed effectively until we are willing to get our hands *dirty*. We do that when we embrace the call to infiltrate the Babylonian system, which is the subject of the next chapter.

ENDNOTE

1. Is it possible that Paul's instructions on the proper use of the gifts have been used to define Acts 2 instead of Acts 2 illustrating the proper interpretation of Paul's instruction in First Corinthians 12 and 14?

Chapter 16

INFILTRATING
THE SYSTEM

*And again He said, "To what shall I liken the kingdom of God? It is like leaven,
which a woman took and hid in three measures of meal till it was all leavened"*
(Luke 13:20-21).

I ONCE TAUGHT ON THIS passage in a small pastor's conference in a European country. My subject was: *The Infiltrating Power of the Kingdom of God.* Much like light that exposes or salt that preserves, leaven influences its surroundings in a subtle but overpowering way. So it is with the Kingdom of God. I spoke about some of the practical strategies we had taken as a church to infiltrate the social system in our area for the cause of Christ.

We had a young man in our church who was on trial. He had already spent time in prison, and was looking at a possible 20-year sentence. He committed the crime before his recent conversion. Both the judge and the prosecuting attorney admitted this young man's life had been transformed by God. But they wanted some measure of justice for the crime. So they sentenced him to six months in a short-term prison. The Sunday before he left, we laid our hands on him, sending him out as a missionary to a mission field that none of us could get into. As a result of this infiltration, over 60 of the approximate 110 prisoners confessed Christ within a year.

Following my message to the pastors, several leaders met together discussing the concepts I had presented. They broke from their huddle to inform me that I was in error. "Leaven always refers to sin," they said, "and this parable shows how the Church will be filled with sin and compromise in the last days." They saw it as a warning, not a promise.

Although I do not dishonor my brothers,[1] I reject this survivalist posture—it disarms and distracts us from the true mind of Christ: one of great triumph. The mistake my brothers made is twofold:

1. They mistook the Church for the Kingdom. They are not the same. The Church is to live in the realm of the *King's domain*, but it in itself is not the Kingdom. While sin does infect the Church, the Kingdom is the realm of God's rule. Sin cannot penetrate and influence that realm.

2. Their predisposition to see a weak, struggling Church in the last days has made it difficult to see the promise of God for revival. It is impossible to have faith where you have no hope. Such approaches to understanding Scripture have crippled the Church.

IT'S OUR TURN

Without a revelation of what God intends to do with His Church, we cannot move in overcoming faith. When the main goal of our faith is keeping us safe from the devil, our faith becomes inferior to what God expects. Jesus had in mind more for us than survival. We are destined to overcome.

Every conversion plunders hell. Every miracle destroys the works of the devil. Every God encounter is an *invasion of the Almighty* into our desperate condition. This is our joy.

The original flame of Pentecost, the Holy Spirit Himself, burns within my soul. I have a promise from God. I am a part of a company of people destined to do greater works than Jesus did in His earthly ministry. Why is it so hard to see the Church with significant influence in the last days? It was God who determined that the Bride should be spotless and without wrinkle. It was God who declared, "Behold darkness will cover the earth, but His glory will appear upon you" (Isa. 60:2 NASB). It was God who calls us, His Church, overcomers (see Rev. 12:11).

The parable about leaven illustrates the subtle but overwhelming influence of the Kingdom in any setting into which it is placed. In these days, God has planned to put us into the darkest of situations to demonstrate His dominion.

A jeweler often places a diamond on a piece of black velvet. The brilliance of the gem is clearer against that background. So it is with the Church. The dark condition of the world's circumstances becomes the backdrop upon which He displays His glorious Church! "Where sin abounded, grace abounded much more" (Rom. 5:20).

To illustrate the principle of infiltrating a dark world system, we will look at two Old Testament heroes who give prophetic insight for today's overcoming Church.

DANIEL AS LEAVEN

Daniel was probably around 15 years old when we begin his story. He was taken away from his family, made a eunuch, and put into the king's service. He, along with Shadrach, Meshach, and Abednego, were chosen because they were "good looking, gifted in all wisdom, possessing knowledge and quick to understand, who had ability to serve in the king's palace, and whom they might teach the language and literature of the Chaldean's" (Dan. 1:4).

Daniel started as a trainee in Nebuchadnezzar's court, but later was promoted to an advisor of foreign kings. He grew above all others in wisdom, and became a counselor to the king. Because of his excellence in service and power, the king considered him ten times better than all the others (see Dan. 1:20).

To more accurately understand the setting, remember that Daniel is now a part of one of the most demonically inspired kingdoms to ever rule the earth. He is deeply embedded into that system. He is numbered with the magicians, astrologers, and sorcerers. While God considered him to be His man, he was just another spiritualist to the king...at least for a season. What a strange group of people to be associated with, especially when you consider that we're talking about Daniel, a prophet without blemish. His unwillingness to be defiled is legendary, raising the high-water mark for generations of prophets to follow.

Babylon was a sophisticated society, with enough distractions to keep any Hebrew in the constant tension between devotion to God and an unhealthy love for this world. When you add strong idolatrous worship and the demonic presence it brings, you have a deadly combination that would undermine the faith of any casual Christian. Daniel, on the other hand, was absolute in his devotion to God, and uncompromising in his purpose. He sought for excellence in his position as *leaven*. If you want to find someone with a reason for bitterness, you've just found him—taken away from his family, made into a eunuch, and forced to serve among the cultists. Greatness in God is often on the other side of injustice and offense. Daniel made it over this hurdle, but not because he was great. He was victorious because of his devotion to the One who is great!

THE POWER OF HOLINESS

Daniel discovered early on the power of holiness. He was unwilling to eat the king's delicacies. Separation to God is demonstrated in personal lifestyle, not associations. He could not control his surroundings. So often the Church gets this backward. Many in the Church live the same way as those in the world, but they will not associate with unbelievers so as not to be defiled. Many Christians prefer to work in a Christian business, attend Christian meetings, and isolate themselves from the very people we are left on the planet to touch in His name. This is the logical product of survival theology. The Kingdom is the realm of the Spirit of God demonstrating the lordship of Jesus. And it's a Spirit-empowered life that has the affect of leaven in a dark world.

THE ULTIMATE CHALLENGE

The ultimate challenge came to all the king's wise men when he asked them not only to interpret a dream he just had, but also tell him what the dream was! When they couldn't, he ordered all the wise men killed. In the process, they sought to kill Daniel and his friends. Daniel asked for an audience with the king. He believed God would enable him to bring the word of the Lord. Before he told the king the dream and it's interpretation, he taught him a virtue of the Kingdom of God called humility. Daniel stated, "This secret has not been revealed to me because I have more wisdom than anyone living, but for our sakes who make known the interpretation to the king, and that you may know the thoughts of your heart" (Dan. 2:30). In other words, it's not because I am great or gifted; it's because God wants us to live, and He wants you to have this message. He then interprets the dream as a servant.

So much of today's Kingdom theology is focused on us ruling, in the sense of believers becoming the heads of corporations and governments. And, in measure, it is true. But our strong suit has been, and always will be, service. If in serving we get promoted to positions of rulership, we must remember that *what got us there will keep us useful*. In the Kingdom, the greatest is the servant of all. Use every position to serve with more power.

PROMOTION CHALLENGED

The Hebrew four were promoted as a result of Daniel's prophetic gift. Please note that there is no mention of Daniel operating in this gift before this crisis. Something similar happened to an evangelist friend of mine while still in his youth. He was invited to speak in a church in Canada. When he got off the plane, the pastor met him with a surprised look on his face, saying, "You're not Morris Cerullo!" The Pastor had a great hunger for signs and wonders to be restored to his church, and thought he had booked a week of meetings with Morris Cerullo. The shocked pastor asked the young man if he had a signs and wonders ministry. He answered, "No." The pastor, looking at his watch said, "You've got four hours to get one," and then took him to the hotel. Out of desperation, the young evangelist cried out to God, and God honored his cry. That night was the beginning of the signs and wonders ministry that has marked his life to this day. God orchestrated these circumstances so that both Daniel and this young evangelist would earnestly pursue spiritual gifts.

Infiltrating the system often involves our willingness to bring spiritual gifts into our world. These gifts actually work better in the world than in the confines of church meetings. When we practice the gifts only in the church, they lose their sharp edge. Invading the world system with His dominion keeps us sharp and gets them saved.

SALVATION BY ASSOCIATION

The rest of the wise men, comprised of magicians, astrologers, etc., were spared because of Daniel. The presence of the Kingdom saves the lives of people who have not earned it through personal obedience. Such is the power of righteousness—it protects those around it.

Promotion does not go unchallenged. Just when you think you have been placed into a position of influence, something will happen to totally rock your boat. Nebuchadnezzar made a golden image that stood 90 feet tall. All in his kingdom were to worship this thing. But the Hebrew children would not. There is a distinction between submission and obedience. Sometimes we are to go against the command of our leaders—but even then, only with submissive hearts.

THE SYSTEM INVADED

An additional lesson from Daniel's life as leaven is found in chapter 4. He has been given the interpretation to another dream. It is about the judgment of God against Nebuchadnezzar. Remember, this is the leader of a demonically inspired kingdom—one that required idolatry! Men of lesser character would have rejoiced in God's judgment. Not Daniel. His response to his master was: "My lord, may the dream concern those who hate you, and its interpretation concern your enemies" (Dan. 4:19).

What loyalty! His devotion was not based on the character of his king. It was based on the character of the One who assigned him the position of service. Some would have had an *I told you so* response to their boss if God judged them in the same way. The world has seen our *holier than thou* attitude, and they're not impressed. It's time they see a loyalty that is not based on genuine goodness. Responses like Daniel's become noticed. They display the Kingdom in its purity and power. They are revolutionary.

The closing verses of chapter 4 record what is possibly the greatest conversion of all time: that of Nebuchadnezzar. He was the darkest ruler ever to live. His final recorded words are: "Now I, Nebuchadnezzar, praise and extol and honor the King of heaven, all of whose works are truth, and His ways justice. And those who walk in pride, He is able to put down" (Dan. 4:37). He was saved from hell because of the leavening power of the Kingdom of God. The system was invaded, righteousness was established, power was displayed, and people were saved.

For massive worldwide revival to reach it's dominating potential, it must be taken out of the four walls of the church and launched into the *marketplace* (see Mark 6:56). Quietly, powerfully, decisively invade through service; and when you run into a person with an impossibility, let him know the reality of heaven is within arm's reach! And "let your peace come upon it" (Matt. 10:13).

JOSEPH AS LEAVEN

God had spoken to Joseph about his purpose in life through dreams. Sharing them with his family got him in trouble. His brothers were already jealous because he was his father's favorite. They later captured him and sold him into slavery.

God prospered him wherever he went because he was a man of promise. As a great servant, he obtained favor in Potiphar's house. When Potiphar's wife tried to seduce him, he said no. She then lied and had him put in prison, where he again prospered. While circumstances had gone from bad to worse, God was establishing the qualities of leaven in His man.

While in prison, he met a butler and a baker who worked for the king. They each had a dream, but were sad because they didn't understand them. Joseph responded, "Do not interpretations belong to God? Tell them to me, please." Joseph had obviously not become bitter against God, and used his gift to interpret their dreams. For the butler it was good news, and he was freed. But the baker was executed.

Sometime later, Pharaoh had two troubling dreams. The butler remembered Joseph's gift, and he was brought before the king. When asked to interpret the king's dream, Joseph replied, "It is not in me." Such a humble heart keeps us useful to God.

Joseph interpreted the dreams and then operated in the gift of wisdom by giving the king counsel as to what to do next. The king honored him by putting him second in command over the entire Egyptian Empire.

Joseph gives us one of the best illustrations of forgiveness in the Bible. His brothers come to him (unknowingly) because of famine in their land. When he finally reveals who he is, and the obvious fulfillment of his dreams, he says, "But now, do not therefore be grieved or angry with yourselves because you sold me here; for God sent me before you to preserve life" (Gen. 45:5).

Notice that Joseph did not forget what happened to him. The notion that we are expected to forget what someone has done to us causes us more damage than good. Suppression simply hides a wound from view. Incubating the wound causes the infection to worsen.

LEARNING FROM THEIR EXAMPLE

Infiltrating the system involves both purity and power. Purity is seen in the character of these men as they demonstrated loyalty and forgiveness beyond reason. Power was released through the use of their gifts.

To be effective as leaven in the *Babylonian system*, we must rethink our understanding of these subjects. God's people must find a heart to see others succeed. Anyone can wish good upon someone who conforms to his or her beliefs and disciplines. But the ability to express loyalty and forgiveness before someone is saved may be the key to touching that individual's heart.

Personal integrity is the backbone of all life and ministry, and our credibility is founded on this one thing. We can be gifted beyond measure. But if we can't be trusted, the world will turn a deaf ear to our message. Integrity is holiness, and holiness is the nature of God. Yieldedness to the Holy Spirit is at the heart of the integrity issue.

TAKING IT TO THE MARKETPLACE

"Wherever He entered, into villages, cities, or the country, they laid the sick in the marketplaces, and begged Him that they might just touch the hem of His garment. And as many as touched Him were made well" (Mark 6:56).

Any gospel that doesn't work in the marketplace, doesn't work. Jesus invaded every realm of society. He went where people gathered. They became His focus, and He became theirs.

We see businessmen use the gifts of the Spirit to identify the needs of their co-workers and customers. A young teammate laid hands on the star running back of his high school football team after he had been knocked out of the game with a serious leg injury. After the running back was healed, he returned to the game acknowledging God had healed him!

A young girl with sugar diabetes was suffering from insulin shock. Her Christian friend prayed for her on the way to the nurse's office. When the mother picked her up from school and took her to the doctor, they found she no longer had diabetes.

A 10-year-old asked her mom to take her to the mall so she could find sick people to pray for. Students set up a sign at their table at our local coffee shop. It says, *"Free Prayer."* People not only got prayer, they received a prophetic word that brought them to a greater awareness of God's love.

Teams of people bring hot meals to our local hotels to touch the needy. A hotel owner gave us a room for a season just so we would have a place to pray for the many sick patrons.

Some invade the bars looking for people who need ministry. The gifts of the Spirit flow powerfully in these environments. In my brother's ministry, grandmas go into the bars in San Francisco. While he stands to the side for their safety, the women sit at a table with a soda and pray. One by one people come to their table asking for prayer. It's common for them to kneel and weep as they discover God's love for them.

Yards in the poorest communities are mowed and cleaned, while others clean the insides of the homes. Some go house to house looking to pray for the sick. Miracles are the norm.

Skateboarders are touched by other skateboarders who look to bring them into an encounter with the God of all power. If people are there, we go there. Under the bridges, out in the vacant lots, we look for the homeless.

We bus the neediest to the church for a holiday banquet. Our families adopt a table, setting it with their finest china, crystal, and silverware. The most broken of our community are brought to the church to be treated as heaven's treasure. They are fed, clothed, and ministered to for their most basic natural and spiritual needs.

Not only does Jesus care for the down and outer, but He also loves the up and outer. The wealthy are some of the most broken of our cities. But we must not serve them for their money! They are accustomed to people becoming friends to get something from them.

Parents become Little League coaches. Some lead after-school programs in our public schools. Others volunteer at a local hospital, or become trained as chaplains for the police department or local high schools. People visit their sick neighbors, seeing God do the impossible.

Where does life take you? Go there in the anointing and watch the impossibilities bow to the name Jesus.

JURY DUTY WITH THE HOLY SPIRIT

Buck was a man who fully embraced taking the gifts into the marketplace. He was selected for jury duty. As soon as he sat down, the Lord spoke to him: "Justice must prevail." When the trial phase was finally over and the jury began to deliberate, they found themselves divided as to the interpretation of the law. Buck explained the issues in such a remarkable way that the others thought he had studied law. He used that opportunity to share his testimony. He was once a great science student, but his mind had been ravished by a lifestyle of drug addiction. Jesus healed his mind as he memorized Scripture. His testimony won the hearts of some jurists, but drove others away.

When it was time to cast their verdict, they were evenly divided. So the deliberations carried over to the next day. Their point of contention was the definition of a *criminal*. The man being tried fit six of the seven qualifications needed for him to be considered guilty. The seventh was questionable. So Buck brought a rose in a vase the next day of deliberations. Everyone thought it was a nice gesture. He let them argue for a while and then asked them, "What is this on the table?" They looked at him like he was stupid, and said, "A rose!" He asked them if they were sure, and they said yes.

He pressed them further asking, "What are the parts that make up a rose?" They listed the petals, stem, leaves, thorns, etc. So he asked them, "Do you see all those parts of this rose?" They responded, "Yes, everything but the thorns." So he asked, "Is it still a rose without those thorns?" They said, "Yes!" To which he stated, "And this man is a criminal!"

They got the message. The gift of wisdom had been in operation without their knowing it. Now all but two agreed he was guilty. It was still a hung jury. When the judge asked each juror if they believed they could come to an agreement, they all said no. That is, except Buck. In his heart were the words, *"justice must prevail."* The judge then gave them 30 minutes to work through their disagreement. As soon as they entered the room for deliberation, the word of the Lord came to Buck. He pointed to one of the two jurors and said, "You say he's innocent because..." Buck proceeded to expose a secret sin in the juror's life. He then turned to the other and did the same. They both looked at each other and said, "I'll change my vote if you change yours!"

Buck first brought the gift of wisdom into the deliberations. It helped to bring clarification that benefited even unbelievers. He then brought a word of knowledge, something that he could not have known in the natural, to expose the sin in two people who had rejected God's dealings. In the end, the will of God prevailed in the situation—*justice!*

Being involved in the supernatural through spiritual gifts is what makes the invasion effective. The Kingdom of God is a Kingdom of power! We must be in pursuit of a fuller demonstration of the Spirit of God. Pray much and take risks.

The ultimate example of this invasion is Jesus. In Him, the supernatural invaded the natural.

Vision, defined by the dreams of God, equip us with undying courage. Such is the purpose of the next and final chapter.

ENDNOTE

1. Please understand, there is a great difference between despising a doctrine and rejecting a brother or sister in the Lord. Phariseeism is born when we think it's OK to reject people in order to protect ideas.

Chapter 17

THIS PRESENT REVIVAL

What God has planned for the Church in this hour is greater than our ability to imagine and pray. We must have the help of the Holy Spirit to learn about these mysteries of the Church and God's Kingdom. Without Him we don't have enough insight even to know what to ask for in prayer.

UNDERSTANDING WHAT IS ABOUT to come is important, but not to equip us to plan and strategize more effectively. On the contrary, it's important to understand God's promise and purpose for the Church so that we might become dissatisfied—so that we will become desperate. Intercession from insatiable hunger moves the heart of God as nothing else can.

Revival is not for the faint of heart. It brings fear to the complacent because of the risks it requires. The fearful often work against the move of God—sometimes to their death—all the while thinking they are working for Him. Deception says that the changes brought about by revival contradict the faith of their fathers. As a result, the God-given ability to create withers into the laborious task of preserving. The fearful become curators of museums instead of builders of the Kingdom.

Others are ready to risk all. The faith of their fathers is considered a worthy foundation to build upon. They have caught a glimpse of what could be and will settle for nothing less. Change is not a threat, but an adventure. Revelation increases, ideas multiply, and the stretch begins.

"The Lord God does nothing unless He reveals His secret counsel to His servants the prophets" (Amos 3:7 NASB). God's activities on earth begin with a revelation to mankind. The prophet hears and declares. Those with ears to hear respond and are equipped for change.

In order to understand who we are and what we are to become, we must see Jesus *as He is*. We are about to see the difference between the Jesus who walked the streets healing the sick and raising the dead, and the Jesus who today reigns over all. As glorious as His life was on earth, it was the *before* side of the Cross. Christianity is life on the resurrection side of the Cross.

This shift in focus will come in these last days. It must happen if we are to become what He has purposed for us.

Religion (which is "form without power") will be more and more despised in the hearts of those who truly belong to Him. Revelation creates an appetite for Him. He doesn't come in a "no frills" model. There's no economy class Holy Spirit. He only comes fully equipped. He is loaded, full of power and glory. And He wants to be seen as He is, in us.

A GREATER CONCEPT

The power of one word from His mouth can create a galaxy. His promises for the Church are beyond all comprehension. Too many consider them to be God's promise either for the Millennium or heaven, claiming that to emphasize God's plan for now instead of eternity is to dishonor the fact that Jesus has gone to prepare a place for us. Our predisposition toward a weak Church has blinded our eyes to the truths of God's Word about us. This problem is rooted in our unbelief, not in our hunger for heaven. Jesus taught us how to live by announcing, "The Kingdom of God is at hand!" It is a present reality affecting the *now*.

We lack understanding of who we are because we have little revelation of who He is. We know a lot about His life on earth. The Gospels are filled with information about what He was like, how He lived, and what He did. Yet that is not the example of what the Church is to become. What He is today, glorified, seated at the right hand of the Father, is the model for what we are becoming!

Consider the opening statement: *What God has planned for the Church in this hour is greater than our ability to imagine and pray.* Such statements cause some to fear the Church will not be balanced. Many say that we must be careful over how much emphasis we put on what we are to become *in the now.* Why? For the most part, it is a fear of disappointment that creates such caution. Fear of disappointment has justified our unbelief. What is the worst that could happen if I pursued what is reserved for eternity? God could say, *No!* We make a big mistake to think we can figure out what has been reserved for heaven, from this side of heaven.

Because many fear excess, mediocrity is embraced as balance. Such fear makes complacency a virtue. And it's the fear of excess that has made those that are resistant to change appear noble minded. Excess has never brought an end to revival. William DeArteaga states, "The Great Awakening was not quenched because of its extremists. It was quenched because of the condemnation of its opponents."[1] He also says, "Divisions occur whenever the intellect is enthroned as the measure of spirituality—not because spiritual gifts are exercised, as many charge."[2] I pay no attention to the warnings of possible excess from those who are satisfied with lack.

This generation is a generation of risk takers. And not all the risks taken will be seen as real faith. Some will come to light as steps of foolishness and presumption. But they must be taken just the same. How else can we learn? Make room for risk takers in your life that don't *bat a thousand.* They will inspire you to the greatness available in serving a great God.

The local steelhead fishermen say, "If you don't get your rig snagged on the bottom of the river now and then, you're not fishing deep enough." While I don't want to honor presumption or error, I do want to applaud passion and effort. Our obsession with perfection has given place to some of our greatest blemishes. When I taught my sons to ride a bike, I took them to the park where there was lots of grass. Why? Because I wanted them not to get hurt *when* they fell. It was not a question of *if*. The addiction to perfection has given place to a religious spirit. People who refuse to step out and be used by God become the critics of those who do. Risk takers, the ones who thrill the heart of God, become the targets of those who never fail because they seldom try.

THE COMING GLORIOUS CHURCH...

The following is a *partial* list of things that are mentioned in Scripture about the Church that have yet to be fulfilled. Jesus intends for us to become mature before He returns. Each of these passages provides a prophetic glimpse into the heart of God for us right now.

Wisdom of God

That now the manifold **wisdom** *of God might be made known by the church to the principalities and powers in the heavenly places, according to His eternal purpose...* (Ephesians 3:10-11).

Wisdom is to be displayed by us NOW! It is clear that God intends to teach the spirit realm about His wisdom through those made in His image—us.

Solomon was the wisest man ever to live, apart from Jesus who is wisdom personified (see I Cor. 1:30). The queen of Sheba came to examine Solomon's wisdom. "And when the queen of Sheba had seen the wisdom of Solomon, the house that he had built, the food on his table, the seating of his servants, the service of his waiters and their apparel, his cup bearers and their apparel, and his entryway by which he went up to the house of the Lord, there was no more spirit in her" (2 Chron. 9:4). She acknowledged that his wisdom was far greater than she ever imagined. The depth of his wisdom was actually identified by these three attributes: *excellence, creativity, and integrity.* When she saw it in action, it took her breath away!

The wisdom of God will again be seen in His people. The Church, which is presently despised, or at best ignored, will again be reverenced and admired. The Church will again be a praise in the earth (see Jer. 33:9).

Let's examine the three elements belonging to Solomon's wisdom:

Excellence is the high standard for what we do because of who we are. God is extravagant, but not wasteful. An excellent heart for God may appear to be wasteful to those on the outside. For example: In Matthew 26:8, we find Mary pouring out an ointment upon Jesus that cost a full year's income. The disciples thought it would be put to better use if it would have been sold and the money given to the poor. In Second Samuel 6:14:-16 and 23, King David humbled himself before the people by taking off his kingly garments and dancing wildly before God. His wife, Michal, despised him for it. As a result, she bore no children to the day of her death—either from barrenness or from the lack of intimacy between her and her husband, David. It was a tragic loss caused by pride. In both situations outsiders considered the extravagant actions of these worshippers to be wasteful. God is good. Excellence comes from viewing things from His perspective.

In pursuing this virtue, we do all to the glory of God, with all our might. A heart of excellence has no place for the poverty spirit that affects so much of what we do.

Creativity is not only seen in a full restoration of the arts, but is the nature of His people in finding new and better ways to do things. It is a shame for the Church to fall into the rut of predictability and call it tradition. We must reveal who our Father is through creative expression.

The Church is often guilty of avoiding creativity because it requires change. Resistance to change is a resistance to the nature of God. Because the winds of change are blowing, it will be easy to distinguish between those who are satisfied and those who are hungry. Change brings to light the secrets of the heart.

This anointing will also bring about new inventions, breakthroughs in medicine and science, and novel ideas for business and education. New sounds of music will come from the Church, as will other forms of art. The list is endless. The sky is the limit. Arise and create!

Integrity is the expression of God's character seen in us. And that character is His holiness. Holiness is the essence of His nature. It is not something He does or doesn't do. It is who He is. It is the same for us. We are holy because the nature of God is in us. It begins with a heart separated unto God, and becomes evident in the Christ nature seen through us.

If we can keep the soiled hands of religion from the beautiful expression of God's holiness, people will be attracted to the Church as they were to Jesus. Religion is not only boring; it is cruel. It takes the breath out of every good thing. True holiness is refreshingly good.

The queen of Sheba became speechless in response to Solomon's wisdom. It's time for the Church's wisdom to cause the world to become silent again.

Glorious Church

. . .*that He might present her to Himself a **glorious church*** (Ephesians 5:27).

God's original intent for mankind is seen in the passage, "For all have sinned and fallen short of the glory of God" (Rom. 3:23). We were to live in the glory of God. That was the target when God created mankind. Our sin caused the arrow of His purpose to fall short.

The glory of God is the manifested presence of Jesus. Imagine this: a people that are continually conscious of the presence of God, not in theory, but the actual presence of God upon them!

We will be a Church in which Jesus is seen in His glory! It is the Holy Spirit's presence and anointing that will dominate the Christian's life. The Church will be radiant. "The latter glory of this house will be greater than the former" (Hag. 2:9 NASB).

Bride Without Spot or Wrinkle

*...that He might present her to Himself a glorious church, **not having spot or wrinkle** or any such thing, but that she should be holy and without blame* (Ephesians 5:27).

Imagine a beautiful young woman prepared for a wedding. She has taken care of herself by eating right and getting all the exercise she needs. Her mind is sharp and she is emotionally secure and free. By looking at her, you'd never know she had ever done anything wrong. Guilt and shame do not blemish her countenance. She understands and exudes grace. According to Revelation 19:7, she made herself ready. Romance will do that to you. As Larry Randolph puts it, "It's a perversion to expect the groom to dress the bride for the wedding." The Church is to make herself ready. The tools are in place for such an event. The Church must now use them.

The former is a biblical description of the Bride of Christ. When we see how great God is, we'll not question His ability to pull this one off. Paul makes a statement to the church at Corinth that he didn't want to return to them until their obedience was complete. That is the heart of God for the Church. And so, Jesus, *the perfect One*, will return for *the spotless one* when He views our obedience as complete.

Unity of Faith

*...till we all come to the **unity of the faith**...* (Ephesians 4:13).

This that is called the *unity of faith* is the *faith that works through love* mentioned in Galatians 5:6. Love and faith are the two essentials of the Christian life.

Faith comes from the Word of God, specifically *"a word freshly spoken."* Faith is what pleases God. It is active trust in Him as Abba Father. He alone is the source of such faith. It comes as the result of Him speaking to His people. Unity of faith means we will hear His voice together, and demonstrate great exploits. It is a lifestyle, not just a concept—as in having *unity in our ideas about faith.* The exploits of the present and coming revival will surpass all the accomplishments of the Church in all history combined. Over 1 billion souls will be saved. Stadiums will be filled with people 24 hours a day, for days on end, with miracles beyond number: healings, conversions, resurrections, and deliverances too many to count. No special speaker, no well-known miracle worker, just the Church being what God has called her to be. And all this will be the outgrowth of the *unity of faith.*

Revelation Knowledge of the Son

*...till we all come to the unity of the faith and of the **knowledge of the Son of God**...* (Ephesians 4:13).

The apostle John once laid his head on the chest of Jesus. He was called the one whom Jesus loved. Toward the end of his life, on the Isles of Patmos, he saw Jesus again. This time Jesus looked nothing like the one he shared that final meal with. His hair was white like wool, His eyes were a flame of fire, and His feet were like burnished bronze. God felt that this revelation was worthy of a book. It is called: The Revelation of Jesus Christ. The entire Church will receive a fresh revelation of Jesus Christ, especially through that book. This that has been so mysterious will be understood. And that revelation will launch the Church into a transformation unlike any experienced in a previous age. Why? *Because as we see Him, we become like Him!*

If the revelation of Jesus is the primary focus of the Book of Revelation, then we'd also have to admit that worship is the central response. The coming increase in revelation of Jesus will be measurable through new dimensions of worship—corporate throne room experiences.

A Mature Man

...till we all come to the unity of the faith and of the knowledge of the
Son of God, to **a perfect man**... (Ephesians 4:13).

An Olympic athlete will never get to the games by gifting alone. It's the powerful combination of a gift brought to its full potential through discipline. That is the picture of the Church becoming a mature man. It is singular, meaning we all function together as one. All its members will work in perfect coordination and harmony, complementing each other's function and gift, according to the directions given by the head. This was not a promise to be fulfilled in eternity. While I don't believe that this is speaking of human perfection, I do believe there is a maturity of function, without jealousy, that will develop as His presence becomes more manifest. We need to embrace this as possible because He said it is.

Filled With the Fullness of God

...to know the love of Christ which passes knowledge; that you may be
filled with all the fullness of God (Ephesians 3:19).

Imagine a house with many rooms. This house represents our life. Every room that we allow His love to touch becomes filled with His fullness. That is the picture of this verse. The Church will know the love of God by experience. This will go beyond our ability to comprehend. That intimate love relationship with God will help us to receive all that He has desired to release since the beginning of time.

...till we all come to the unity of the faith and of the knowledge of the
Son of God, to a perfect man, to the measure of the stature of the fullness
of Christ (Ephesians 4:13).

The experiential love of God, and the corresponding fullness of the Spirit, is what is necessary to bring us to the full *stature of Christ—Jesus will be accurately seen in the Church, just as the Father was accurately seen in Jesus.*

Gifts of the Spirit Fully Expressed

*And it shall come to pass in the last days, says God, that I will pour out of My Spirit on **all flesh**; your **sons** and your **daughters** shall prophesy, your **young** men shall see visions, your **old** men shall dream dreams. And on My **menservants** and on My **maidservants** I will pour out My Spirit in those days; and **they** shall prophesy* (Acts 2:17-21).

This passage quoted from Joel 2 has never been completely fulfilled. It had initial fulfillment in Acts 2, but its reach was far greater than that generation could fulfill. First of all, *all flesh* was never touched by that revival. But it will happen. In the coming move of God, racial barriers will be broken, as will the economic, sexual, and age barriers. The outpouring of the Spirit in the last generation will touch every nation on the earth, releasing the gifts of the Spirit in full measure upon and through His people.

First Corinthians 12–14 is a wonderful teaching on the operation of the gifts of the Spirit. But it is so much more. It is a revelation of a body of believers who live in the realm of the Spirit that is essential for last days' ministry. These manifestations of the Holy Spirit will be taken to the streets where they belong. It is there that they reach their full potential.

This generation will fulfill the cry of Moses for all of God's people to be prophets. We will carry the Elijah anointing in preparing for the return of the Lord in the same way that John the Baptist carried the Elijah anointing and prepared the people for the coming of the Lord.

Greater Works

...He who believes in Me, the works that I do he will do also; and **greater works** *than these he will do, because I go to My Father* (John 14:12).

Jesus' prophecy of us doing greater works than He did has stirred the Church to look for some abstract meaning to this very simple statement. Many theologians seek to honor the works of Jesus as unattainable, which is religion fathered by unbelief. It does not impress God to ignore what He promised under the guise of honoring the work of Jesus on the earth. Jesus' statement is not that hard to understand. *Greater* means "greater." And the *works* He referred to are signs and wonders. It will not be a disservice to Him to have a generation obey Him, and go beyond His own *high-water mark*. He showed us what one person could do who has the Spirit without measure. What could millions do? That was His point, and it became His prophecy.

This verse is often explained away by saying it refers to *quantity* of works, not *quality*. As you can see, millions of people should be able to surpass the sheer number of works that Jesus did simply because we are so many. But that waters down the intent of His statement. The word greater is *mizon* in the Greek. It is found 45 times in the New Testament. It is always used to describe "quality," not quantity.

Thy Kingdom Come

Your kingdom come. Your will be done on earth as it is in heaven (Matthew 6:10).

He's not the kind of Father who gives us a command to ask for something without fully intending to answer our request. He directs us to pray this prayer because it is in His heart to fulfill it. The safest prayers in existence are the ones He tells us to pray. His answer will be *beyond all we could ask or think*. And it is *"according to the power that works in us"* (Eph. 3:20).

Jesus said that He would be returning after the gospel of the Kingdom is preached in all the world—then the end would come (see Matt. 24:14). The present-day understanding of *preaching the gospel of the Kingdom* means to preach a message that will bring as many people to conversion as possible. But what did preaching the gospel of the Kingdom mean to Jesus? Every instance in which He either did it, or commanded it, miracles followed. The message was to be a declaration of His lordship and dominion over all things, followed by demonstrations of power, illustrating that His world is invading ours through signs and wonders. Consider what is meant by this promise: there will be a generation of *believers* that will preach as He did, doing what He did, in every nation of the world before the end comes! That is quite a promise.

The present reality of the Kingdom will become manifest and realized in the everyday life of the believer. That world will break into this one at every point where the Christian prays in faith. The lordship of Jesus will be seen, and the bounty of His rule will be experienced. While the full expression of His Kingdom may be reserved for eternity, it has never entered our minds what God would like to do before then. It's time to explore that possibility.

THE EXPLOSIVE CHURCH

Wouldn't it be wonderful to have churches so explosive in the supernatural that we would have to find ways to calm them down? That's what Paul had to do with the Corinthian church. The instructions about the gifts of the Spirit were given to a people who had so much they needed to organize it. "Let everything be done decently and in order" (1 Cor. 14:40). You can't organize what you don't have. *Everything* has to be done before you can add a structure to make it more effective. Order is a poor substitute for power. But if you have much power, you'll need good order. *Only in that case* will order add a new dimension to the role of power in the Church.

LOVING PEOPLE, NOT THEIR IDEAS

In discussing the present move of God with a cessationist,[3] he told me that I was under deception because of my pursuit of a gospel of power. He informed me that all miracles ended with the death of the last of the 12 apostles. He further stated that the miracles of healing, the testimonies of restored families, the new zeal for the Scriptures, and the passion to give a witness of God's love to others was probably a work of the devil. I told him that his devil was too big and his God was too small. In order to feel good about our present condition, the Church has created doctrines to justify weaknesses. Some have even made those deficiencies seem like strengths. These are doctrines of demons! While I love and honor people who believe such things, I feel no need to honor such nonsense.

We are the most to be pitied if we think we've reached the fullness of what God intended for His Church here on earth. All Church history is built on partial revelation. Everything that has happened in the Church over the past 1,900 years has fallen short of what the early Church had and lost. Each move of God has been followed by another, just to restore what was forfeited and forgotten. And we still haven't arrived to the standard that they attained, let alone surpassed it. Yet, not even the early Church fulfilled God's full intention for His people. That privilege was reserved for those in the last leg of the race. It is our destiny.

As wonderful as our spiritual roots are, they are insufficient. What was good for *yesterday* is deficient for *today*. To insist that we stay with what our fathers fought for is to insult our forefathers. They risked all to pursue something fresh and new in God. It's not that *everything* must change for us to flow with what God is saying and doing. It's just that we make too many assumptions about the *rightness* of what presently exists. Those assumptions blind us to the revelations still contained in Scripture. In reality, what we think of as the *normal Christian life* cannot hold the weight of what God is about to do. Our wineskins must change. There is very little of what we now know as Church life that will remain untouched in the next ten years.

REACHING THE MAXIMUM

It has never entered the mind what God has prepared for us while on this earth. His intent is grand. Instead of limiting ourselves by our imagination and experience, let's press on to a renewed hunger for things yet to be seen. As we pursue the Extravagant One with reckless abandon, we will discover that our greatest problem is the resistance that comes from between our ears. But faith is superior. And it's time for us to make Him unconcerned about whether or not He'll find faith on the earth.

The Kingdom is in the now! Pray for it, seek it first, and receive it as a child. It is within reach.

A FINAL LESSON FROM A CHILD

In a recent meeting on the coast of northern California we had a remarkable level of breakthrough in the miraculous, especially for North America. Deafness, blindness, arthritis, and many other afflictions were healed through God's saving grace. There were between 40 and 50 healings in this meeting of about 200 people, as Jesus once again demonstrated His dominion over all things.

One notable miracle happened to a 3-year-old boy named Chris, who had clubfeet. He had sores on the tops of his feet where they would rub on the carpet in his effort to walk. When those in attendance were released to pray for the sick,[4] several from our team gathered around this child. Immediately, God began to touch him. When they were through praying, they put him down on the floor. For the first time in his life his feet were flat on the ground! He stared in amazement at his feet, reaching down, he touched the sores. One of his little friends whispered to him, "Run!"

He suddenly took off and ran in a circle exclaiming, "I can run!" Needless to say there was much rejoicing in the house that night.

We returned home and watched the video of that evening over and over again. We were so thrilled with the miracle that it took us awhile to notice that Chris was intently trying to tell us something. My wife, who was holding the camera, had asked him, "What happened to you?"

Looking into the camera, he answered, "Jesus big! Jesus big!"

In our excitement, we unknowingly changed the subject and asked about his feet.[5] Those who saw the miracle gave us the details. But as we watched the tape, we heard his testimony, "Jesus big! Jesus big!" The only thing we can figure is that he had an encounter with Jesus who came and healed him.

CONCLUSION

This story, like all the others contained in this book, is about the goodness of God. It is *the testimony of Jesus*. The Book of Revelation reveals this principle, "The testimony of Jesus is the spirit of prophecy" (Rev. 19:10). A testimony prophesies what is possible again. It declares another miracle is now available. It illustrates to all who will listen, the nature of God and His covenant with mankind. All He looks for is someone who will add his or her faith to the testimony given. Because He is no respecter of persons, He will do for you what He did for another. Because He is the same today as yesterday, He is willing to do again what He did long ago.

Two weeks after Chris's miracle, I showed his video to our church. Our people were very encouraged. The next day two of our young men went to the mall and saw an elderly woman with a cane. When they asked to pray for her, she wasn't interested, until she heard Chris's story. His testimony prophesied God's goodness to her, and she became hungry for prayer. As they laid hands on her, the tumor on her knee disappeared. By word of knowledge they told her that God was also healing her back. When she touched her back, she discovered that the tumor she hadn't told them about was also gone!

On another Sunday, I taught on the power of the testimony, and used Chris's story as an illustration. There was a family visiting from Montana with a similar need; their little girl's feet turned inward at about 45 degrees, causing her to trip over them when she ran. When her mother heard the testimony of Jesus healing the clubfeet, she said in her heart, *I'll take that for my daughter!*[6] Following the service she picked up her child from our nursery and discovered that her daughter's feet were perfectly straight! The testimony *prophesied*, the mother *believed*, and the daughter was *healed*.

His invasion continues, and will continue without end!

> *Of the increase of His government and peace there will be no end* (Isaiah 9:7).

> *The kingdoms of the world have become the kingdoms of our Lord and of His Christ, and He shall reign forever and ever!* (Revelation 11:15)

ENDNOTES

1. William DeArteaga, *Quenching the Spirit,* (Creation House, 1996), 55.

2. Ibid., 19.

3. An individual who believes miracles stopped after the first-century Church was born.

4. We train every believer to pray for the sick. It's not healthy for the church when the sick are prayed for only by the pastor.

5. How profound—a child wanted to talk about Jesus, the One the sign pointed to, and we were so fascinated with the miracle that we didn't notice what he was trying to say.

6. She understood the power of the testimony is the spirit of prophecy. Prophecy has the ability to cause!

DEVOTIONAL

Day I

THE NORMAL
CHRISTIAN LIFE

———————⟡———————

For the kingdom of God is not in word but in power (I Corinthians 4:20).

TODAY'S DEVOTION

OUR CHURCH'S DELIBERATE PURSUIT of the poor and the miracles is common. [Working miracles] is closer to the normal Christian life than what the Church *normally* experiences. The lack of miracles isn't because it is not in God's will for us. The problem exists between our ears. As a result, a transformation—*a renewing of the mind*—is needed, and it's only possible through a work of the Holy Spirit that typically comes upon desperate people.

[Our church members] are ordinary people who serve an extravagant Father. [The only] great person involved [is] Jesus. All the rest of us simply make room for God, believing Him to be good 100 percent of the time. The risks that [we take are] more than God [can] pass up....

The company of people who have joined this quest for an authentic gospel—*the gospel of the Kingdom*—is increasing. Loving God and His people is an honor. We will no longer make up excuses for powerlessness because powerlessness is inexcusable. Our mandate is simple: raise up a generation that can openly display the raw power of God. [We are on a] quest for the King and His Kingdom.

(Quote From *When Heaven Invades Earth,* Pages 28)

QUESTIONS

1. What do you think helps create an *opportunity* for a miracle to happen?

2. In your opinion, why do contemporary local churches find signs and wonders to be less frequent than what the churches in the first century experienced?

3. How have miracles affected your life? Have you experienced a miracle or seen one? If so, was there an atmosphere for the supernatural? What was it like?

4. Who needs miracles in your sphere of influence? Be specific to name the person and the specific miracle needed. In your view, what is necessary to bring about each miracle?

5. Explain why salvation is the biggest miracle of all. Regarding the list you wrote for #4 above, are there any who need salvation? How might this miracle come to them?

6. The author tells us, "Loving God and His people is an honor." Have you ever thought of this as an honor? By adopting this attitude, how could Christians change the way they are viewed by those outside the Kingdom?

MEDITATION

"The lack of miracles isn't because it is not in God's will for us. The problem exists between our ears" (*When Heaven Invades Earth,* Page 28).

What miracles do you desire to see God perform through you?

What do you think is your biggest obstacle to seeing these manifest? Pray for the Holy Spirit to bring your mind into submission to His wisdom and will.

Day 2

COMMISSION
RESTORED

Then God blessed them, and God said to them, "Be fruitful and multiply; fill the earth and subdue it; have dominion over the fish of the sea, over the birds of the air, and over every living thing that moves on the earth" (Genesis 1:28).

TODAY'S DEVOTION

THE BACKBONE OF KINGDOM AUTHORITY and power is found in the *commission*. Discovering God's original commission and purpose for mankind can help fortify our resolve to a life of history-changing significance. To find that truth we must go back to the beginning.

Man was created in the image of God and placed into the Father's ultimate expression of beauty and peace: the Garden of Eden. Outside of that garden it was a different story. It was without the order and blessing contained within and was in great need of the touch of God's delegated one—Adam.

Adam and Eve were placed in the garden with a mission. God said, "Be fruitful and multiply; fill the earth and subdue it" (Gen. 1:28). It was God's intention that as they bore more children, who also lived under God's rule, they would be extending the boundaries of His garden (His government) through the simplicity of their devotion to Him. The greater the number of people in right relationship to God, the greater the impact of their leadership. This process was to continue until the entire earth was covered with the glorious rule of God through man.

(Quote From *When Heaven Invades Earth*, Page 30-31)

QUESTIONS

1. Why do you think God chose to delegate His authority on earth?

2. Do you think mankind (Adam and Eve) were fully prepared to handle their delegated authority? Why or why not?

3. The author tells us that simple devotion was all that was necessary for God's government to be extended. What are your thoughts as to how this can be true?

4. As God's delegated authority, what impact have you made to defeat darkness?

5. Do you feel as if you are one who subdues the earth, or are you subdued by it?

6. In what ways have you accepted your *commission* from the Lord? Are you resolved to a life of history-changing significance? What does this mean to you?

MEDITATION

"In Genesis chapter I we discover it's not a perfect universe....It's obvious why the rest of the planet needed to be subdued—it was under the influence of darkness (see Gen. 1:2). God could have destroyed the devil and his host with a word, but instead He chose to defeat darkness through His delegated authority—those made in His image who were lovers of God by choice" (*When Heaven Invades Earth,* Page 31).

As someone who was created in the image of God, how can you use that image to subdue the earth?

Day 3

WE ARE BORN
TO RULE

*And Jesus came and spoke to them, saying, "All authority has been given to
Me in heaven and on earth. Go therefore and make disciples of all the nations,
baptizing them in the name of the Father and of the Son and of the Holy Spirit"*
(Matthew 28:18-19).

TODAY'S DEVOTION

IN REDEEMING MAN, Jesus retrieved what man had given away....The
original plan was never aborted; it was fully realized once and for all in the
resurrection and ascension of Jesus. We were then to be completely restored
to His plan of ruling as a people made in His image. And as such we would
learn how to enforce the victory obtained at Calvary....

We were born to rule—rule over creation, over darkness—to plunder
hell and establish the rule of Jesus wherever we go by preaching the gospel
of the Kingdom. *Kingdom* means *King's domain*. In the original purpose of
God, mankind ruled over creation. Now that sin has entered the world,
creation has been infected by darkness, namely, disease, sickness, afflicting

spirits, poverty, natural disasters, demonic influence, etc. Our rule is still over creation, but now it is focused on exposing and undoing the works of the devil. We are to give what we have received to reach that end. If I truly receive power from an encounter with the God of power, I am equipped to give it away. The invasion of God into impossible situations comes through a people who have received power from on high and learn to release it into the circumstances of life.

(Quote From When Heaven Invades Earth, Pages 33)

QUESTIONS

1. The author tells us that Jesus retrieved what man had given away. What was it that man gave away? At what cost?

2. How does a person increase his rule over darkness?

3. Have you ever "plundered hell"? What types of things might this include?

4. What does it take for us to expose and undo the works of the devil? What spiritual gifts might we use to do this?

5. Have you received power from an encounter with God? Is this power specialized in any specific arena? How can you expand it?

6. Do you readily release the power you have received into the circumstances of your life? What holds you back? What do you think is necessary to have a greater release?

MEDITATION

"We are often more convinced of our *unworthiness* than we are of His *worth*. Our *inability* takes on greater focus than does His *ability*. But the same One who called *fearful Gideon* a Valiant Warrior and *unstable Peter* a Rock has called us the Body of His beloved Son on earth. That has to count for something" (*When Heaven Invades Earth*, Page 36).

Who do you relate to the most...Gideon or Peter? What ability do you find in Jesus that makes up for your inability?

Day 4

REPENT TO SEE

Therefore, leaving the discussion of the elementary principles of Christ, let us go on to perfection, not laying again the foundation of repentance from dead works and of faith toward God (Hebrews 6:1).

TODAY'S DEVOTION

JESUS THE MESSIAH CAME…full of surprises. Only the contrite in heart could keep up with His constant *coloring outside the lines* and stay unoffended. His purpose was revealed in His primary message: "Repent, for the kingdom of heaven is at hand" (Matt. 4:17). Now there's something that caught them completely off guard; He brought His world with Him!

Repentance means much more than weeping over sin, or even turning from those sins to follow God. In fact, turning from sin to God is more the *result* of true repentance than it is the actual act. Repentance means you *change your way of thinking.* And it's only in changing the way we think that we can discover the focus of Jesus' ministry—the Kingdom.

This is not just a heavenly mandate to have happy thoughts. Obeying this command is possible only for those who surrender to the grace of God. The renewed mind is the result of a surrendered heart.

Repentance is often defined as *doing an about-face*. It implies that I was pursuing one direction in life and I change to pursue another. Scripture illustrates it like this, "Repentance from dead works...faith toward God" (Heb. 6:1). Faith then is both the crown and the enabler of repentance.

(Quote From *When Heaven Invades Earth*, Pages 37-38)

QUESTIONS

1. Why do you think Jesus "colored outside the lines"? Do you think you imitate Him in this way? Why or why not?

2. What does repentance mean to you? What takes place in your heart when you truly repent?

3. How easy is it to change your way of thinking about something of which you have always been sure? When you repent of something, how does it change your mind?

4. Why is the heart involved in order to renew the mind? How does this work?

5. How is obedience possible only for those who have a surrendered heart? How does someone surrender to God's grace?

6. How does faith enable repentance? Is God asking you to repent of some sin or disobedience? How does your faith need to grow in order to truly repent?

MEDITATION

"Hidden sin is the *Achilles' heel* of the Church in this hour. It has kept us from the purity that breeds boldness and great faith" (*When Heaven Invades Earth*, Page 38).

Are there people in your life who you can count on to help you identify your hidden sins?

Find one or two who can give you a current assessment of your *Achilles' heel.*

Ask God to forgive you for these, even if you still do not see them yourself.

Ask for boldness and great faith to have their work in your life.

Day 5

DOMINION
REALIZED

*But if I cast out demons by the Spirit of God, surely the kingdom of God
has come upon you* (Matthew 12:28).

TODAY'S DEVOTION

THE ENEMY'S ATTEMPT to anchor our affections to the things that are
visible is easily resisted when our hearts are aware of the presence of His
world. Such awareness aids us in the task of being *co-laborers* (see I Cor. 3:9)
with Christ (see I Cor. 3:9)—*destroying the works of the devil* (see I John 3:8).

If the Kingdom is *here and now*, then we must acknowledge it's in the
invisible realm....

The unseen world has influence over the visible. If the people of God
will not reach for the Kingdom at hand, the realm of darkness is ready to
display its ability to influence. The good news is that *"His* [the Lord's]
kingdom rules over all" (Ps. 103:19). Jesus illustrated this reality in Matthew
12:28, saying, "If I cast out demons by the Spirit of God, surely the kingdom of God has come upon you." There are two things to notice....First,

Jesus worked only through the Spirit of God; and second, the Kingdom of God came upon someone in his deliverance. Jesus caused the collision between two worlds: the world of darkness and the world of light. Darkness *always* gives way to light! And in the same way, when the dominion of God was released through Jesus to that man, he became free.

(Quote From *When Heaven Invades Earth*, Pages 38-39, 42)

QUESTIONS

1. How aware are you of the "presence of His world"? Why is this awareness a "heart" issue and not just a "mind" issue?

2. How does the awareness of God's world in our world help us to be *co-laborers* with Christ? Do you think of yourself as one who destroys the works of the devil? Why or why not?

3. How have you seen the invisible realm of the Kingdom of God? Have you seen it when others around you had not? What do you do when you see this realm?

4. In light of the fact that the world has so many difficult issues and there are multitudes who deny the existence of God, how do you explain Psalm 103:19: *"His kingdom rules over all"*?

5. Just as Jesus worked only through the Spirit of God, we need to do likewise as His agents. Evaluate your dependence upon the Spirit and how you operate as His agent in your daily life.

6. The collision between the world of darkness and the world of light will have repercussions for those who experience it. What was your world of darkness like and what happened when light invaded it? Who needs to hear your testimony this week? Today?

MEDITATION

"*Grace* is different from the *Law* in that the favor comes *before* the obedience. Under grace the commandments of the Lord come fully equipped with the ability to perform them…to those who hear from the heart (see James 1:21-25). Grace enables what it commands" (*When Heaven Invades Earth,* Page 42).

Do you feel the grace upon you when you choose to obey in a way that is normally difficult for you?

Take time to praise the God who enables you to obey all His commands.

Day 6

FAITH—ANCHORED IN THE UNSEEN

---

*Now faith is the substance of things hoped for,
the evidence of things not seen* (Hebrews 11:1).

TODAY'S DEVOTION

FAITH HAS ITS ANCHOR in the unseen realm. It lives *from* the invisible *toward* the visible. Faith actualizes what it realizes. The Scriptures contrast the life of faith with the limitations of natural sight (see 2 Cor. 5:7). Faith provides eyes for the heart.

Jesus expects people to see from the heart. He once called a group of religious leaders *hypocrites* because they could discern the weather but couldn't discern the times. It's obvious why Jesus would prefer people to recognize the *times* (spiritual climate and seasons) over natural weather conditions, but it's not quite so apparent why He would consider them hypocrites if they didn't.

Many of us have thought that the ability to see into the spiritual realm is more the result of a special gift than an unused potential of everyone. I remind you that Jesus addresses this charge to the Pharisees and Sadducees. The very fact that they, of all people, were required to see is evidence that everyone has been given this ability. They became blind to His dominion because of their own corrupted hearts and were judged for their unfulfilled potential....

Faith...is the nature of life in this family. Faith sees. It brings His Kingdom into focus. All of the Father's resources, all of His benefits, are accessible through faith.

(Quote From *When Heaven Invades Earth,* Pages 45-46)

QUESTIONS

1. Due to the fact that faith has its anchor in the unseen realm, how do you describe faith to an unbeliever?

2. What do you think the author means when he says, "Faith actualizes what it realizes"? What does this statement have to do with how you approach matters that you face in your daily life?

3. How does a person "see from the heart"? What spiritual gifts do we use when we recognize the times and seasons in our lives?

4. How would you rate your ability to see into the spiritual realm? What can you do to stimulate the unused potential you still possess?

5. What types of corruption do you face that can make you blind to Jesus' dominion? What steps might you take to avoid and/or divert from that corruption when it comes your way?

6. If "faith is the nature of life in this family," as a member of the family, what must you do to cultivate the culture of faith? What kind of commitment do you need to make?

MEDITATION

"Jesus told us that He only did what He *saw* His Father do. Such an insight is vital for those who want more. The power of His actions—for instance, the mud in the eye of the blind—is rooted in His ability to see" (*When Heaven Invades Earth*, Page 46).

Look up several Scriptures that speak of the focus of our spiritual eyes—Matthew 6:33; Colossians 3:2; Second Corinthians 4:18.

Pray that the principles of these verses would be like corrective laser surgery to your spiritual eyes.

Day 7

FAITH FROM A RELATIONSHIP

By faith we understand that the worlds were framed by the word of God, so that the things which are seen were not made of things which are visible (Hebrews 11:3).

TODAY'S DEVOTION

FAITH IS BORN of the Spirit in the hearts of mankind. Faith is neither intellectual nor anti-intellectual. It is superior to the intellect. The Bible does not say, *With the mind man believes!* Through faith, man is able to come into agreement with the mind of God....

The Holy Spirit lives in my spirit. That is the place of communion with God. As we learn to receive from our spirits, we learn how to be Spirit led.

"By faith, we understand" (Heb. 11:3). Faith is the foundation for all true intellectualism. When we *learn to learn* that way, we open ourselves up to grow in true faith because faith does not require understanding to function.

I'm sure that most of you have had this experience—you've been reading the Bible, and a verse *jumps out at you.* There is great excitement over this verse that seems to give so much life and encouragement to you. Yet, initially you couldn't teach or explain that verse if your life depended on it. What happened is this: Your spirit received the life-giving power of the Word from the Holy Spirit (see 2 Cor. 3:6). When we learn to receive from our spirit, our mind becomes the student and is therefore subject to the Holy Spirit. Through the process of revelation and experience, our mind eventually obtains understanding. That is biblical learning—the spirit giving influence to the mind.

(Quote From *When Heaven Invades Earth,* Pages 50-51)

QUESTIONS

1. Describe how you view faith in regard to your mind and intellect. How do you see the tug-of-war that plays between the intellect and your faith? How can it be a win/win outcome?

2. We know that God's wisdom is beyond man's wisdom; so why do we rely on our minds so much? What can help us come into agreement with the mind of God?

3. Take stock of your current place of communion with God. Does it flow easily, or do you find life scarce? Does the Spirit of God find a welcome domain with your spirit? Do you move together as one?

4. The author tells us, "Faith is the foundation for all true intellectualism." Explain this in terms of how you understand the truth of the Kingdom of God.

5. When you read the Bible, does the Holy Spirit provide life-giving power to the words you read? How does this work? What lets you know that it is the Holy Spirit speaking?

6. To become a student of the Holy Spirit, how is humility involved? What is your understanding of the process of revelation and experience, and their impact on your understanding?

MEDITATION

"Faith is the mirror of the heart that reflects the realities of His world into ours. It is the substance of the unseen realm. This wonderful gift from God is the initial earthly manifestation of what exists in His Kingdom. It is a testimony of an invisible realm called the Kingdom of God. Through prayer we are able to pull that reality into this one—that is how faith functions" (*When Heaven Invades Earth*, Page 51).

Take some time to reflect on the realities of God's world and how they have invaded your world.

Pray specifically for areas that need the reality of the Kingdom of God today.

Day 8

A SUPERIOR REALITY

Set your mind on things above, not on things on the earth (Colossians 3:2).

TODAY'S DEVOTION

MY FAITH IS NOT just an abiding faith; it is active. It is aggressive by nature. It has focus and purpose. Faith grabs hold of the reality of the Kingdom and forcefully and violently brings it into a collision with this natural one. An inferior kingdom cannot stand.

One of the more common things people tell me when I'm about to pray for their healing is, *I know God can do it.* So does the devil. At best, that is hope...not faith. Faith knows He will.

For one who has faith, there is nothing impossible. There are no impossibilities when there is faith...and there are no exceptions....

"So then faith comes by hearing, and hearing by the word of God" (Rom. 10:17). Notice it does not say, *faith comes from having heard.* The whole nature of faith implies a relationship with God that is current. The emphasis is on hearing...in the now!...

What this world needs is for the Church to return to a *show and tell* message of the Kingdom of God. They need an anchor that is greater than everything they can see. The world system has no answers to the world's increasing problems—every solution is only temporary.

(Quote From *When Heaven Invades Earth*, Pages 55-57)

QUESTIONS

1. Define "abiding faith" and "active faith." How does an active faith become aggressive? Does this describe your faith?

2. Does "forceful" and "violent" describe your faith? Do you have collisions with the natural world? How is the natural world inferior to God's Kingdom?

3. Explain the difference between hope and faith. Which characterizes your worldview for the most part? How can you increase your faith level on a daily basis?

4. If "there are no impossibilities when there is faith," why do you think there are so few miracles? Why does the Church seem so impotent?

5. The progression of faith as stated in Romans 10:17 elevates the importance of the Word of God, "So then faith comes by hearing, and hearing by the word of God." Is there a difference between reading and hearing? How do you think this relates to Hebrews 4:12, "For the word of God is living and powerful..."?

6. Is the Kingdom of God something that most Christians choose to "show and tell"? How can Christians change their mind-set to understand the permanence of the Kingdom solutions to today's problems and the temporary nature of the world system?

MEDITATION

"People of great faith are hard to live with. Their reasoning is *otherworldly*" (*When Heaven Invades Earth*, Page 55).

In what ways have you found people of great faith difficult to live with?

Does your description resemble yourself in any way? Does *otherworldly* mean to be so heavenly minded that we are no earthly good?

How can we be "in the world but not of it"?

Day 9

THE CLUSTER
BOMB EFFECT

Nor give place to the devil (Ephesians 4:27).

TODAY'S DEVOTION

FAITH IS NOT the absence of doubt; it's the presence of belief. I may not always feel that I have great faith. It's a mistake for me to ever examine my faith. I seldom find it. It's better for me to obey *quickly*. After it's over I can look back and see that my obedience came from faith.

When the corporate level of faith grows, it has what I call a *cluster bomb effect*, where innocent bystanders get touched by the miracle-working power of God....

Corporate faith pulls on heaven in marvelous ways. His world becomes manifest all around us....

But power is not in the number of people in attendance. It's the number of people in agreement. Exponential power (see Deut. 32:30) is the product of the *unity of faith*....

An automobile may have several hundred horsepower. But the car will go nowhere until the clutch is released, connecting the power contained in the running motor and transferring that power to the wheels. So it is with faith. We have all the power of heaven behind us. But it is our faith that connects what is available to the circumstances at hand. Faith takes what is available and makes it actual.

(Quote From *When Heaven Invades Earth*, Pages 57-58, 60)

QUESTIONS

1. If "faith is not the absence of doubt," how do we get rid of doubts? Do you find that thoughts of doubt come into your mind when you pray for miracles?

2. If faith is "the presence of belief," how do we make faith operational in our daily lives? What fights against you to keep you from surrounding yourself with faith wherever you go?

3. What has your experience been in terms of the corporate working of faith? Have you ever experienced "innocent bystander" touches of God's power? What brings these types of corporate anointing?

4. What comes to mind when you think about the Kingdom of God becoming manifest on the earth? Is your picture filled with a serene sedentary group of people enjoying the "best" earth has to offer, or is it painted with hard work, violence, and corporate revolution? Which picture do you choose to be part of?

5. Why do you think power increases exponentially when people unify their faith? What scriptural principle is at work?

6. As you trace your history, how do you see your faith connecting to the power of heaven? What are your hopes for the future of your connection?

MEDITATION

The author tells us, "Rest is the climate that faith grows in (see Heb. 3:11–4:11)." But he also says, "Faith may quietly press in, or it may cry out very loudly, but it is always violent in the spirit world" (see Matt. 11:12) (*When Heaven Invades Earth*, Pages 59-60).

Where are you in the tension between rest and violence?

How does Jesus want to bring balance to your life and encourage you forward?

Day 10

PRAYING
HEAVEN DOWN

※

In this manner, therefore, pray: Our Father in heaven,
hallowed be Your name (Matthew 6:9).

TODAY'S DEVOTION

THE LORD'S MODEL PRAYER provides the clearest instruction on how we bring the reality of His world into this one. The generals of revival speak to us from ages past, saying, *If you pray, He will come!*

Biblical prayer is always accompanied by radical obedience. God's response to prayer with obedience always releases the nature of heaven into our impaired circumstances.

Jesus' model reveals the only two real priorities of prayer: First, intimacy with God that is expressed in worship—*holy is Your name.* And second, to bring His Kingdom to earth, establishing His dominion over the needs of mankind—*Your Kingdom come....*

Let me highlight one more thought that will help us to better understand the purpose behind prayer. As disciples, we are both citizens and ambassadors of another world. This world is our assignment, but not our home. Our purpose is eternal. The resources needed to complete the assignment are unlimited. The only restrictions are those between our ears. ...

An outline of Matthew 6:9-13 gives us the Kingdom approach to prayer:

1. Praise and worship

2. Praying for heaven on earth

    a.   Heaven's effect on material needs

    b.   Heaven's effect on personal relationships

    c.   Heaven's effect on our relationship to evil

3. Praise and worship

(Quote From *When Heaven Invades Earth*, Pages 64-65, 69)

QUESTIONS

1. How does the Lord's Prayer help us "bring the reality of His world into this one"? Has this been so in your experience?

2. Do you feel that the Lord comes when you pray? What is necessary for you to sense His presence during your prayer time?

3. The author gives us a progression—biblical prayer; radical obedience; release of heaven into our impaired circumstances. Comment on this progression in terms of your personal experience.

4. The first priority of prayer is to minister to God out of an intimate personal relationship. How much of your prayer time is spent in worship? What are the ways in which you hallow His name?

5. The second priority of prayer is to bring the reality of His rulership (the Kingdom) to earth. How do you pray His Kingdom come? Where do you need His Kingdom to reign in your life currently?

6. As ambassadors of another world, we are to remember our purpose is eternal. Having an eternal perspective can change how we view our daily interaction with others and our mundane chores. In what ways can you put this eternal perspective to use in your life?

MEDITATION

"If you want anything from God, you will have to pray into heaven. That is where it all is. If you live in the earth realm and expect to receive from God, you will never get anything" (Albert Hibbert, Smith Wigglesworth: *The Secret of His Power*, (Tulsa, OK: Harrison House, Inc., 1982), 47). (*When Heaven Invades Earth*, Page 63).

Consider this quote from Smith Wigglesworth in terms of how you currently pray.

If you are not to live in the earth realm, where are you to live? How do you arrive there?

Day 11

REPRESENTING
ANOTHER WORLD

For our citizenship is in heaven, from which we also eagerly wait for the Savior, the Lord Jesus Christ (Philippians 3:20).

TODAY'S DEVOTION

WHEN WE PRAY FOR His Kingdom to come, we are asking Him to super-impose the rules, order, and benefits of His world over this one until this one looks like His....[God's] world collides with the world of darkness, and His world always wins. Our battle is always a battle for dominion—a conflict of kingdoms....

God has chosen to work through us. We are His delegated authority on planet earth, and prayer is the vehicle that gives occasion for His invasion. Those who don't pray allow darkness to continue ruling. The enemy's greatest efforts at deceiving the Church are centered on the purpose and effect of prayer.

"For our citizenship is in heaven, from which we also eagerly wait for the Savior, the Lord Jesus Christ" (Phil. 3:20). Paul spoke these words to the church at Philippi, a Roman city in the country of Macedonia. It enjoyed a Roman culture and

the rule and protection of Roman government, all while living in Macedonia. Philippians understood very well Paul's charge about being citizens of another world. Paul spoke, not about going to heaven someday, but about living as citizens of heaven today…specifically *from heaven toward earth.*

We have the privilege of representing heaven *in* this world, so that we might bring a manifestation of heaven *to* this world.

(Quote From *When Heaven Invades Earth,* Pages 71-72)

QUESTIONS

1. Our society wants to whitewash the collision God's world has with ours by compromising Kingdom values with humanism. How do you recognize when compromise threatens your convictions? What should we do about it?

2. If God's world always wins in the fight over darkness, why do we see so much darkness in the world today? What is stopping us from seeing a greater degree of victory? What is our responsibility in this?

3. What role does prayer play in the war of the worlds (God's versus darkness)? What has your prayer life done toward this cause? How can you influence others to join their prayers with yours in order to bring victory to this world?

4. As a citizen of heaven, what are we waiting for (see Phil. 3:20)? What does living as "citizens of heaven today" on earth look like? What affect can it have?

5. God has asked us to do the following jobs. Describe how you are currently fulfilling each one and where you need to grow the most.
    *   ambassador
    *   invasion force
    *   infiltrator
    *   citizen
    *   warrior

MEDITATION

"When we pray for His Kingdom to come, we are asking Him to superimpose the rules, order, and benefits of His world over this one until this one looks like His" (*When Heaven Invades Earth*, Page 71).

If you were to pick one area where you feel God's Kingdom needs to be superimposed as soon as possible, what would it be?

Are there other people you know who have this same burden?

Could you join with them in corporate prayer to allow exponential power to make its impact? Plan to contact them and pray in unity.

Day 12

EMBASSY LIFESTYLE

Every place that the sole of your foot will tread upon I have given you...
(Joshua 1:3).

TODAY'S DEVOTION

As AMBASSADORS, WE LIVE in one world while representing another. An embassy is the headquarters of an ambassador and his or her staff. It is actually considered a part of the nation it represents. So it is with the believer/ambassador. The Bible promises: *"Every place that the sole of your foot will tread upon I have given you"* (Josh. 1:3).

Just as ambassadors of the United States have an income based on the standard of living of this nation regardless of what nation they serve in, so also ambassadors of the Kingdom of God live according to the economy of heaven, though they are still on earth. All of our King's resources are at our disposal to carry out His will. That is how Jesus could speak of the carefree life—*consider the sparrow* (see Matt. 6:26).

As an ambassador, the military of the Kingdom I represent is at my disposal to help me carry out the King's orders. If as a representative of a nation my life is threatened, all of my government's military might is prepared to do whatever necessary to protect and deliver me. So it is with heaven's angelic host. They *render service for those who would inherit salvation* (see Heb. 1:14).

(Quote From *When Heaven Invades Earth,* Pages 72-73)

QUESTIONS

1. What are the types of considerations United States ambassadors must give as they represent our country, yet respect and live in another culture? What types of considerations must we entertain as ambassadors of the Kingdom of God while living in this world?

2. Make a list of the places where your feet tread in a typical day. How can you make your "embassy" real in these places? What kind of awareness will you need?

3. If all of our King's resources are at our disposal, how should we be stewards of His resources? What should our mind-set be so that we won't be unbalanced—thinking ourselves in poverty, or spending as if there was no tomorrow?

4. Who are the "military of the Kingdom"? How does the Lord's armed forces work on our behalf? What types of protection might they give? What kinds of deliverance might they provide? Have you called on the angelic host to help you at times? What kinds of service did they render?

5. As you consider your life as an ambassador, remember the protocol that is given to respect and honor diplomats. Do you think there is a respect for Kingdom diplomats in the spiritual world? In the earthly realm? Why or why not?

6. How carefree are you? (See Matthew 6:26.) What concerns do you have that make it difficult to experience the resources of the King?

MEDITATION

The author shares, "This *ambassador mentality* is one I first picked up from Winkey Pratney. When he boards a plane, he reminds himself that while others may represent IBM and XEROX, he is there representing another world. I have followed his example and practiced this principle for close to 30 years. It has helped me to keep a clear perspective on the eternal purpose of every outing" (*When Heaven Invades Earth*, Page 73).

How might you prepare your mind every day to have an *ambassador mentality*?

Day 13

THE KINGDOM
AND THE SPIRIT

To know the love of Christ which passes knowledge; that you may be filled with all the fullness of God (Ephesians 3:19).

TODAY'S DEVOTION

JOHN THE BAPTIST was the *high-water mark* for all under the Old Covenant. But the least in this new era were born to surpass Him through their relationship with the Holy Spirit....

Likewise, salvation was not the ultimate goal of Christ's coming. It was the immediate target...the marker in the lane. Without accomplishing redemption, there was no hope for the ultimate goal—which was to fill each born-again person with the Holy Spirit. God's desire is for the believer to overflow with Himself, that we might *"be filled with all the fullness of God"* (Eph. 3:19). The resulting fullness of the Spirit was different than anyone had ever before experienced. For that reason, the greatest of all Old Testament prophets could confess: "I need to be baptized by You," meaning, "I need Your baptism...the one I was assigned to announce!"

The baptism in the Holy Spirit makes a lifestyle available to us that not even John had access to. Consider this: We could travel off of this planet in any direction at the speed of light, 186,000 miles a second, for billions of years, and never begin to exhaust what we already know to exist. All of that rests in the palm of His hand. And it's this God who wants to fill us with His fullness. That ought to make a difference!

(Quote From *When Heaven Invades Earth,* Pages 77, 79-80)

QUESTIONS

1. Explain the difference between the Old Covenant and the New Covenant. What made John the "high-water mark" for the Old Covenant? Why was this mark less than what God intended for us?

2. How does a person develop a relationship with the Holy Spirit? Describe your current relationship with the Spirit of God. How has He shaped your world internally and externally?

3. How does salvation in Jesus Christ open the door for the Holy Spirit to fill a person? What has been your experience with receiving salvation and the infilling of the Holy Spirit?

4. When Ephesians 3:19 tells us to "be filled with all the fullness of God," what does this mean? How can any imperfect person on earth be filled with God? What does this mean for your life?

5. How does it make you feel to consider that the same God, who holds the universe in the palm of His hand, wants to have intimate communion with you?

6. Knowing that the Almighty God desires to fill us should keep our egos in a true balance...humble but bold, full of faith and yet full of submission. Instead of evaluating your "self-worth," evaluate your "God-worth."

MEDITATION

"Somehow, I always thought that the baptism in the Holy Spirit was a one-time event; I received my prayer language and that was it. The Bible teaches differently. In Acts 2 we find 120 being baptized in the Spirit in the upper room. Yet, in Acts 4 we find some of the same crowd being *refilled*. Some have put it this way: one baptism, many fillings. Why? We leak" (*When Heaven Invades Earth*, Page 72).

Take some moments to reflect on where your leaks are. How can they be patched?

Day 14

THE VALUE OF
HIS PRESENCE

And lo, I am with you always, even to the end of the age (Matthew 28:20b).

TODAY'S DEVOTION

BY FAR THE GREATEST GIFT ever received by us is the Holy Spirit Himself. Those who discover the value of His presence enter realms of intimacy with God never previously considered possible. Out of this vital relationship arises a ministry of power that formerly was only a dream. The incomprehensible becomes possible because He is with us.

I will be with you is a promise made by God to all His servants. Moses heard it when he faced the challenge of delivering Israel from Egypt (see Exod. 3:12). Joshua received this promise when he led Israel into the Promised Land (see Josh. 1:9). When Gideon received the call of God to be a deliverer for Israel, God sealed it with the same promise (see Judg. 6:16). In the New Testament, this promise came to all believers through the Great Commission (see Matt. 28:19). It comes when God has required something of us that is humanly impossible. It's important to see this. It's the presence of God that links us to the impossible. I tell our folks, *He is in me for my sake, but He's upon me for yours.* His presence makes anything possible!

God doesn't have to try to do supernatural things. He is supernatural. He would have to try to not be. If He is invited to a situation, we should expect nothing but supernatural invasion.

(Quote From *When Heaven Invades Earth*, Page 83)

QUESTIONS

1. How has the Holy Spirit increased your intimacy with God? In what ways has this changed your devotional time?

2. Has a new level of power accompanied your increase of intimacy? Power to do what?

3. When the Lord Jesus said He would always be with us, what did He mean? Have you felt Jesus with you in most of your walk? Why or why not?

4. Have you faced a challenge and needed deliverance? How did God bring deliverance? Was Jesus' presence a factor in your deliverance?

5. Have you had to lead others into a new area (on the job or in ministry or in the home) and needed courage to proceed? How did God build your leadership? Was Jesus' presence a factor in your ability to lead?

6. How has God worked the supernatural on your behalf or on behalf of someone you know? How do you explain to others how God supercedes the impossible and makes things possible?

MEDITATION

"Following the leading of the Holy Spirit can present us with [a] dilemma. While He never contradicts His Word, He is very comfortable contradicting our understanding of it....But to follow Him, we must be willing to follow off the map—to go beyond what we know. To do so successfully we must recognize His presence above all" (*When Heaven Invades Earth*, Page 85).

How easily do you follow the Holy Spirit "off the map"?

Do you recognize His presence quickly?

Day 15

THE ANOINTING
AND THE
ANTICHRIST SPIRIT

Jesus said to them, "My food is to do the will of Him who sent Me, and to finish His work" (John 4:34).

TODAY'S DEVOTION

IT WOULD SEEM THAT with all the significance attached to the name "Jesus," anyone desiring to undermine His work of redemption might be referred to as "Anti-Jesus," not "Anti-Christ." Even religious cults recognize the value of Jesus the man. At the very least, cults consider Him to be a teacher or a prophet and possibly "a" son of God. This horrendous error provides us with an understanding of why *antichrist* was the name given to this spirit of opposition. The spirits of hell are at war against the anointing, for without the anointing mankind is no threat to their dominion.

Jesus' concern for mankind was applauded. His humility was revered, but it was the anointing that released the supernatural. And it was the supernatural invasion of God Himself that was rejected by the religious leaders.

This anointing is actually the person of the Holy Spirit upon someone to equip them for supernatural endeavors. So revered is the Holy Spirit in the Godhead, that Jesus said, "Anyone who speaks a word against the Son of Man, it will be forgiven him; but whoever speaks against the Holy Spirit, it will not be forgiven him, either in this age or in the age to come" (Matt. 12:32).

(Quote From *When Heaven Invades Earth*, Page 89)

QUESTIONS

1. Do you readily perceive when an antichrist spirit is at work? In what ways have you observed this? Why do so many people buy into the philosophy of antichrist?

2. Why do cults and others recognize Jesus as a teacher or a prophet? Why can't this be true? How does the spirit of antichrist take Jesus' anointing out of the picture?

3. How does our anointing threaten the dominion of the spirits of hell? Do you think of yourself as a threat? How much of a threat are you? Where do you need to become more of a threat?

4. Why do you think the supernatural acts of Jesus were rejected by the religious leaders in His day? Do you think the supernatural is rejected today? Why or why not?

5. How does the Holy Spirit equip someone for supernatural endeavors? How have you been equipped? Do you utilize that equipping regularly?

6. Why do you think the Holy Spirit is to be so revered? Explain Matthew 12:32 as you would to someone who doesn't understand the working of the Holy Spirit.

MEDITATION

"To fulfill His mission, Jesus needed the Holy Spirit.... If the Son of God was that reliant upon the anointing, His behavior should clarify our need for the Holy Spirit's presence upon us to do what the Father has assigned.... We must be clothed with the Holy Spirit for supernatural ministry" (*When Heaven Invades Earth*, Page 88).

Just like the Old Testament priests, our anointing qualifies us for ministry. Do you think most Christians qualify their ministry with education and/or position, or do they really see the anointing as their qualification?

What place does training and equipping have in seeing God's purposes fulfilled through us?

How do you view your ministry currently? Are you anointed?

Day 16

THE REALM
BEYOND REASON

"For My thoughts are not your thoughts, nor are your ways My ways," says the Lord. "For as the heavens are higher than the earth, so are My ways higher than your ways, and My thoughts than your thoughts" (Isaiah 55:8-9).

TODAY'S DEVOTION

FOLLOWING THE ANOINTING...is very similar to Israel following the cloud of the Lord's presence in the wilderness. The Israelites had no control over Him. He led, and the people followed. Wherever He went, supernatural activities took place. If they departed from the cloud, the miracles that sustained them would be gone. Can you imagine what would have happened if our fear-oriented theologians had been there? They would have created new doctrines explaining why the supernatural ministry that brought them out of Egypt was no longer necessary to bring them into the Promised Land. After all, now they had the tablets of stone. Then, as today, the real issue is the priority we place upon His presence. When that's intact, the supernatural abounds, but without it we have to make up new doctrines for why we're OK as we are.

In New Testament terms, being a people focused on His presence means that we are willing to live beyond reason. Not impulsively or foolishly, for these are poor imitations for real faith. The realm beyond reason is the world of obedience to God. Obedience is the expression of faith, and faith is our claim ticket to the God realm....His nature is powerful and righteous, but His ways cannot be controlled. He is unpredictable.

(Quote From *When Heaven Invades Earth,* Pages 90-91)

QUESTIONS

1. If you had been an Israelite in the wilderness, how would you have felt being at the Lord's mercy for everything you needed? Do you think their lack of control is why they continually questioned what the Lord was doing?

2. Have you ever wanted the Lord to tell you what, where, when, and how to do something? The Israelites had these answers, but they rebelled at the Lord's directives anyway. Do you think you would rebel if the Lord told you something that you didn't agree with? Why or why not?

3. What are some of the arguments you have heard that discount the supernatural activities of God, whether past or present? Why do you believe in God's supernatural power? What is your testimony to His power?

4. The cloud of God's presence marked the spot of His supernatural care for His people, the Israelites. How does the cloud of God's presence mark the spot of His supernatural care for His people today? Have you witnessed this presence and accompanying miracles? Describe your experience.

5. Does your rational mind ever keep you from realizing His presence at times? How does a world beyond reason work? How can you be sure it is real?

6. Explain the connection between obedience and faith. Do you find obedience difficult in any areas of your life? Is your faith affected in these same areas? What can you do to increase obedience and your faith?

MEDITATION

"Every time we follow the leading of the Holy Spirit, we fly in the face of the antichrist spirit. While the foolishness of some who claim to be Spirit-led have made this adventure more difficult, we nevertheless are assured of succeeding if it is truly our passionate desire. He'll not give a stone to anyone who asks for bread" (*When Heaven Invades Earth*, Page 94).

Take time to pray that the Lord will help you follow and obey the leading of the Holy Spirit. Ask Him to increase your passion to be Spirit-led.

Day 17

TEACHING INTO
AN ENCOUNTER

*Do you not believe that I am in the Father, and the Father in Me? The words that
I speak to you I do not speak on My own authority; but the Father who
dwells in Me does the works* (John 14:10).

TODAY'S DEVOTION

JESUS ESTABLISHED THE ultimate example in ministry by combining the
proclamation of the gospel with signs and wonders. Matthew records this
phenomenon this way: "And Jesus went about all Galilee, teaching in their
synagogues, preaching the gospel of the kingdom, and healing all kinds of
sickness and all kinds of disease among the people" (Matt. 4:23)....

The Gospel of John records how this combination of words and supernatural works takes place, "The words that I speak to you I do not speak
on My own authority; but the Father who dwells in Me does the works"
(John 14:10). It's apparent that we speak the word, and the Father *does the
works*—miracles!

As men and women of God who teach, we must require from ourselves *doing, with power!* And this *doing* must include a breaking into the impossible—through signs and wonders.

Bible teachers are to instruct in order to explain *what they just did,* or *are about to do.* Those who restrict themselves to mere words limit their gift, and may unintentionally lead believers to pride by increasing knowledge without an increased awareness of God's presence and power. It's in the trenches of Christlike ministry that we learn to become totally dependent upon God. Moving in the impossible through relying on God short-circuits the development of pride.

(Quote From *When Heaven Invades Earth,* Pages 97-98)

QUESTIONS

1. If Jesus gave us the "ultimate example in ministry by combining the proclamation of the gospel with signs and wonders," why do you think we aren't able to continue in His footsteps? How does the partnership of the Word and wonders work?

2. When you speak the Word of God, on whose authority do you speak? How do you know that authority exists? What effect does the Word of God have?

3. When you do the works of God, on whose authority do you act? How do you know that authority exists? What effect does a true work of God have?

4. If we are to require ourselves to go about *"doing, with power,"* what must happen in the faith realm? What will equip us to extend our borders in the miraculous?

5. How can Bible teachers unintentionally lead believers into pride? Have you experienced this firsthand? What is the danger

of knowledge without the awareness of God's presence and power?

6. Dependence upon God is the key to our encounters with the Almighty. How does relying on God short-circuit the development of pride?

MEDITATION

"Any revelation from God's Word that does not lead us to an encounter with God only serves to make us more religious. The Church cannot afford 'form without power,' for it creates Christians without purpose" (*When Heaven Invades Earth*, Page 97).

How true is this for you? For your local church? How can this change?

Day 18

GOD IS BIGGER THAN HIS BOOK

———◆———

You are wrong because you know neither the Scriptures nor God's power
(Matthew 22:29 AMP).

TODAY'S DEVOTION

IN THIS PASSAGE Jesus rebukes the Pharisees for their ignorance of the Scriptures *and* God's power. His rebuke comes within the context of *marriage* and *resurrection,* but is aimed at the ignorance infecting every area of their lives.

What was the cause? They didn't allow the Scriptures to lead them to God. They didn't understand...not really understand. The word *know* in this passage speaks of "personal experience." They tried to learn apart from such an experience. They were the champions of those who spent time studying God's Word. But their study didn't lead them to an encounter with God. It became an end in itself.

The Holy Spirit is the *dunamis* of heaven. An encounter with God is often a power encounter. Such encounters vary from person to person according to God's design. And it's the lack of power encounters that lead to a misunderstanding of God and His Word. Experience is necessary in building a true knowledge of the Word. Many fear experience because it *might* lead away from Scripture. The mistakes of some have led many to fear experiential pursuit. But it is illegitimate to allow fear to keep us from pursuing a deeper experience with God! Embracing such fear causes a failure to the other extreme, which is culturally more acceptable, but significantly worse in eternity.

(Quote From *When Heaven Invades Earth*, Pages 103-104)

QUESTIONS

1. Do you think there are modern-day "Pharisees" within the Church who do not allow the Scriptures to lead them to God? What makes the ultimate difference to gain true understanding? How does this lead you to pray for the Church?

2. How does someone have a "personal experience" with God? How does a personal experience lead to understanding? Do you wonder at great preachers who find seemingly "new" truths hidden within Scriptures you have read many times? Is this because they allow the Scriptures to lead them into a personal experience and as a result they receive insight? How does this happen?

3. What place does study of God's Word have in the life of the believer? What is its limitation? What place does it have in your life?

4. Describe what a "power encounter" with God is like. Have you had one (or more) of these encounters? What makes them bring truth to light?

5. Why do people fear experiences? Are they justified by what they have experienced or seen others do? How can we avoid this pitfall?

6. What should replace any fear we have of power encounters with God? What are the risk factors if we *don't* have these encounters? What are the risks if we *do* have them?

MEDITATION

"The Bible is the absolute Word of God. It reveals God; the obvious, the unexplainable, the mysterious, and sometimes offensive. It all reveals the greatness of our God. Yet it does not contain Him. God is bigger than His book" (*When Heaven Invades Earth*, Page 104).

Take time to praise God for His Word. Give Him glory for its directives for your life. Then worship the Lord for who He is in all of His greatness.

Day 19

THE WORKS OF
THE FATHER

*And He who sent Me is with Me. The Father has not left Me alone,
for I always do those things that please Him* (John 8:29).

TODAY'S DEVOTION

FOR HUNDREDS OF YEARS the prophets spoke of the Messiah's coming.
They gave over 300 specific details describing Him. Jesus fulfilled them all!
The angels also gave witness to His divinity when they came with a mes-
sage for the shepherds: "For there is born to you this day...a Savior, who
is Christ the Lord" (Luke 2:11). Nature itself testified to the arrival of the
Messiah with the star that led the wise men (see Matt. 2:1). Yet with this
one statement, "Unless I do the works of the Father, do not believe Me"
(John 10:37), Jesus put the credibility of all these *messengers* on the line.
Their ministries would have been in vain without one more ingredient to
confirm who He really was. That ingredient was *miracles.*

Jesus gave people the right to disbelieve it all if there was no demonstration of power upon His ministry. I hunger for the day when the Church will

make the same statement to the world. *If we're not doing the miracles that Jesus did, you don't have to believe us....*

Jesus displayed the Father's heart. All His actions were earthly expressions of His Father in heaven....Jesus continues to point the way to the Father. It has now become our job, by means of the Holy Spirit, to discover and display the Father's heart: giving life, and destroying the works of the devil.

(Quote From *When Heaven Invades Earth*, Pages 109-110, 112-113)

QUESTIONS

1. The criteria Jesus gave in order to believe Him was fairly simple...He had to do the works of the Father. What are the works of the Father? How can someone recognize them when they see them?

2. Why does a demonstration of power bring credibility to ministry? Does this mean that anyone who does miracles is doing the work of the Father? Why or why not?

3. Why do miracles express the Father's heart? If the Church is to express the Father's heart to the world, it seems logical then, that they are to perform miracles. In your opinion, what is stopping the Church from doing this?

4. What types of miracles destroy the works of the devil? Explain. When a miracle happens, how does life and light go forth into darkness?

5. How adept are you at displaying the love of God through miracles? Where might you grow to increase your effectiveness in this arena? Create a plan to challenge yourself to greater dependence upon the Father for these kinds of works.

6. The author emphasizes how important doing the works of the Father is, by comparing all the credentials Jesus had (prophetic voices, angelic witnesses, and nature's testimonials), to this one overarching credential. In your opinion, why did God bother to do all these other proofs of Jesus' divinity? Do you see their purpose within the context of His greatest credential?

MEDITATION

"We can travel the globe and preach the gospel, but without a personal revelation of the Father's heart we're carrying around secondhand news—a story without a relationship. It might save people because it is truth, but there is so much more" (*When Heaven Invades Earth*, Page 114).

What is your personal revelation? Can you relate it easily if asked?

Day 20

EVERYONE IS
A CANDIDATE

*So Jesus said to them again, "Peace to you! As the Father has sent Me,
I also send you"* (John 20:21).

TODAY'S DEVOTION

IN THE SAME WAY that Jesus revealed the Father's heart to Israel, so the
Church is to *be a manifestation* of the Father's heart to the world....

Everyone in our community is a target for God's love. There are no
exceptions. The testimonies of radical transformation come from every sector of society and every conceivable place— school, work, home, the malls
and stores, and even the parks, streets, and homeless camps. Why? There is
a growing company of people who have the Father's business in mind. They
consciously take Him wherever they go....Every believer has a part to play
in carrying out this privileged assignment.

We have the privilege of rediscovering God's original purpose for His
people. We who long for this must pursue Him with reckless abandon. The
following is a list of things to do to help make your pursuit practical:

1. Prayer...

2. Study...

3. Read...

4. Laying on of hands...

5. Associations...

6. Obedience...

Jesus said, "As the Father sent Me, I also send you." He did the works of the Father, and then passed the baton on to us.

(Quote From *When Heaven Invades Earth*, Pages 114-117)

QUESTIONS

1. Bringing the Father's heart to the world is quite a mission statement! How best would you be able to do this? What would be your first priority? Second? Third?

2. Imagine a bull's-eye in a heart shape painted on each person you have the opportunity to speak to during your day. Who would be the most difficult to target? Who would be easiest? Who might repel your love when you give it? How will you respond, whether the love is received or not?

3. Are you called to express the Father's love to a specific group of people or within a certain ministry? Is the love of God your motivation for what you do, or is there another agenda? Check your heart and be sure you are truly doing what the Father's will is.

4. Consciously taking God with us everywhere we go takes preparation and spontaneous focus. What do you think the preparation might entail? How can you remind yourself to be constantly aware of the Lord's Kingdom throughout your conversations and work?

5. Look at the list of six items that the author has given to help make your pursuit practical. Rate yourself on each one on a scale of 1-10 with 10 being the highest. Where do you need to improve? What steps will you take to do so?

6. When Jesus passed the baton to us, He literally sent us to do what He did. That means we are to continue the race with the same attitude, obedience, substance, and power. How do you think the Church can do this and successfully win the race? How will we know victory is achieved?

MEDITATION

"We are the carriers of His presence, doers of His will. Giving what we have received releases Him into situations previously held in the grip of darkness. That is our responsibility and privilege" (*When Heaven Invades Earth*, Page 114).

Let the Lord "knight" you into His special service today. Spend time in prayer preparing to accomplish great exploits for His Kingdom.

Day 21

POWERLESSNESS: UNNECESSARY AND UNBALANCED

Heal the sick, cleanse the lepers, raise the dead, cast out demons. Freely you have received, freely give (Matthew 10:8).

TODAY'S DEVOTION

WHILE CHARACTER MUST BE at the heart of our ministries, power revolutionizes the world around us. Until the Church returns to Jesus' model for true revolutionaries, we will continue to be recognized by the world merely as nice people—while it is overcome with disease and torment, on its way to hell.

Some Christians actually have considered it to be more noble to choose *character* over *power*. But we must not separate the two. It is an unjustifiable, illegitimate choice. Together they bring us to the only real issue—obedience.

Once, while teaching a group of students about the importance of signs and wonders in the ministry of the gospel, a young man spoke up, saying,

"I'll pursue signs and wonders when I know I have more of the character of Christ in me." As good as that may sound, it comes from a religious mind-set, not a heart abandoned to the gospel of Jesus Christ. In response to this student's comment, I opened to the Gospel of Matthew and read the Lord's charge: "Go therefore and make disciples of all nations...teaching them to observe all things that I have commanded you" (Matt. 28:19). I then asked him, "Who gave you the right to determine when you are ready to obey His command?"

(Quote From *When Heaven Invades Earth*, Pages 119-120)

QUESTIONS

1. In your own words, explain the place character has in ministry. Why has the character of well-known evangelists and preachers been at the center of controversies? How should we pray for those who have risen to prominence?

2. How does "power revolutionize the world around us"? What testimony does power make to the lost of the world? As a revolutionary of the Lord Jesus, where is your power? Is it demonstrating itself regularly? Does it leave a testimony wherever you go?

3. If you had to choose between character or power, which would you choose? Why? Why is this an unjustifiable, illegitimate choice? Why do we need both of these to obey?

4. Why do those who want character *before* signs and wonders build a religious mind-set in themselves? What makes a heart abandoned to the gospel of Jesus Christ?

5. Because the Lord is our Commander, we don't choose when we will obey. That means we might not think we are ready when He asks us, but we must obey anyway. Is this a step of faith? What makes us choose obedience over the questions in our minds?

6. Make a list of the Christians who are prominent in your world. Some may be local, some national. Pray each day this week for them to have the character to back up a ministry marked by power.

MEDITATION

"Many believers have made it their primary goal in life to be well-respected citizens of their communities. Good character enables us to be solid contributors to society, but most of what is recognized as a Christian lifestyle can be accomplished by people who don't even know God. Every believer should be highly respected *and more*. It's the *and more* part that we're often lacking" (*When Heaven Invades Earth*, Page 119).

Take some time to consider what you are lacking. How could God use you if you were highly respected *and more*?

Day 22

CLOTHED
WITH POWER

$\text{\textbeta}\!-\!\!\!\!\!\!\bullet\!\!\!\!\!\!-\!\text{\textbeta}$

And suddenly there came a sound from heaven, as of a rushing mighty wind, and it filled the whole house where they were sitting (Acts 2:2).

TODAY'S DEVOTION

SO GREAT WAS THE disciples' need for power to become witnesses that they were not to leave Jerusalem until they had it. That word *power* (*dunamis*) speaks of the miracle realm. It comes from *dunamai*, which means "ability." Think about it—we get to be clothed with *God's ability!*

The remaining 11 disciples were already the most trained people in signs and wonders in all of history....And it was those 11 who had to stay until they were clothed with *power from on high*. When they got it they knew it. This power came through an encounter with God.

Some, because of their fear of error, have said it's improper to seek for an experience with God. After all, many deceived groups have come from those who based their beliefs on experiences in conflict with Scripture. Under the guidance of such attitudes, fear becomes our teacher. But why aren't those same individuals afraid of belonging to the doctrinally stable camps that are powerless? Is this deception any less dangerous than that of the power abuser? Will you bury your gifts and tell the Master when He comes that you were afraid of being wrong? Power and character are so closely aligned in Scripture that you cannot be weak in one without undermining the other.

(Quote From *When Heaven Invades Earth,* Page 124)

QUESTIONS

1. The disciples needed power even though they had firsthand training from an incarnate Jesus. What kind of power do you think we need? From where do we get our firsthand training? What kind of training is necessary to help us become witnesses?

2. Consider for a moment the concept of you being clothed with God's ability. What does this mean in terms of potential? What does this mean in terms of responsibility?

3. The disciples received their power in a most dramatic way in Acts 2. Do you think people receive power this dramatically with every encounter of God? Why or why not? What do you think should accompany all encounters with God?

4. What is "fear of error"? Are you familiar with any error in beliefs concerning the power of God? How can we be sure we don't fall into error? Are there principles from the Word that help guide us? What are they?

5. Do you know of groups who have doctrinal stability but are powerless? What are these groups afraid of? How can we be sure we don't become powerless?

6. In your understanding, how can you become balanced in using your gifts freely, yet not abusing them? In what ways are

character and power aligned in Scripture? How do these help safeguard each other?

MEDITATION

"If [God] is to be free to move in our lives, we will constantly be involved in impossibilities. The supernatural is His natural realm. The more important the Holy Spirit becomes to us, the more these issues will be paramount in our hearts" (*When Heaven Invades Earth*, Page 125).

How natural is the supernatural in your life?

Does God bring you lots of impossibilities so that you can overcome them and bear testimony to His power?

How well do you *flow* with the Holy Spirit?

Day 23

PRAYER—THE GATEWAY TO POWER

For Christ did not send me to baptize, but to preach the gospel—not with words
of human wisdom, lest the cross of Christ be emptied of its power
(I Corinthians I:I7 NIV).

TODAY'S DEVOTION

JESUS SAID THAT we must receive the Kingdom like a child. The life of power is at home in the heart of a child. A child has an insatiable appetite to learn. Be childlike and read the works of those who have succeeded in the healing ministry....We have grown fat on the theories of classroom Christians. We must learn from those who *just do it!*...

If we teach, preach, or witness and nothing happens, we must go back to the drawing board—our knees. Do not make excuses for powerlessness. For decades the Church has been guilty of creating doctrine to justify their lack of power, instead of crying out to God until He changed them. The lie they came to believe has given rise to an entire branch of theology that has infected the Body of Christ with a fear of the Holy Spirit. It deceives under the guise of staying undeceived. The Word must go forth with power. Power is the realm of the Spirit. A powerless Word is *the letter* not *the Spirit*. And we all know, "The letter kills, but the Spirit gives life" (2 Cor. 3:6). Lives must be changed in our ministry of the Word. Keep in mind that conversion is the greatest and most precious miracle of all.

(Quote From *When Heaven Invades Earth*, Pages 129-130)

QUESTIONS

1. What do you think Jesus meant when He said we must receive the Kingdom like a child? Are we to be innocent? Are we to be cute? What does He really expect from an adult who would receive the Kingdom like a child?

2. Are you a learner? Do you have an insatiable appetite to learn? Do you have a teachable spirit? Do you have the humility to be taught by those God chooses to instruct you?

3. Who are the people you know who have successful healing ministries? If you don't know any, ask your pastor or someone you respect to recommend people, books, or tapes for your instruction. Be sure these people do not just talk about healing as a theory but actually see healing miracles in their ministry.

4. When you fail at teaching, preaching, or witnessing, do you quickly go to your knees in prayer? Have you ever rationalized why your words had no effect? What do these self-justifications do to keep you from the real Source of power?

5. When you believe your own rationalizations, you believe a lie. How do you break through the lies that build up in your life and wake up to what really is wrong? Why do you think crying out to God banishes pride from your life? How can God change your mind-set?

6. Why do you think many people are fearful of the Holy Spirit? Why do many find it easier to follow the letter of the law and not the Spirit of the law? Why is change so disconcerting to many people? Is there an issue of control? Are there any other issues at work here?

MEDITATION

"We hear a lot about what the anointing costs. Without question, walking with God in power will cost all who give themselves to this mandate. But the absence of power is even more costly" (*When Heaven Invades Earth*, Page 132).

Has the absence of power personally cost you anything? Has it hurt your ministry or witness?

What price do you need to pay to receive power from on high?

Day 24

THE HIGH COST
OF LOW POWER

---

*If I had not done among them the works which no one else did, they would have
no sin; but now they have seen and also hated both Me and My Father*
(John 15:24).

TODAY'S DEVOTION

REVIVAL IS THE ATMOSPHERE in which Christ's power is most likely to
be manifested. It touches every part of human life, breaking into society
with sparks of revolution. Such glory is costly, and it is not to be taken
lightly. Nevertheless, a powerless Church is far more costly in terms of
human suffering and lost souls. During revival, hell is plundered and heaven
is populated. Without revival, hell is populated...period. Let me illustrate
the necessity of signs and wonders in our quest to see our cities transformed
and the glory of God fill the earth. Without [them], the world suffers, God
is grieved, and we are the most to be pitied....

A primary purpose of the miracle realm is to reveal the nature of God.
The lack of miracles works like a thief, stealing precious revelation that is

within the grasp of every man, woman, and child. Our debt to mankind is to give them answers for the impossible, and a personal encounter with God. And that encounter must include great power.

We are to be a witness for God. To give *witness* is to "represent." This actually means to *re-present* Him. Therefore, to re-present Him without power is a major shortcoming. It is impossible to give an adequate witness of God without demonstrating His supernatural power.

(Quote From *When Heaven Invades Earth*, Pages 133-134)

QUESTIONS

1. Give a description of what you think "revival" is. What are its components? How do you know that it is truly revival? Have you ever experienced revival? What was involved? What kind of revolution does it spark?

2. What is the cost of revival and the accompanying glory? Do you think most Christians are willing to pay the price? Why or why not?

3. How do signs and wonders help transform cities? How do they usher in the glory of God? Have you seen a community impacted by miracles? How could this happen?

4. How does the lack of signs and wonders make the world suffer? How does this lack grieve God? Have you experienced any of these negative repercussions?

5. Explain how miracles reveal the nature of God. Do they make God more real to you? If so, in what way? What part of God's character becomes real through seeing the miraculous?

6. How are miracles a witness of God and His Kingdom? In what ways do they represent Him? If there is no power accompanying our words, how do we have an inadequate witness?

MEDITATION

"Power exposes sin and brings people to a decision. When power is missing, we are not using the weapons that were in Jesus' arsenal when He ministered to the lost. The outcome? Most remain lost. Power forces people to be aware of God on a personal level, and it is demanding in nature" (*When Heaven Invades Earth*, Pages 135-136).

Has the power of God ever exposed sin in your life? Did it bring you to a decision? Describe the demand that power puts on the life of a believer.

Day 25

MIRACLES REVEAL HIS GLORY

This beginning of signs Jesus did in Cana of Galilee, and manifested His glory; and His disciples believed in Him (John 2:11).

TODAY'S DEVOTION

JESUS ATTENDED A wedding where they ran out of wine. As yet He hadn't performed any of the wonders for which He would later become known. Mary knew who her son was and what was possible....Her faith just made room for the extravagance of God! Jesus followed this with the miracle of turning the water into wine....

Jesus again looked to see what the Father was doing and now noticed that He was turning water into wine. So Jesus followed His lead and did the miracle. [Mary's] faith so touched the heart of the Father that He apparently changed the chosen time to unveil Jesus as the miracle worker. Faith moves heaven, so that heaven will move earth.

According to John 2:11, this demonstration of God's power released the glory of God into that location. Signs and wonders do that. They release the glory of God into our cities. The need—be it physical sickness, poverty, oppression, etc.—represents the impact of darkness. The miracle displaces darkness and replaces it with light—glory. When miracles are absent, so is the glory of God, which is the manifested presence of Jesus.

(Quote From *When Heaven Invades Earth*, Pages 139-140)

QUESTIONS

1. The first known miracle that Jesus performed was changing water into wine. Would it have been your choice for how Jesus would usher in His supernatural ministry? Are our misconceptions often blocks to participation in the miraculous?

2. How did Mary's faith change whether a miracle would be performed that day or not? Do you think she had seen other miracles and knew He was able to perform them? What kind of evidence do you need in order for your faith to engage?

3. How easy is it for you to tap and see what the Father is doing? What blocks your view? What enables it? How strong is your faith in this area?

4. The author tells us, "Faith moves heaven, so that heaven will move earth." Why is this true? How does this happen? Is God changing His mind when we exercise faith? Why or why not?

5. The miracle at the wedding ushered a season of power in Cana. Why do you think this happened? What kind of effect do you think it had on the citizens? On the local government? On the social welfare of the people?

6. From your answers to the questions in #5, draw some conclusions as to what changes might occur if miracles took place in your church this Sunday. How would it affect your community?

MEDITATION

"How will the glory of God cover the earth? I believe that, at least in part, it will be through a people who walk in power, bringing the testimony of Jesus to the nations of the world. There will be a generation that will catch this and will invade the world system with this living testimony of who Jesus is!" (*When Heaven Invades Earth*, Page 140).

How determined are you to be part of the testimony that will bring the glory of God?

Have you caught the vision of walking in power? Will you commit to being part of heaven's invasion on earth by being a living testimony?

Day 26

HOW DO WE GET THE POWER?

Behold, I send the promise of My Father upon you; but tarry in the city of Jerusalem until you are endued with power from on high (Luke 24:49).

TODAY'S DEVOTION

JESUS COMMANDED THE most highly trained individuals in the supernatural to ever walk the earth to "wait in Jerusalem for what the Father has promised" (Acts 1:4)....The baptism of fire would give them their own ongoing encounter that would help to keep them at the center of God's will *when* persecution came.

The baptism of the Holy Spirit is an immersion into the *dunamis* of heaven. The ability to pray in tongues is a wonderful gift given through this baptism. I pray in tongues constantly, and am grateful for such a gift from God. But to think that speaking in tongues is *the* purpose for such a holy invasion is embarrassingly simplistic. It would be the same as saying that when Israel crossed the Jordan River it was the same as possessing the Promised Land. Yes, they were in it, they could see it, but they did not possess it! Their river crossing gave them the legal access to the possession. This wonderful Spirit baptism has given us such an access. But to stand on the banks proclaiming *it's all mine*, is foolishness at best. Such ignorance has caused great numbers of people to halt their pursuit once they've received their spiritual language. They have been taught they are now full of the Holy Spirit.

(Quote From *When Heaven Invades Earth*, Pages 145-146)

QUESTIONS

1. Do you like it when you are told to "wait"? Why or why not. When Jesus asked the disciples to "wait," what test did the disciples face? Did they understand what the Father had promised...in other words, did they know what they were waiting for? What spiritual empowerment are you waiting for?

2. What is an "ongoing encounter"? How did the disciples' baptism create this? Have you had a baptism of fire? If so, has it empowered an "ongoing encounter"?

3. How does an "ongoing encounter" with God help to keep a person in the center of God's will when persecution comes? Why is this so crucial to our ongoing witness and impact on the world?

4. How are the ability to pray in tongues and *dunamis* interconnected? What do you think the purpose of speaking in tongues is?

5. Spirit baptism gives us access to what? Describe what we receive immediately and what we receive when we continue to grow in *dunamis*.

6. What are to be our pursuits after the baptism of the Holy Spirit? What must we do to gain our pursuits? How do we know if we are growing in these or not?

MEDITATION

"A glass is only full when it overflows. Fullness can only be measured by overflow. The fullness of God ought to do more for me than give me a supernatural language. If that's all there was, I'd have no complaint. It's a glorious gift from God. But His purposes bring us into more, to a divine partnership in which we become co-laborers with Christ" (*When Heaven Invades Earth*, Page 146).

Are you full of God? Do you have a regular overflow that is measurable? What does your partnership with God look like?

OUR DEBT TO THE WORLD: AN ENCOUNTER WITH GOD

—◦—

If the household is worthy, let your peace come upon it. But if it is not worthy, let your peace return to you (Matthew 10:13).

TODAY'S DEVOTION

GOD'S COVENANT PROMISE, "I will be with you," has always been linked to mankind's need for courage to face the impossible. There is no question that the presence of God is what brings us great comfort and peace. But the presence of God was always promised to His chosen ones to give them assurance in the face of less than favorable circumstances.

He is the great treasure of mankind. He always will be. It is this revelation that enabled the revolutionary exploits of the apostle Paul. It's what strengthened a king named David to risk his life in order to transform the system of sacrifice and worship. Moses needed this assurance as the man who was sent to face Pharaoh and his demon-possessed magicians. They all needed incredible confidence to fulfill their callings....

The Great Commission provides more interesting reading for those who remember what kind of men God was giving His charge to—greedy, prideful, angry, and self-centered. Yet Jesus called them to change the world. What was the one word of assurance that He gave them before departing from sight? "I will be with you always..." (see Matt. 28:19-21)....

The presence of God is to be realized in the anointing. Remember, anointing means *smeared*—it is God covering us with His power-filled presence. Supernatural things happen when we walk in the anointing!

(Quote From *When Heaven Invades Earth*, Pages 149-151)

QUESTIONS

1. What is the connection between the presence of God and peace? How does this work? What is your peace like—intermittent or constant? How does your answer reflect the presence of God in your life?

2. What is the true test as to whether you have peace or not? When unfavorable circumstances enter your life, does peace reign? When you are faced with challenges, what emotions can rise to the surface that are not God's choice? What are the negative thoughts that may come?

3. How did you come to discover that God is the great treasure of your life? Has this revelation made a difference in how you live each day? Have you done any revolutionary exploits that resemble Paul's? Have you received strength and helped transform anything within the Church? Have you received assistance to face opposition square in the face?

4. What kind of confidence does the presence of God bring? Do you find that you are more confident than a year ago? Why or why not? How does confidence grow within us?

5. If Jesus was not uncomfortable trusting His disciples with the job of changing the world, do you think He is uncomfortable trusting you with your commission? Truthfully, do you believe Jesus can overcome your shortcomings and still use you to do His Kingdom work?

6. Describe what the "anointing" is to you. If the "presence of God is to be realized in the anointing," how does your description come to bear on the presence of God? Describe what being "smeared" by God means to you. How does this smearing affect your daily life?

MEDITATION

"Why do some walk with a greater sense of God's presence than others? Some people place high value on the presence of God, and others don't. The ones who do enjoy fellowship throughout their day with the Holy Spirit are extremely conscious of how He feels about their words, attitudes, and activities. The thought of grieving Him brings great sorrow. It's their passion to give Him preeminence in everything. That passion brings that believer into a supernatural life—one with the constant activity of the Holy Spirit working through them" (*When Heaven Invades Earth*, Page 150).

Reflect on which of these sentences describe you and which do not. Where do you want to go from here?

Day 28

JESUS PASSED
THE BATON

---

*Most assuredly, I say to you, he who believes in Me, the works that I do he will
do also; and greater works than these he will do, because I go to My Father*
(John 14:12).

TODAY'S DEVOTION

FOR US TO BECOME all that God intended, we must remember that Jesus'
life was a model of what mankind could become if it were in right relationship with the Father. Through the shedding of His blood, it would be possible for everyone who believed on His name to do as He did and become
as He was. This meant then that every true believer would have access to the
realm of life that Jesus lived in.

Jesus came as the light of the world. He then passed the baton to us,
announcing that we are the light of the world. Jesus came as the miracle
worker. He said that we would do "greater works" than He did (see John
14:12). He then pulled the greatest surprise of all, saying, "Right now the
Holy Spirit is with you, but He's going to be in you"(see John 14:17). Jesus,

who illustrates to us what is possible for those who are *right with God*, now says that His people are to be the tabernacle of God on planet earth. Paul affirms this revelation with statements such as, "Do you not know that you are the temple of God?" (I Cor. 3:16), and "you are a dwelling place of God" (Eph. 2:22).

(Quote From *When Heaven Invades Earth*, Page 155)

QUESTIONS

1. As you look at the life of Jesus, what are the striking aspects of His relationship with His Father that inspire you? List the results of the relationship between Jesus and His Father that speak most to you. Based on your answers, what would be the next steps toward a more intimate relationship with the Father?

2. Jesus is our model of Kingdom expansion. How does belief in His name bear weight on how much we become like Him? Describe the realm of life that is then open to us as believers.

3. Just as Jesus was the light of the world, we are to be the same. To be the light of the world, what would be your mission statement? What is your strategy to be the light wherever you go?

4. Just as Jesus was the miracle worker, we are to do greater miracles than He did. How is this possible? What kind of grade would you give the contemporary Church in doing greater things than Jesus did? Explain why you graded the Church the way you did.

5. After Jesus ascended, the Holy Spirit changed positions. Instead of being "with" us, He now is "in" us. Explain the difference between "with" and "in" in terms of the process, the results, and the relationship.

6. Trace the place where God has dwelled on earth: Moses' tabernacle...David's tabernacle...the temple in Jerusalem...

our bodies. How does each dwelling place show the plan of God's relationship to man?

MEDITATION

"What was the initial revelation of the house of God? It has the presence of God, a gate to heaven, and a ladder with angels ascending and descending upon it. Why is this important to understand? This revelation shows the resources that are at our disposal to carry out the Master's plan. This principle of being the stewards of the heavenly realm then becomes more than the assignment of the individual, and becomes the privilege of an entire Church for the sake of their entire city" (*When Heaven Invades Earth*, Page 156).

How does the understanding that you have all of God's resources at your disposal make you feel?

Because they are to be used to carry out the Master's plan, how is your stewardship vital?

How does your personal assignment affect your local church's assignment?

Day 29

ENTERING THE TWILIGHT ZONE

Bless the Lord, you His angels, who excel in strength, who do His word, heeding the voice of His word (Psalm 103:20).

TODAY'S DEVOTION

I TRAVEL TO MANY CITIES that are spiritually very dark. When you enter such cities you can feel the oppression. Considering what I represent to that city, it would be wrong for me to focus on the darkness. I don't ever want to be impressed with the devil's work. I come as a *house of God*. As such I contain a gate to heaven, with a ladder providing angelic activities according to the need of the moment. Simply put, *I am an open heaven!* This does not apply to a select few. On the contrary, this revelation is about the house of God and the principles of the house apply to all believers. But few realize or implement this *potential* blessing. With an open heaven I become a vehicle in the hand of God to release the resources of heaven into the calamities of mankind. Angels are commissioned to carry out the will of God. "Bless the Lord, you His angels, who excel in strength, who do His word, heeding the voice of His word" (Ps. 103:20). He is more eager to invade this world than we are to receive the invasion. And angels play an integral part.

They respond to His command and enforce His Word. But the *voice of His word* is heard when the Father speaks to the hearts of His people.

(Quote From *When Heaven Invades Earth*, Pages 157-158)

QUESTIONS

1. The author relays how he travels to cities that are spiritually dark. How would he feel the oppression he speaks of? Have you ever felt oppression? Did it overwhelm you or keep you from a strong spiritual connection?

2. Why do you think the author tells us that it would have been wrong for him to focus on darkness when he felt oppression? How can it deter us from great works that the Lord wants to do? Are you able to overcome darkness? How?

3. As a gate to heaven, you have authority to do what? Do you see yourself as someone who provides access to another dimension? How can people's needs be met in the spontaneity of the moment because of this open heaven?

4. How does God use you as a vehicle to release the resources of heaven into the calamities of mankind? Is this an issue of money only? What other resources are available to you? Is this confined to what you personally have, or are there other resources available?

5. Have you ever thought of God planning an "invasion" of planet earth? What factors would inhibit the invasion? Why aren't people ready to receive God's invasion?

6. Consider the statement, "The voice of His word is heard when the Father speaks to the hearts of His people." What does this

mean to you? How does this voice speak to the angels? How does it release resources to earth?

MEDITATION

"Angels await the people of God speaking His word. I believe angels pick up the fragrance of the throne room through the word spoken by people. They can tell when a word has its origins in the heart of the Father. And, in turn, they recognize that word as their assignment" (*When Heaven Invades Earth*, Page 158).

This is a beautiful portrayal of how angels receive assignments. How is mankind involved in this process?

Is it weighty to think of your connection with angelic assignments?

Day 30

OUR IDENTITY
IN THIS WORLD

Love has been perfected among us in this: that we may have boldness in the day of judgment; because as He is, so are we in this world (I John 4:17).

TODAY'S DEVOTION

WHILE MOST OF THE CHURCH is still trying to become as Jesus was, the Bible declares, "As He is, so are we in this world" (I John 4:17)....

The "as He is, so are we" declaration is far beyond what any of us could have imagined; especially in light of the glorified description of Jesus in Revelation I. Yet, the Holy Spirit was sent specifically for this purpose, that we might attain "to the measure of the stature of the fullness of Christ" (Eph. 4:13). The Holy Spirit came with the ultimate assignment at the perfect time. During Jesus' ministry, it was said, "The Holy Spirit was not yet given, because Jesus was not yet glorified" (John 7:39). The Holy Spirit comforts us, gives us gifts, reminds us of what Jesus has said, and clothes us with power. But He does all this to *make us like Jesus.* That is His primary mission. So why didn't the Father send Him until Jesus was glorified? Because without Jesus in His glorified state there was no *heavenly model of what we were to become!* As a sculptor looks at a model and fashions the clay into its likeness, so the Holy Spirit looks to the glorified Son and shapes us into His image. *As He is, so are we in this world.*

(Quote From *When Heaven Invades Earth,* Pages 163-164)

QUESTIONS

1. Explain what you think First John 4:17 means to your life. How does the fact that Jesus is no longer incarnate impact what you are to become?

2. How does Jesus' glorified description in Revelation I impact you? List the verses that describe Him and make personal notes regarding each one.

3. What is the "stature of the fullness of Christ"? How do you "measure" up? What part of the fullness of Christ is easily seen in your life? How does this measure testify to God's glory?

4. What is the true mission of the Holy Spirit in our lives? What is His strategy? What tools does He use to accomplish His mission? How is this possible?

5. If the Holy Spirit is as a sculptor and we are as the clay, how moldable and pliable are you in the hands of the Master Potter? Do you fashion easily into the shape He desires, or do you resist? Perhaps there are specific areas of more resistance than others. If so, what are they? What might you do to become more pliable?

6. How can you be more like Jesus to this world? Because many are looking for something other than the glorified Christ, you will need to think in terms outside this world. How will you take on a Jesus model and move in power and authority?

MEDITATION

"Jesus became poor so that I could become rich. He suffered with stripes to free me from affliction, and He became sin so I might become the righteousness of God (see 2 Cor. 5:21). Why then should I try to become *as He was*, when He suffered so I could become *as He is?* At some point, the reality of the resurrection must come into play in our lives—we must discover the power of the resurrection for all who believe (see Eph. 1:21; 3:20)" (*When Heaven Invades Earth*, Pages 164-165).

Consider why you should become as He is. Is the resurrection an everyday consideration in your life?

BECOMING LIKE HIM

━━━━━━━━━━━━━━❈❈❈━━━━━━━━━━━━━━

Then Mary said, "Behold the maidservant of the Lord! Let it be to me according to Your word." And the angel departed from her (Luke 1:38).

TODAY'S DEVOTION

As He is, so are we in this world. The revelation of Jesus in His glorified state has at least four overwhelming characteristics that directly affect the coming transformation of the Church; these must be embraced as a part of God's plan in these final hours.

Glory—This is the manifested presence of Jesus....He lives in all believers, but the glory of His presence comes to rest on only a few. It is sometimes seen and frequently felt. He is returning for a glorious Church. It is not an option....

Power—To be *as He is* involves being a continuous expression of power. The baptism in the Holy Spirit clothes us with this heavenly element....It is the *power of salvation*—for the body, soul, and spirit....

Triumph—Jesus conquered all things: the power of hell, the grave, sin, and the devil....Every name and power has been placed under His feet. He calls us His body—and this body has feet....This victory doesn't mean we live without battles; it simply means our victory is secured....

Holiness—Jesus is perfectly holy—separate *from* all that is evil, *unto* all that is good. Holiness is the language through which the nature of God is revealed....Holiness in the Church reveals the beauty of God.

(Quote From *When Heaven Invades Earth*, Pages 168-170)

QUESTIONS

I. Mary believed the angel and then lived out her assignment. It was that simple...or was it? Trace the difficulties Mary faced in those months and years after the angelic visitation. She had to continuously go back to the reality of the visitation and remind herself of her assignment. What is your assignment? What difficulties have you faced that force you to revisit your call to it?

2. In your opinion, how does *glory* directly affect the coming transformation of the Church? How does it affect your transformation?

3. In your opinion, how does *power* directly affect the coming transformation of the Church? How does it affect your transformation?

4. In your opinion, how does *triumph* directly affect the coming transformation of the Church? How does it affect your transformation?

5. In your opinion, how does *holiness* directly affect the coming transformation of the Church? How does it affect your transformation?

6. Summarize how these four overwhelming characteristics affect the Church as a whole in terms of its transformation. Then summarize how the total impact of the above four characteristics impact your own transformation.

MEDITATION

"At some point we must rise up to the high call of God and stop saying things about ourselves that are no longer true. If we're going to fully come into what God has for us in this last days' revival, we will have to come to grips with the issue of being more than *sinners saved by grace*. Maturity comes from faith in the sufficiency of God's redemptive work that establishes us as sons and daughters of the Most High" (*When Heaven Invades Earth*, Page 168).

How can we see ourselves as not just sinners saved by grace but heirs of God?

What does it take for us to believe we are precious in God's sight even when we don't feel it?

Day 32

WARRING
TO INVADE!

———————— ✦ ————————

To execute on them the written judgment—this honor have all His saints
(Psalm 149:9).

TODAY'S DEVOTION

FOR TOO LONG the Church has played defense in the battle for souls.... This may come as a surprise, but I don't care what the devil plans to do. The Great Commission puts me on the offensive. I've got the ball. And if I carry the ball effectively, his plans won't matter....

Spiritual warfare is unavoidable, and ignoring this subject won't make it go away. Therefore, we must learn to battle with supernatural authority! The following principles are often overlooked insights:...

1. The safest place in this war is obedience....

2. Never allow anything to distract you from this point of strength....

3. When we refuse fear, the enemy becomes terrified....

4. Submission is the key to personal triumph....

5. The Church is on the attack. That's why the *gates of hell*, the place of demonic government and strength, *will not prevail* against the Church....

6. It is His delight to have us enforce the triumph of Jesus....

7. Praise honors God. But it also edifies us and destroys the powers of hell!...

This is by no means a complete list. It's just enough to turn our perspective of spiritual warfare from one that is religious and carnal, to one that has a Kingdom mind-set.

(Quote From *When Heaven Invades Earth*, Pages 173-177)

QUESTIONS

1. Why do you think the Church has been on the defense and not on the offense in the battle for souls? Do you think the Church has focused on what the devil's plans are versus what God's are? What needs to change?

2. To be on the offensive means that we attack first...right? How do we know where to attack? What to attack? How to attack? With what weapons? How do we get our military strategy?

3. What do you think it means to "battle with supernatural authority"? How can we learn how to do this?

4. Look over the list of seven principles the author shares. Comment on each one in terms of your experience and ability in each area.

5. Look over the list again and find Scriptures that will help you gain strength in each.

6. Finally, make a point to memorize your Scriptures over the next seven weeks so that you are ready to pursue the enemy instead of allowing the enemy to pursue you.

MEDITATION

"We were born in a war. There are no time-outs, no vacations, no leaves of absence. The safest place is in the center of God's will, which is the place of deep intimacy. There He allows only the battles to come our way that we are equipped to win" (*When Heaven Invades Earth*, Page 177).

Even though war is inevitable, how comforting it is to know we can win every one. How is this possible? Is it probable?

HOW TO MISS
A REVIVAL

For the hearts of this people have grown dull. Their ears are hard of hearing,
and their eyes they have closed, lest they should see with their eyes and hear
with their ears, lest they should understand with their hearts and turn,
so that I should heal them (Matthew 13:15).

TODAY'S DEVOTION

HISTORY IS FILLED WITH people who prayed for a visitation of God and missed it when it came. And this happened even though some had a strong relationship with God. Many believers have a blindness that the world doesn't have. The world knows its need. But for many Christians, once they are born again, they gradually stop recognizing their need. There is something about desperation for God that enables a person to recognize whether or not something is from God. Jesus spoke of this phenomenon, saying, "For judgment I have come into this world, that those who do not see may see, and that those who see may be made blind" (John 9:39).

The testimony of history and the record of Scripture warn us of the possibility of this error. "Therefore let him who thinks he stands take heed lest he fall" (1 Cor. 10:12). Matthew says it's the dull of heart who can't see (see Matt. 13:15). A dull knife is one that has been used. The implication is that the *dull of heart* had a history in God, but did not keep current in what God was doing. We maintain our *sharp edge* as we recognize our need and passionately pursue Jesus. This *first love* somehow keeps us safely in the center of God's activities on earth.

(Quote From *When Heaven Invades Earth,* Page 180)

QUESTIONS

1. Why do you think so many have missed a visitation from God after they had spent time on their knees praying for it? Doesn't a strong relationship with God prevent such things? Why or why not?

2. Why do you think "recognizing our need" is so important to the believer? How desperate are you for God?

3. Explain the meaning of John 9:39. Who do the "blind" refer to here? Who are the ones who can see? Why did Jesus say such things?

4. In First Corinthians 10:12, it speaks about a person "who thinks he stands." What does this mean? A person of this description might have fallen prey to what types of sins? How do you think you can avoid these sins?

5. What does "dull of heart" mean? Why does this condition prevent spiritual sight? How can someone keep "current" with what God is doing? Is this a current events exercise or something else?

6. How sharp is your edge? How do you fan the flame of your first love? What part of your relationship with God may need some fanning currently?

MEDITATION

"Revival is central to the message of the Kingdom, for it is in revival that we more clearly see what His dominion looks like and how it is to affect society. Revival, at its best, is Thy Kingdom come. In a way, revival illustrates the normal Christian life" (*When Heaven Invades Earth*, Page 179).

Have you ever read about past revivals? Research the Internet or read a book that describes some of the greatest revivals and the people who preached during them. Consider what they preached and apply it to today's world.

Day 34

CLOSE ENCOUNTERS

<hr>

Now to Him who is able to do exceedingly abundantly above all that we ask or think, according to the power that works in us (Ephesians 3:20).

TODAY'S DEVOTION

THINK ABOUT THE Acts 2 experience of the disciples. Notice the elements of this Spirit-directed service:

1. They were praying.

2. They were in unity.

3. They all spoke in tongues.

4. Unbelievers heard those tongues.

5. People were saved.

Consider the Acts 2 company's predicament: they just had an encounter with God without a chapter and verse to explain what just happened. Peter, under the direction of the Holy Spirit, chose to use Joel 2 as the proof-text to give the needed backbone to their experience. Joel 2 declares there would be an outpouring of the Holy Spirit involving prophecy, dreams, and visions. The outpouring happened as promised in Acts 2, but it had none of the things mentioned by Joel. Instead, it had the sound of wind, fire, and tongues. It was God who used this passage to support this new experience.

The very fact that this seems like an improper interpretation of Scripture should reveal to us that it is we who often approach His book incorrectly. The Bible is not a book of lists that confine or corral God. The Word does not contain God—it reveals Him. Joel 2 revealed the nature of God's work among man. Acts 2 was an illustration of what God intended by that prophecy.

(Quote From *When Heaven Invades Earth*, Pages 185-186)

QUESTIONS

1. Look at the five elements of the Spirit-directed service in Acts 2. How many of these depict your local church? Should this happen each and every worship service? Why or why not? Is there a system we are to employ, or will each Spirit-led service have differences?

2. If you had been one of the disciples and experienced the outpouring of Acts 2, how would you have reacted? Would an explanation be necessary to you right then and there? Why or why not? Would believers need an explanation later to understand what had happened? Why or why not?

3. Read Joel 2:28-29. Look at the people groups mentioned here. Why were each used as examples of where God would pour out His Spirit? Does this help validate the ones He chose to use in Acts 2? Does this help validate why He would choose you and your local church? How?

4. What is the difference between confining or corralling God and explaining what God does? Where do you cross the line between these two? What do we have to avoid when we give explanation for how God is working?

5. The link between Joel and Acts provides an example of how the Old and New Testaments work together to bring principles of God's Word to us. Explain how this is true with these two passages. Are there others you can cite that are not exact quotes of each other but help clarify how the Lord works? If so, give examples.

6. "The Word does not contain God—it reveals Him." What does this mean to you? How does this give room to experience God each time you read the Word?

MEDITATION

"We miss God when we live as though we have Him figured out. We have the habit of making Him look like us. In fact, if we think we understand Him we have probably conformed Him into our image. There must remain mystery in our relationship with this One who has purposed to work beyond our capacity to imagine. To endeavor to know Him is to embark on an adventure in which questions increase" (*When Heaven Invades Earth*, Page 187).

Think about your relationship with God. Is there mystery involved in it? Do you see your relationship as an adventure? Do questions increase because of your growing intimacy?

Day 35

INFILTRATING
THE SYSTEM

*And again He said, "To what shall I liken the kingdom of God?
It is like leaven, which a woman took and hid in three measures of
meal till it was all leavened"* (Luke 13:20-21).

TODAY'S DEVOTION

WITHOUT A REVELATION of what God intends to do with His Church, we cannot move in overcoming faith. When the main goal of our faith is keeping us safe from the devil, our faith becomes inferior to what God expects. Jesus had in mind more for us than survival. We are destined to overcome.

Every conversion plunders hell. Every miracle destroys the works of the devil. Every God encounter is an *invasion of the Almighty* into our desperate condition. This is our joy.

The original flame of Pentecost, the Holy Spirit Himself, burns within my soul. I have a promise from God. I am a part of a company of people destined to do greater works than Jesus did in His earthly ministry. Why is it so hard to see the Church with significant influence in the last days?

It was God who determined that the Bride should be spotless and without wrinkle. It was God who declared, "Behold darkness will cover the earth, but His glory will appear upon you" (Isa. 60:2 NASB). It was God who calls us, His Church, overcomers (see Rev. 12:11).

The parable about leaven illustrates the subtle but overwhelming influence of the Kingdom in any setting into which it is placed. In these days, God has planned to put us into the darkest of situations to demonstrate His dominion.

(Quote From *When Heaven Invades Earth*, Pages 190-191)

QUESTIONS

1. Why do we need a revelation of what God intends to do with His Church? What does this have to do with moving in overcoming faith?

2. How can the devil become a distraction to the direction of your faith? How easy is it to replace a mind-set of "survival" with a mind-set toward "overcoming"? Have you been able to do it? What do you think are the necessary steps to change anyone's mind-set?

3. Explain how conversions plunder hell and miracles destroy the works of the devil. If these are the military invasion strategy of God, why doesn't the Church have more success in the campaign? What part are you playing in this invasion?

4. The Church is supposed to be influential in the last days. Is it currently? Why or why not? What can improve its influence? What will the Church need to become involved in, to a greater capacity, for there to be effective influence?

5. Isaiah 60:2 says that God's glory will come upon us. How does this happen? How are you bringing God's glory into the darkness?

6. Instead of despairing over the darkness of the times, we are to see our opportunity to have greater influence. Why will this be true? Are you ready to negotiate the darkness in order to bring dominion? Why or why not?

MEDITATION

"A jeweler often places a diamond on a piece of black velvet. The brilliance of the gem is clearer against that background. So it is with the Church. The dark condition of the world's circumstances becomes the backdrop upon which He displays His glorious Church! 'Where sin abounded, grace abounded much more' (Rom. 5:20)" (*When Heaven Invades Earth*, Page 191).

Think about your local church as a jewel in your community of black velvet. How well does it display God's glorious Church? What do people think about your church in your community?

How is your church seen by other churches? How can we help display our local churches so that God's brilliance will be easily seen?

Day 36

THE POWER
OF HOLINESS

*And He said to them, "Go into all the world and preach the gospel
to every creature"* (Mark 16:15).

TODAY'S DEVOTION

So MUCH OF TODAY's Kingdom theology is focused on us ruling, in the
sense of believers becoming the heads of corporations and governments.
And, in measure, it is true. But our strong suit has been, and always will be,
service. If in serving we get promoted to positions of rulership, we must
remember that *what got us there will keep us useful.* In the Kingdom, the greatest
is the servant of all. Use every position to serve with more power....

Infiltrating the system often involves our willingness to bring spiritual gifts
into our world. These gifts actually work better in the world than in the
confines of church meetings. When we practice the gifts only in the church,
they lose their sharp edge. Invading the world system with His dominion
keeps us sharp and gets them saved....

The presence of the Kingdom saves the lives of people who have not earned it through personal obedience. Such is the power of righteousness—it protects those around it.

Promotion does not go unchallenged. Just when you think you have been placed into a position of influence, something will happen to totally rock your boat.... There is a distinction between submission and obedience. Sometimes we are to go against the command of our leaders—but even then, only with submissive hearts.

(Quote From *When Heaven Invades Earth*, Pages 193-195)

QUESTIONS

1. In order to lead, what does the Lord ask us to do? In order to be the greatest, what does He tell us to be? In order to be the first, what does the Lord require? Are we not to be ambitious? What place does ambition have?

2. How does servant leadership work? What are its requirements? What are its results? Are their any promises of promotion?

3. How do you "serve with more power"? Consider this thought another way—how can you get more power to serve? Who are the people who look up to you either in the home, in ministry, or in the business world? Do they see you as a servant? Take some time to ask them to evaluate the quality of your servanthood.

4. Our spiritual gifts are not to be used within the four walls of the church; we are to take these to the marketplace. In what ways can you use spiritual gifts where you work or live? They do not have to be identified as spiritual gifts, but actually means of infiltrating the system. Have you ever used a spiritual gift in a "secular" environment that brought special insight or success?

5. If we serve where we are positioned, God uses the power of our righteousness. How can this serve the people who work or live with us? Can this power affect the financial status of the corporation or house where we serve? Can this power affect the work climate? Explain.

6. Have you received promotion in ministry or on the job and experienced an immediate attack that challenged it? What happened? Is there a way to challenge leaders and peers without throwing submission out the window? How can this be done?

MEDITATION

"For massive worldwide revival to reach its dominating potential, it must be taken out of the four walls of the church and launched into the *marketplace* (see Mark 6:56). Quietly, powerfully, decisively invade through service; and when you run into a person with an impossibility, let him know the reality of heaven is within arm's reach!" (*When Heaven Invades Earth*, Pages 195-196).

How do you view your Great Commission? Is it easy to be a witness? Does your holiness find power readily available when needed?

TAKING IT TO
THE MARKETPLACE

Wherever He entered, into villages, cities, or the country, they laid the sick in the marketplaces, and begged Him that they might just touch the hem of His garment. And as many as touched Him were made well (Mark 6:56).

TODAY'S DEVOTION

ANY GOSPEL THAT doesn't work in the marketplace, doesn't work. Jesus invaded every realm of society. He went where people gathered. They became His focus, and He became theirs.

We see businessmen use the gifts of the Spirit to identify the needs of their co-workers and customers. A young teammate laid hands on the star running back of his high school football team after he had been knocked out of the game with a serious leg injury. After the running back was healed, he returned to the game acknowledging God had healed him!...

A 10-year-old asked her mom to take her to the mall so she could find sick people to pray for. Students set up a sign at their table at our local coffee shop. It says, *"Free Prayer."* People not only got prayer, they received a prophetic word that brought them to a greater awareness of God's love....

Skateboarders are touched by other skateboarders who look to bring them into an encounter with the God of all power. If people are there, we go there. Under the bridges, out in the vacant lots, we look for the homeless.

(Quote From *When Heaven Invades Earth*, Pages 198-199)

QUESTIONS

1. "Any gospel that doesn't work in the marketplace, doesn't work." What does this mean? Do you think this is true? Explain your answer.

2. Think through the strata of society that Jesus invaded. Name people from these different social groups who were changed by bumping elbows with Jesus. Are these people representative of society today? Are we to bump elbows with them as Jesus did?

3. Jesus was focused on the people who gathered around Him. He considered all their needs. What are the needs of the people who are gathered around you at home, in ministry, in the marketplace? What do you do about these needs? What did Jesus do?

4. As Jesus focused on the people around Him, they began to focus on Him. Who have you led to Christ? Do you help people focus on the Lord by your acts of prayer, generosity, or service on their behalf?

5. The author gives examples of Christians who made a difference to the people around them. Ask the Lord to reveal who is the next priority of focus in your ministry in the marketplace. Begin to pray consistently for that person and allow the Lord to reveal

acts of service or generosity that you might be able to do that will bring focus to Jesus.

6. No matter what religion they believe or don't believe, people across the world recognize God's love. When they see Mother Teresa or missionary agencies provide care in critical moments, they are not afraid to receive a "bless you" from the one ministering to them. Is there someone in your sphere of influence who has a crisis that is in need of a miracle? From prayer for a miracle to acts of kindness, are you able to find a way to minister a "bless you" to them in their hour of need?

MEDITATION

"Not only does Jesus care for the down and outer, but He also loves the up and outer. The wealthy are some of the most broken of our cities. But we must not serve them for their money! They are accustomed to people becoming friends to get something from them.... Where does life take you? Go there in the anointing and watch the impossibilities bow to the name Jesus" (*When Heaven Invades Earth*, Page 199).

Think about what the author has said here and consider the impossibilities before you. Grab the anointing and watch those impossibilities bow to the name of Jesus.

Day 38

THIS PRESENT
REVIVAL

To the intent that now the manifold wisdom of God might be made known by the
church to the principalities and powers in the heavenly places, according to
the eternal purpose which He accomplished in Christ Jesus our Lord
(Ephesians 3:10-11).

TODAY'S DEVOTION

UNDERSTANDING WHAT IS about to come is important, but not to equip
us to plan and strategize more effectively. On the contrary, it's important
to understand God's promise and purpose for the Church so that we might
become dissatisfied—so that we will become desperate. Intercession from
insatiable hunger moves the heart of God as nothing else can.

Revival is not for the faint of heart. It brings fear to the complacent
because of the risks it requires. The fearful often work against the move of
God—sometimes to their death—all the while thinking they are working
for Him. Deception says that the changes brought about by revival contradict the faith of their fathers. As a result, the God-given ability to create

withers into the laborious task of preserving. The fearful become curators of museums, instead of builders of the Kingdom.

Others are ready to risk all. The faith of their fathers is considered a worthy foundation to build upon. They have caught a glimpse of what could be and will settle for nothing less. Change is not a threat, but an adventure. Revelation increases, ideas multiply, and the stretch begins.

(Quote From *When Heaven Invades Earth*, Pages 203-205)

QUESTIONS

Think on Ephesians 3:10-11 in terms of the following phrases:

1. Manifold wisdom of God.

2. Known by the church.

3. To the principalities and powers in the heavenly places.

4. Eternal purpose.

5. Which He accomplished in Christ Jesus. For each phrase explain:

   - What you think it means.

   - What impact it has on the world.

   - What potential it has for your community.

   - What demand it has for your life.

   - Why it requires faith and courage.

   - What change will be needed of the participants.

MEDITATION

"What God has planned for the Church in this hour is greater than our ability to imagine and pray. We must have the help of the Holy Spirit to learn about these mysteries of the Church and God's Kingdom. Without Him we don't have enough insight even to know what to ask for in prayer" (*When Heaven Invades Earth*, Page 203).

Has God ever stirred your imagination beyond your normal scope of thinking?

Have you ever felt like you were dreaming His dream and making it yours?

Spend time asking the Lord to share His heart and desires with you so you might add your faith to the dream and watch it come *to life!*

Day 39

GLORIOUS CHURCH

That He might present her to Himself a glorious church, not having spot or wrinkle or any such thing, but that she should be holy and without blemish (Ephesians 5:27).

TODAY'S DEVOTION

WISDOM IS TO BE DISPLAYED by us NOW! It is clear that God intends to teach the spirit realm about His wisdom through those made in His image—us....

The wisdom of God will again be seen in His people. The Church, which is presently despised, or at best ignored, will again be reverenced and admired....

Excellence is the high standard for what we do because of who we are. God is extravagant, but not wasteful. An excellent heart for God may appear to be wasteful to those on the outside....Excellence comes from viewing things from His perspective....

Creativity is not only seen in a full restoration of the arts, but is the nature of His people in finding new and better ways to do things....We must reveal who our Father is through creative expression....This anointing will also bring about new inventions, breakthroughs in medicine and science, and novel ideas for business and education....

Integrity is the expression of God's character seen in us. And that character is His holiness. Holiness is the essence of His nature. It is not something He does or doesn't do. It is who He is. It is the same for us. We are holy because the nature of God is in us.

(Quote From *When Heaven Invades Earth*, Pages 206-208)

QUESTIONS

1. Define what "wisdom" means to you. How does God's wisdom come to mankind? How can we teach the spirit realm about His wisdom?

2. Imagine...the Church "will again be reverenced and admired." Is this possible? Explain your answer. What must the Church do to change its reputation? How must society change to accept the clear message the Church reveals?

3. What message does excellence in the Church speak to unbelievers? How will God's excellence create a new standard for all other excellence? Will we be criticized by those who don't understand God's perspective?

4. How does creativity within the Church bring a witness to the lost? How does this creativity manifest itself? How can the Church go beyond imitating the world's creativity and actually forge new paths?

5. In a dog-eat-dog environment, how will integrity make the Church stand above the rest? Won't Christians just get stepped on in the marketplace by those who play the political games to

succeed? How will Christians' integrity make a way through the agendas of others?

6. Holiness is usually viewed as being a goody-two-shoes. How will society begin to see holiness for what it really is? Will they recognize the nature of God in us and desire it for themselves? What will bring about their desire?

MEDITATION

"We will be a Church in which Jesus is seen in His glory! It is the Holy Spirit's presence and anointing that will dominate the Christian's life. The Church will be radiant.... She will be a Bride without spot or wrinkle" (*When Heaven Invades Earth*, Page 209).

What must you do to increase the Holy Spirit's presence and the anointing in your life?

How will your local church need to prioritize what it does to foster these throughout the congregation?

Day 40

REACHING THE
MAXIMUM

Of the increase of His government and peace there will be no end, upon the throne of David and over his kingdom, to order it and establish it with judgment and justice from that time forward, even forever. The zeal of the Lord of Hosts will perform this (Isaiah 9:7).

TODAY'S DEVOTION

ALL CHURCH HISTORY is built on partial revelation. Everything that has happened in the Church over the past 1,900 years has fallen short of what the early Church had and lost. Each move of God has been followed by another, just to restore what was forfeited and forgotten. And we still haven't arrived to the standard that they attained, let alone surpassed it. Yet, not even the early Church fulfilled God's full intention for His people. That privilege was reserved for those in the last leg of the race. It is our destiny.

As wonderful as our spiritual roots are, they are insufficient. What was good for *yesterday* is deficient for *today*. To insist that we stay with what our fathers fought for is to insult our forefathers. They risked all to pursue something fresh and new in God. It's not that *everything* must change for us to flow with what God is saying and doing. It's just that we make too many assumptions about the *rightness* of what presently exists. Those assumptions blind us to the revelations still contained in Scripture. In reality, what we think of as the *normal Christian life* cannot hold the weight of what God is about to do. Our wineskins must change. There is very little of what we now know as Church life that will remain untouched in the next ten years.

(Quote From *When Heaven Invades Earth,* Page 215)

QUESTIONS

I. Why does the Church have only partial revelation? Does God withhold His thoughts? Do we have problems hearing Him? What is the cause of our dilemma?

2. Why have we seen cycles of revival and forfeiture? Do you think there is a way to continue revival from one generation to the next? Do you think that is what our generation is supposed to do for the next?

3. What are your spiritual roots? Are there those in your family who have passed a heritage of the love of Christ to you? How have those roots affected your spiritual journey? What are their limitations?

4. Have you had an experience in revival or an increased anointing at any time in your life? If so, what made it so vibrant? Have you ever wanted to return to those feelings and experiences? Why doesn't God continue the same expressions and experiences throughout our journey? Why are we to pursue something fresh and new?

5. What do you think must change for us to flow with what God is saying and doing? What do you think it means when the author says, "We make too many assumptions about the rightness of

what presently exists"? What are the assumptions the Church has made?

6. How does someone change a "wineskin"? What does this mean to you personally? How does the Church view their wineskin? What currently constitutes the "norm" for the Christian experience? Do you think God will dramatically make changes in that norm?

MEDITATION

"It has never entered the mind what God has prepared for us while on this earth. His intent is grand. Instead of limiting ourselves by our imagination and experience, let's press on to a renewed hunger for things yet to be seen. As we pursue the Extravagant One with reckless abandon, we will discover that our greatest problem is the resistance that comes from between our ears. But faith is superior. And it's time for us to make Him unconcerned about whether or not He'll find faith on the earth" (*When Heaven Invades Earth*, Page 216).

Flip through the pages of this book and highlight any comments, questions, or answers that you need to follow up on in the coming days. Take a protracted time to pray over your part in seeing Heaven invade Earth!

ABOUT BILL JOHNSON

BILL JOHNSON is a fifth-generation pastor with a rich heritage in the Holy Spirit. Together, Bill and his wife serve a growing number of churches that have partnered for revival. This leadership network has crossed denominational lines, building relationships that enable church leaders to walk successfully in both purity and power.

Bill and Brenda (Beni) Johnson are the senior pastors of Bethel Church in Redding, California. All three of their children and spouses are involved in full-time ministry. They also have nine wonderful grandchildren.

Recommended Reading

A Life of Miracles by Bill Johnson

Basic Training for the Prophetic Ministry by Kris Vallotton

Basic Training for the Supernatural Ways of Royalty by Kris Vallotton

Developing a Supernatural Lifestyle by Kris Vallotton

Dreaming With God by Bill Johnson

Face to Face by Bill Johnson

Here Comes Heaven by Bill Johnson and Mike Seth

Loving Our Kids On Purpose by Danny Silk

Purity: The New Moral Revolution by Kris Vallotton

Momentum by Bill Johnson and Eric Johnson

Release the Power of Jesus by Bill Johnson

Strengthen Yourself in the Lord by Bill Johnson

The Happy Intercessor by Beni Johnson

The Supernatural Power of a Transformed Mind by Bill Johnson

The Supernatural Ways of Royalty by Kris Vallotton and Bill Johnson

The Ultimate Treasure Hunt by Kevin Dedmon

When Heaven Invades Earth by Bill Johnson

Hosting the Presence by Bill Johnson

DESTINY IMAGE PUBLISHERS, INC.

"Promoting Inspired Lives."

VISIT OUR NEW SITE HOME AT
WWW.DESTINYIMAGE.COM

FREE SUBSCRIPTION TO DI NEWSLETTER

Receive free unpublished articles by top DI authors, exclusive
discounts, and free downloads from our best and newest books.
Visit www.destinyimage.com to subscribe.

Write to: Destiny Image
P.O. Box 310
Shippensburg, PA 17257-0310

Call: 1-800-722-6774

Email: orders@destinyimage.com

For a complete list of our titles or to place an order
online, visit www.destinyimage.com.

FIND US ON **FACEBOOK** OR FOLLOW US ON **TWITTER**.

www.facebook.com/destinyimage   **facebook**
www.twitter.com/destinyimage   **twitter**